Platonic Studies of Greek Philosophy

SUNY Series in Philosophy
Robert Cummings Neville, Editor

Platonic Studies of Greek Philosophy
Form, Arts, Gadgets, and Hemlock

Robert S. Brumbaugh

State University of New York Press

Published by
State University of New York Press, Albany

© 1989 State University of New York

For information, address State University of New York
Press, State University Plaza, Albany, N.Y., 12246

Library of Congress Cataloging in Publication Data

Brumbaugh, Robert Sherrick, 1918–
    Platonic studies of Greek philosophy : form, arts, gadgets, and
hemlock / Robert S. Brumbaugh.
        p.   cm.—(SUNY series in philosophy)
    Includes index.
    ISBN 0–88706–897–9. ISBN 0–88706–898–7 (pbk.)
    1. Plato. 2. Aristotle. 3. Philosophy, Ancient. I. Title.
II. Series.
B395.B772 1988
184—dc19

88–8578
CIP

10 9 8 7 6 5 4 3 2 1

Contents

Foreword

In my second year of graduate school, 1961–62, I was assigned to be one of the half dozen or more teaching assistants for Robert Brumbaugh's freshman course in Ancient Philosophy. We TAs, of course, were preoccupied with covering the terror of the beginning teacher with the bravado necessary to appear authoritative, if not wise, to smart Yalies. Perhaps it was that bravado that caused us to take a somewhat superior attitude toward Professor Brumbaugh's lectures. They were all so . . . obvious. *Anybody* could see the points he drew from the texts. Brumbaugh's history of philosophy seemed to us supercritical graduate students to be just a parade of ideas that lay plainly in the texts.

Then, at my first job after graduate school, I discovered that those ideas were not only not obvious until pointed out, but that they were almost wholly new and original. Furthermore, they were by and large convincing to my new colleagues, even in my casual "surely you've heard this before" articulation. On the basis of "my" profound and original scholarship I was assigned to teach history of philosophy. This seemed to call for a radical reevaluation of Brumbaugh's ideas. So I spoke with my erstwhile teaching assistant partners at the next philosophers' convention, and discovered they had had the same surprizing experience. We all had found that what had seemed so obvious in graduate school was taken to be profound and original in the larger philosophic communities. Indeed, it was giving us the status of learned experts in a field most of us had taken for granted in our studies. That status, of course, is very precious to assistant professors and I, at least, have been slow to give credit where it's due.

It now gives me mature pleasure to confess my sources by introducing this volume by Robert Brumbaugh. Within it are displayed all the virtues that have made him such an influential teacher for so many years to so many students. Perhaps the chief of those virtues is an uncanny, even if ordinarily unnoticed, habit of calling almost simultaneously to mind all levels of philosophical generalization. On the one

1

hand there are glorious generalizations (see "All the Great Ideas") and on the other there are philological arguments based on the frequency of the *men . . . de* construction. In between are analyses of the logic of arguments, reconstructions of the intent and strategy of Plato's and Aristotle's writings, critical evaluations of the philosophers' positions, discussions of the social context of philosophy in the ancient world, an overall interpretation of the history of philosophy, and a critical appraisal of our own culture and what it might learn from ancient Greek thought. And these different modes are all cheek to jowl, run by us so breathlessly that we don't realize we've been hit by a wholesale education in the subject of Platonic themes. Despite its occasional passages of heavy apparatus, this book is best enjoyed as philosophical *belles lettres*, a work that takes us into the fast and amazing mind of one of our most original thinkers. If the reader wonders whether I mean Plato or Brumbaugh, either answer will do.

With remarkable coherence, the essays here fall into five groups of increasing generality. Part I is a study of the *Republic*, focusing on Books V–VII in which Plato discusses his four approaches to or indications of the Form of the Good that true dialecticians should know: the analogy of the sun, the allegory of the cave, the divided line, and the ideal curriculum. Brumbaugh analyzes these as if they were the central panel of a pediment on a Greek temple, framed on either side with the discussions of the state in Books II–IV and Books VIII–IX, and of practical concerns of justice in Books I, IX, and X. Without reifying Platonic mathematicals, Brumbaugh then shows how mathematics really does play the orienting and organizing role in Plato's thought that Plato said it should. This portion of the text is in part an updating of Brumbaugh's first major book, *Plato's Mathematical Imagination*.

Part II deals with Platonic dialogues other than the *Republic*, and it fairly sparkles with imaginative brilliance. Chapter 8, on the myth of Atlantis and Plato's account in the *Critias*, is a bravura display of a wide array of philosophic genres: textual analysis, reconstruction of argument, interpretation of the cultural situation, and critical application of ancient ideas to contemporary life.

Part III is about Aristotle and his modifications of Platonism. Chapter 11 in that Part on the unity of the *Metaphysics* is an extraordinarily important article for studies of Aristotle. Whereas most accounts of the difference between Plato and Aristotle are written by Aristotelians, this one tells the story from the Platonic side, and everything seems subtly different.

Part IV has as its thesis the importance of technology and gadgets for Plato's thinking. Although Plato may have rejected mechanistic thinking as a model for guiding life and the polis, he was fascinated with the crafts and his world was full of technology to an extent far greater than imagined a few years ago. In many respects, the chapters here are the most charming, recounting Brumbaugh's own experiences in Greece as his discovery of Greek technology changed his view of Plato's polis.

Part V focuses themes of directly contemporary relevance, and finds resources for understanding them in Plato's world: feminism, literary style and theory, and the place of philosophy in a world of power struggles. Brumbaugh points out that the greatest significance of the trial of Socrates is that it induced Plato to become a philosopher rather than a politician: how that consequence has made history!

It must be said that the discipline of history of philosophy generally attracts Aristotelian-minded thinkers, bent on finding the *isms* and *ologies* of the philosophic movements. Convinced that categories are concretely in the things, such Aristotelian thinkers almost invariably commit the fallacy of misplaced concreteness, and any living thinkers subjected to their analysis squirm at the violence done to the self-perceived richness of their own thought. One thinks of the effects of the historical writings of Richard McKeon, Brumbaugh's teacher, or more recently of Walter Watson's *The Architecture of Meaning.*

A Platonist such as Brumbaugh, however, convinced of the independent reality of forms, can *play* with conceptual patterns as tools for interpreting the slippery sliding flow of concrete thought. As Brumbaugh once said about John Wild's passionate defense of concreteness, for a true Platonist the concrete never hardens. Precisely because no concrete thing is ever fully identical with a form, no finite set of forms is ever fully adequate to becoming's Mixture (as Plato put it in the *Philebus*). Consequently, philosophic interpretation consists in coming at the text from as many angles as possible, regarding none as exhaustive but searching for the next zany perspective that can open up a whole new stratum of meaning. Readers of this volume will find a Platonic history of philosophy of extraordinary brilliance, most brilliant when its angles of analysis are most zany. They will also discover on reflection that the trendy deconstructionist search for the "diffarent" is little more than old fashioned Platonism topped with German *Angst* and French hoopla. A Platonic form is exactly what constitutes "differance" in context. To say that a concrete item in the realm of becoming is a confusion of several incompatible forms, none of which is adequately expressed for long, is a plain Platonic way of denying a "transcendental signifier," without the gratuitous anticlericalism of the French appropriation of Heidegger's dubious analysis of "onto-theology." Furthermore, in the hands of a master scholar such as Brumbaugh, the Platonic approach to history can very well establish sound truths about the texts, even if none is the whole truth. The inventiveness of the interpreting reader is not free license, as the more casual deconstructionists sometimes claim, but rather the work of finding or imagining a new point of view, a new formal scheme, from which to question the text. Whether the forms can indeed be found in the text is a question to which there are valid scholarly answers. Although a Platonist's imagination should be as zany as possible, his or her scholarly responsibility is as hardnosed as any Aristotelian's. Brumbaugh's work is the paradigm, as shown in this volume.

There is an essential element of Brumbaugh's Platonism that finds no parallel in deconstructionist, Aristotelian, or other current approaches to the history of philosophy, save that of process thought. For Plato, forms are not merely structures but values and norms. As Brumbaugh shows in scores of ways here, forms don't just sit there in things. By virtue of their very structure they give things value. Because of their forms, things have importance and interest. Brumbaugh guides the readers' tour through ancient Greece by showing first *how* things are interesting, and then what makes them interesting. To an Aristotelian devoted to structural completeness, Brumbaugh's Platonic tour might at first seem too much like a little of this, a little of that, and then on to a little of something else. After a while, even the Aristotelian catches on that the jumps in angle of vision are a subtle systematic weaving of a comprehensive *appreciation* of the matter. Though the language is perhaps anachronistic, I suspect a fair Platonic alternative to the Aristotelian ideal of knowledge as possession in mind of the forms of things, is a dialectical habit of culturing of one's habits by detailed appreciation of the worths of things. For a Platonist, the structural element of form is instrumental to the form's conveying of value on the things participating in it. And knowledge at base is appreciation relative to action.

One more general point about Brumbaugh's approach needs to be remarked. Without fanfare, without Hegel's Cunning of Reason or even much Labor of the Notion, Brumbaugh displays the cultural importance of gaining a systematic, comprehensive vision of things. Of course, there can be many such visions of things, and Brumbaugh nearly always advocates four; the more visions of the whole the better. How to relate and choose among competing synoptic visions was the topic of Brumbaugh's brilliant *Plato on the One*. Our cultural problem, however, is not that we have a surfeit of comprehensive visions but rather our poverty of them. The systematic spirit has been so tromped in our century that systematic philosophy has almost had to hide in the closet. Only Whitehead and his students have successfully pursued the task. Brumbaugh here not only shows that system is important, but he shows how to do it. He is a master of the little idea that defines a whole and sets it in focus. Although the ostensible topic of this book is history of philosophy, my own conviction is that "Platonic Themes" means speculative philosophy in the grand tradition.

As I began with an anecdote about Brumbaugh as a teacher, let me end by recalling a point that Brumbaugh makes frequently about teaching, usually in discussing the *Meno*, as in this volume. Plato's dialogues often seem verbally inconclusive; yet if analyzed for their dramatic structure, it appears that the characters have changed in accord with Socrates' intent. Thus Meno leaves the conversation a bit more virtuous, Euthyphro with a little less impious confidence, Phaedrus with a better taste in lovers and literature. The same double teaching holds true, I believe, of Brumbaugh's book here. On the surface there are arguments about texts, interpretations, historical situations, and criticism—arguments by which we may be instructed and with which we will agree and disagree according to our various ways of participation in the community of thinkers. The book's cumulative effect, however, is to make us a bit more Platonistic, a bit lighter in our interpretations of things, a bit more imaginative, much more curious, and far more given to delight in speculative vision.

ROBERT CUMMINGS NEVILLE

Acknowledgements

All of these chapters have appeared as articles, or, in a few cases, were presented as lectures. The original appearance is indicated for journal articles in each case. Chapter 2 is a lecture originally given to the Greater Boston Area Colloquium on Ancient Philosophy in 1976; Chapter 13 is a paper originally presented to the Society for Ancient Greek Philosophy in 1963; Chapter 14 is a lecture given to the Colorado State Society for History and Philosophy of Science in 1978. Chapter 17 is part of introductory reading material I prepared, with the aid of an N.E.H. summer grant, for a course in "Four Definitions of Women in Classical Philosophy and Literature," given in 1986; I have copyrighted it as of 1987.

I want to thank Robert Neville for his extraordinarily perceptive and helpful suggestions as editor and fellow Plato admirer; and William Eastman for his tolerant help as Editor. Colleagues and students during my forty-five years of teaching have consistently helped me understand, present, and see the present relevance of the kind of Platonic philosophy I have tried to develop in studies of Plato, of time, and of education. I owe more than I can say to my wife, who has discussed my work and shared travel and leisure with me for our entire joint careers; without her companionship and encouragement, I would never have been able to continue thinking, teaching, and writing.

Introduction

When, in a society, public officials think personal income is more their responsibility than public welfare; when athletes compete for cash, not glory; when there is a proliferation of doctors and lawyers; then that society desperately needs philosophy. This is one message from Plato's *Republic* that any twentieth century reader of newspapers and viewer of television commercials can see the relevance of today. At least, we can see that we need *something;* but what is the "philosophy" that Plato recommends as remedy?

This book is a collection of essays exploring Plato's thought from its central statement in the *Republic* to its apparent revisions after his death by the Lyceum and Academy. Contemporary as the issues and examples often are, it is not about politics, but about the goals and principles that politics, and human living, need as their guide. We run into a controversy over women's rights in what may be meant as a blueprint of utopia, and we confront a controversy over Aristotle's claim that he, not Plato, should provide us with our philosophy. In between, we find Plato defending his own idealism against alternatives that sound strangely like modern positivism, pragmatism, and existentialism in ancient incarnation.

Philosophy, as Plato and most thinkers since have conceived it, is a discipline that sees the world "synoptically." In the complex classical setting in which Plato's thought developed, specializations and special interests at high intensity each tended to go its own way. Political policy had to balance considerations of military necessity, economic advantage, class interest, and local order. The city of Athens itself, in Plato's time, brought together the theater, market, Academy, Acropolis, and Assembly; it was a scene of intense interaction. The trouble was that these special interests and functions—combined with a divided class structure—were in a balanced tension delicately maintained, a balance which often tilted in one direction or another, and exploded on occasion. Plato's *Republic* was a proposal that philosophy educate a group of policy makers who would represent the general welfare and direct the state in the light of public interest. The education necessary for this task was to be "dialectic," a study of reality yielding realistic criteria to make judgments of value. This is the central point of Plato's *Republic*, one of the most often read and discussed documents in Western thought. The *Republic* deals with justice and with the criteria of sound social organization, but reaches far beyond to bring together education, poetry, religion, and psychology in its vision. But when Plato's spokesman, Socrates, is asked to define and give a detailed account of dialectic, he refuses and moves on to another topic. From what Socrates *has* told us, however, I think it is fair to say that the best example, and probably course textbook, of this philosophic higher education would be the *Republic* itself. It compares competing views of human nature and their implications for society; competing views of the best social order; and alternative notions of what constitutes a good human life. As a textbook for philosophy and social science, it holds together admirably well. Further, it is typical of Plato in many of his dialogues to make the dialogue itself illustrate what it is about; and when it is about a method, as the *Phaedrus* is about rhetoric and the *Parmenides* at least in part about deductive logic, the dialogue itself uses the method it discusses.

My essays develop the theme that the *Republic* is itself an example of dialectic. I have concentrated on Books V, VI and VII, where there has been most controversy over the author's intention and the unity of the work. These central Books take on new meaning when put in the context of the dialogue as a whole, which has the tidy symmetry of a classical pediment. The center of the work is the Form of the Good, the criterion of value by which we are to judge competing "hypotheses" concerning human nature, and the arts and institutions these imply.

The next set of essays discuss a connected series of dialogues that follow the *Republic* as successive defenses of the philosophic vision it describes. These dialogues are the *Parmenides*, *Theaetetus*, *Sophist*, and *Statesman*. They evidently extend the earlier work of Plato by new, more technical, explorations of the domains of abstractions, arts and crafts, language, and kinds of knowledge. I think that, in addition, they serve as successive defenses of the philosophy the *Republic* presents and presupposes. If one tries to take away any part of the four-level philosophic scheme on which the *Republic* rests, (the scheme presented by the Divided Line in Book VI), an alternative philosophy results which runs into some form of self-contradiction or inability to explain such evident matters of fact as the existence of mathematical knowledge or the acceptance of the Sophist's refutations as an art. A larger set was planned than those Plato actually wrote out, but it would have gone beyond the group we have only in a final dialogue, The Philosopher. The dialogues of this group actually written remain classics of philosophy, though most scholars may not read them as connected as tightly to the *Republic* as I have tried to show that they are.

Plato's philosophy itself is, of course, a formalism, with a world of forms and a world of things that "share" in them. But after the analytic dialogues that directly follow the *Republic*, Plato's work shows changes of emphasis. One such change shows itself as a new interest in the details of natural science and natural theology, the former in the *Timaeus*, the latter in Book X of the *Laws* and the *Epinomis*. A second change seems to be a modification of the idea of inquiry as a search for pure definition and form, for a *logos*, by the added requirement that the *logos* be accompanied by illustrative *examples*. This need for example to give concreteness to abstract concepts and statements is presented in the *Statesman*, and figures as crucial in the account of a true method of knowing which Plato describes in the *Seventh Letter*, which is now generally though not universally accepted as genuine. One thinks, at this point, of Kant's insistence that knowledge must combine *both* concepts and intuitions.

Some other chapters deal with the fortunes of Plato's thought immediately after Plato. At his death, there was a split in the Academy; Aristotle left, to return later to found his own university, the Lyceum, in Athens. In his lectures on first philosophy he has a good deal to say about what the shortcomings are of Plato and his Academic successors, Speusippus and Xenokrates, and how he himself corrects them. The work in which Aristotle does this the most, the *Metaphysics*, is difficult in the extreme; in fact, some scholars have claimed that it is not a single unified lecture course at all. But I think a look at the historical situation in the Academy, in conjunction with Richard McKeon's general outline of the *Metaphysics* text, helps to clarify both the Academic break and the key point on which Aristotle claimed his superiority to Plato. If I am right, we can also begin to see why Aristotle was so belligerent in his attacks on Platonism, since his own system contained in its new context so many similarities to Plato. If my admittedly speculative account of Aristotle modifying the Platonic scheme of the *Republic* in one direction, and the Academy also modifying it, but in another, is correct, a chapter here comes to its end in the history of ancient Greek philosophy.

But it is *our* history, too. When Plato writes about the evil consequences of legislators who see their bank accounts as their first responsibility, or athletes who think of cash prizes as the true goal of physical grace and athletic training, there is a prescience we should not ignore. And in an age, like ours, of explosively increasing individualism and specialization, we might do well to reread Plato, bearing in mind two of his most central political thoughts: until policy makers are also philosophers, there is little hope for the happiness of mankind; and only the person who can see the picture of all things *in their interconnection, synoptically,* can become a good philosopher.

Recent archaeology has something to say about the context of Plato's thought, which brings out an unexpected explanation for the relevance of his world to our own.

There is still a general impression that Greek philosophy was purely intellectual and Greek culture wholly unmechanical. Accordingly, Plato's relation to the arts and crafts has been construed as an opposition, comparable to that of formalism and mechanism. Thus there is a general feeling that the modern world, with its science and ever-present technology, is not the place for classical thought (not even for the purely intellectual first statements of the atomic theory.) But a look at classical context can change this notion of opposition. In the first place, Plato's criticism of the arts is directed largely against proposals to make all education technical instead of liberal. It does not reflect his constant curiosity about and references to the crafts, nor to the fact that they constitute one indispensable stage of his own schematism of kinds of knowing and stages of education. Indeed, it is by these very arts that we create instantiations of Platonic forms in space and time. (Plato's final work, the model legal code of the *Laws,* is in fact a masterpiece of social technology.) And though there is not the development of labor-saving devices we associate today with applied science, there is a clear sense of mechanical ingenuity in the minor technology that recent archaeology has discovered, a realm of gadgetry.

Thus, in Plato's world it is *presupposed* that ideal forms must find their way into inventions, arts, and crafts. Given an ideal—say of justice or honesty—this sets up two problems: its definition and its implementation. That there is this dimension of implementation to be attended to by philosophy, Plato, through the *Republic,* takes for granted. His future rulers spend three times as long in gaining practical technical experience as they spend on their dialectical education. And later in his works, when Plato turns his attention to the forms as they affect lower levels of his Divided Line, he recognizes the need for inventiveness and the problems posed to technology in more detail.

That Plato's world included appreciation of ingenious mechanism establishes a context which his philosophy presupposed. If the form of time were to find its way down to the marketplace, it needed a complex assist from sundials or water-driven celestial globes. That the application of ideas could not simply be taken for granted became clearer as

Plato and the Academy tried harder to apply them. There is no opposition, then, between the classical and modern view on this score. Only, the classical theorists in the Platonic tradition insisted that the functional connections of levers, weights, and gearing were evidence—both in art and nature—of causally related intelligence and purpose, in opposition to some modern thinkers (and the ancient atomists) who thought "intelligence" was simply itself a complex of cords, tubes, and circuits.

In Plato's dialogue the *Critias,* he draws a picture of the mythical Atlantis, an empire based on vast but relatively mindless technology. It ends sunk beneath the sea. But that is because it is unphilosophical, not primarily because it is gigantic. The moral may be that the forms we think we are imitating may not turn out to be the actual objects of imitation we intended!

Plato's text shows his appreciation of the technology and ingenuity of his surrounding world. His culture was much less alien to our own than the nineteenth-century romantic pictures of classics scholars led us to believe; and twentieth-century archaeology has the evidence to use for a correction. This correction is included in my discussion of Platonic themes because of its bearing on the presence and relevance of Plato to our own century.

We also want to ask what the alternatives to Platonism are. In the classical periods there were three alternatives. To make this relation more concrete, I will present the respective *definitions of women* of the four. This has a double purpose: It gives us a typical case study of the divergence of Platonism from the other systems, and it gives more context to the earlier discussion of the status of women in Book V of the *Republic.* The question of system alternatives is also relevant to the choice of philosophic writing style. But here the issue is simpler. The West has almost uniformly followed as its model either the *dramatic* style of Plato or the *treatise* paradigm of Aristotle. The choice between these two reflects a philosophical, not simply a rhetorical, choice; and as a conclusion to my discussion of content, I hope this point concerning literary form will become clear.

Finally, I have returned to the trial of Socrates, the tragic point in ancient history from which Plato's decision to be a philosopher, not a politician, began. It is natural to return from this event to Plato's account in the *Republic* of his answer to the question "In what kind of world was Socrates a possibility?" It is equally natural to end the discussion of Platonic answers with the questions from which they began.

One moral that I hope has come through my chapters is that there is no question of being either a classics scholar *or* an expert in ancient philosophy. We need four things to understand the Greek philosophers. These are precision in treating their linguistic texts and archaeological contexts, speculative imagination in grasping their ideas, a sense of presence to give these exercises contact with reality, and a sense of relevance as we compare their world and their insights to our own. It seems to me to be the last of these, the sense of relevance, that is moving toward the foreground as scholarly work approaches the twenty-first century.

This is already foreshadowed in Whitehead's epigram that "the safest general characterization of Western philosophy is as a series of footnotes to Plato." Any good teacher of ancient philosophy will probably be stronger in some of these four dimensions than in others, but he or she certainly will be good because there is an appreciation of all four.

Part I

Reinterpreting Plato's Republic

Chapter 1

A New Interpretation of
Plato's Republic

The present chapter offers some new interpretations of the *Republic* for discussion. Each year for the past five, I have started to put aside historical work and to concentrate on pure metaphysics instead; each time, however, there has been just one more idea or interpretation that seemed too potentially important to let go. This time, I stopped to look into volume 2 of James Adam's edition of the *Republic* while transferring books from one case to another, and I saw that the "balance" of the cosmic model in the final myth was also the key to the overall outline of the dialogue itself. Since a dialogue on justice should have justice done it, I decided to put off my transfer of books and interests once more, and to write a new historical footnote to Plato.

I will concentrate, in turn, on three points. The first point is that the device of having action interact with argument, characteristic of the early dialogues, continues in the *Republic* itself. The second point is that a principle of aesthetic symmetry governs the outline of main topics discussed, relating them in such a way that each except the central theme receives two balancing, but not identical, treatments. My third point will be that the *Republic* as a whole is itself an example of the mysterious science of "dialectic," prescribed as the culmination of philosophic study in Book VII, but very tersely described there. Read in this way, the *Republic* puts itself before us as a model both of the justice that it seeks to comprehend and of the dialectical method by which to comprehend it.

The *Republic* has had many interpretations and adventures. Past readers have been so fascinated by individual sections out of context that they have almost universally undersold the unity of the dialogue as a whole.

Nor is there any more agreement as to the central theme than there is as to which section represents the fundamental doctrine. Something about the construction of the dialogue itself makes it possible to select politics, or pleasure, or dialectic, or poetry and education, and come up with a relatively coherent reading.

Why is it that, although we cannot disagree with the judgment that this is one of the truly great works in Western philosophic literature (and it is still, in English and other translations, a philosophic best-seller), there can be such discrepant judgments of what it is about, and of what it says concerning whatever its topic is taken to be?

The answer is that Plato expected that readers would know how to approach philosophic dialogue, and how to recognize traditional symmetry in a topic outline that employed it. These have proved to be very demanding expectations.

I

There seems to be an increasing recognition today that the earlier Platonic dialogues are "self-referential," in the sense that their concrete characters and actions are examples of the abstract topics they discuss. It is not always recognized, however, how closely connected these two dimensions are in presenting a doctrine or in establishing meaning. As a clear example of this interaction, let us look briefly at the discussion of whether virtue can be taught in Plato's *Meno*.

Young Meno, at the outset, assumes that if virtue can be taught, this must be done either didactically, by precept (as Gorgias has taught him), or by influence of an example. In the end, the argument seems plausible that, since anyone who knew what virtue was would want to teach it, but no teachers by either method can be found, virtue is not teachable.

This is the outcome of the argument, which has no doubt depressed school administrators ever since the first papyrus editions came to their attention. But the dialogue is quite another matter; for in fact we see Meno improving in wisdom, courage, temperance, and justice as he talks with Socrates. And this dramatic fact adds another proposition to the set used in the formal summary: "there exists at least one teacher of virtue, Socrates the Athenian." Thus, virtue can, in a sense, be taught—but neither by Sophistic precept nor Anytean example; rather, it can be taught by a third alternative, shared inquiry. And here is a clear case where the concrete drama of the dialogue justifies an added proposition that casts a new light on the apparent inconclusive outcome of the philosophic argument. Similar results have been shown to hold for a majority of the early dialogues.

This aspect of the *Republic* centers on the characters and relations of its three main speakers, Socrates, Glaucon, and Adeimantus. The drama is concerned with choice; as in Prodicus's fable of the choice of Herakles, young men are confronted with a discussion that involves "nothing less than the choice of a way of life." At the outset, the pursuit of justice seems unreasonable when we compare the advantages of injustice for achieving riches and glory. By the very end, however, criteria can be offered that lead to a right choice of lives in the other world, when each must pick the pattern of another incarnation; and the way of justice has been found reasonable, after all.

The three speakers are characterized, both in descriptive asides and by their interests and styles of thought, in a way that invites us to identify each with one of the three "parts of the soul" which are a central concept in the discussion. Glaucon, dear to Socrates, musical, and like the timocratic man in ambitiousness, represents the "spirited" part. He is best able to follow theoretical and abstract construction and discussion: thus the ethical implications of the forms of music, computation of the unhappiness of the tyrant, and the highly speculative account of the good find him as the respondent. Adeimantus seems by contrast to be the spokesman for the legitimate interests and claims of the appetitive part of the soul. He is more concerned with what people think and tell us (particularly the poets) than with such a theoretical construct as his brother's theory. Quite in character, he agrees with Socrates' suggestion that the basis of the state is economic, and indeed he might have accepted a rustic cooperative as his final utopia if brother Glaucon had not found it "a city for pigs." When Adeimantus is talking, the discussion is full of detailed concrete observations of what people say, what they believe, and what actual cities have been like in Greece. For Socrates to have answered his objections verbally, he claims, is not enough; he wants to be genuinely persuaded. Socrates, to do what he hopes, must convince the young men in their own terms that the life of justice is both more honorable and more pleasant than its contrary.

This persuasion is not too easily achieved; in the first half of the *Republic*, objections and interruptions mark the changes of respondent; in the second half, a harmony is beginning to emerge both in the argument itself and in the relations among its participants. And in this way, the final dramatic result personifies justice in the soul, as each speaker takes his place in the final steps of what had been a sharp debate, now transformed into a friendly discussion. The pattern of changes of speaker not only marks a topic outline but goes with a development of character that instantiates the central theme.

II

In addition to its dimension of drama, the *Republic* has an unusual pattern of symmetry in its outline of themes discussed. Comparison of the pattern with the design of a temple pediment seems to me particularly illuminating.

Imagine a triangular frame to be filled in by balancing figures of sculpture. A motif of religion and cosmic justice serves as an open-and-close bracket for the entire discussion. After the prologue, the first book opens with the portrait of Cephalus, who enjoys and personifies the old age of a just man. Commentators have noted that the description of Socrates' aged host, seated on his throne-like chair, wearing garlands, is clearly meant to present a visual image to the reader, as indeed it does. In Book I, Cephalus is wondering about the journey of the soul from life to death; the old myths he has heard take on a new vividness; yet he at least has good hope, since he has never treated god or man unjustly. The *Republic* ends, in Book X, with the myth of Er, in a philosophic poem brought by a messenger who recounts the return of the soul from death to life. If we are to pick visual symbols to represent this thematic balance, we might imagine our triangular pediment frame with Cephalus seated in the lower left, and the goddess Necessity seated on her throne in the lower right.

The next major theme (by "major theme" I will mean a single topic held in focus for more than ten Stephanus pages) is that of poets and poetry, which is central in Books II and III. And, significantly, just before the closing myth in the final book of the *Republic*, Book X, Socrates abruptly and explicitly returns the discussion to this theme of poetry. Once again, if we will, we can visualize two more figures of our pediment: perhaps the good poet as teacher is one, the bad poet being exiled, the other. I am sure we can imagine many other figures that would fit well; what I intend to emphasize is mainly that the A-B thematic pattern in the opening of the dialogue is balanced by the B-A pattern of its close.

For brevity in characterization, I will call the next theme that of the soul. The tripartite structure of the self, and the formal definition of justice as harmony in the soul, is an outstanding focus for this section of the discussion. This third theme is central in Book IV; it returns a second time in the final appraisal of types of soul and life that makes up the second half of Book IX. Here we might think of a design showing the contention of the parts on the left, their cooperation on the right; perhaps the discussion of the *Republic* itself is a good model. In any case, we now have a thematic pattern A-B-C balanced by a concluding pattern C-B-A. And the figure of a pediment begins to be suggestive in a second way: its increasing altitude as we approach the center indicates a dynamic principle of order at work here, moving, with successive topics, from becoming to the higher level of being, toward a world of science and beyond guess or hearsay.

The next theme is introduced by the sharpest dramatic break in the dialogue. This is the rise of the state, in Book V. Plato's own image of his calm guardians in procession to the Acropolis is a good picture for this. The balancing theme is the decline of the state, introduced by the choir of Muses in Book VIII. This is not a calm upward procession but a mad rout from the citadel, jostling and plunging downward. (As I first wrote this, I found myself visualizing something like the blue wall of the Sistine Chapel; and that is not sound classical imagery. But Plato's text has vivid descriptions that offer imagery for this downhill flight. The "king of the hill" battle between competitors "kicking and butting one another with horns and hoofs of iron" is one of the most vivid images in the entire *Republic*.)

This now completes the list of balanced themes, with the pattern A-B-C-D . . . D-C-B-A. What would belong in the center of our pediment? Clearly, on the analogy of other pediment themes where gods and goddesses act to create justice or order, it should be the goddess of Justice herself. At the very vertex, Plato suggests we picture the form of the good by the symbol of the sun. The goddess belongs here too, as symbol of the ordering power of the good. It is this central section, Books VI and VII, which is the axis of symmetry for the rest, and the high point both of the triangular frame and of the becoming-to-being dialectical progression: having "risen to this high place," we must then "go down into the cave."

This collage of Platonic pictures raises two immediate questions: Why is there this strange duplication that says everything twice in reversed order, and why does anyone believe that Plato expected his readers to pursue or recognize such an elaborate latent structural order? The second question is the easier to answer, so I will turn to it first.

Both in sculpture and in epic poetry, the open-and-close pattern was a familiar one, and in the air. But this alone is, I concede, rather vague, and as an answer to the question, will not do. What seems to me to clinch the case for Plato's conscious awareness of this type of "balance" as an aesthetic property is the intrusive description of the physical and mechanical details of the model of the universe which figures in the Myth of Er. A bewildering puzzle to Proclus, who indeed proposed rewriting the whole section; an odd fantasy to A. E. Taylor; the possible ghost of an archaic Pythagorean machine to John Burnet;

the listing has only one suggestive property. If we write down the numbers, one through eight, representing the relative degree (first through eighth) of a given property in each of the nested bowls that spin about in the machine, symmetrical pairs all "balance" by adding to a sum of nine, and the two sets of four on either side of a central axis also (almost) balance, adding to eighteen and eighteen in one figure, seventeen and nineteen in another (see Note, below). And this association of symmetrical balance and posited abstract order is put forward as though its recognition would be obvious to the reader. I am not suggesting anything so bizarre as that the *Republic* is, like the Voynich manuscript attributed to Roger Bacon, a cipher, with the law of nines at its end a key in plain text. I am suggesting, however, that the transfer here of symmetric balance to mechanical imagery does argue a much greater sensitivity to such pattern than a modern reader has. It is nice to have this transparent illustration; but even without it, one can argue from internal indications that the thematic symmetry is deliberate.

We can turn now to the first, more difficult, question: Why is there this duplicated treatment of topics? At first, it may seem that this should not be a problem, since in the other middle dialogues this happens, too—for example, both in the *Symposium* and the *Phaedo*. But in these cases, the first occurrence is on the level of becoming, and the repeated theme is then treated on the level of being, of form. In the *Republic*, however, the paired treatments are on the same level of a being-becoming scale; yet they seem to differ in method, in style, and even in ostensible doctrine.

The suggestion that commends itself is that the difference between an upward and a downward movement of the dialectic accounts for the difference in each case. The initial discussion is each time constructing a formal model by a method that looks for the simplest set of principles underlying complex phenomena; the second treatment tests the adequacy of these principles by confronting them with the full range of empirical data. For the former purpose, one must use a critical method that eliminates whatever is logically irrelevant or inconsistent; but for the latter purpose, we must reintroduce considerations of empirical, existential, relations that are actual, though they may not be logically necessary.

It is remarkable what changes do occur in the account of the individual soul between the open brackets of Book IV and their close in Book IX. In the earlier analysis, the law of contradiction, plus a minimum number of examples, gives us a human race divided by heredity into three species, each one-dimensionally fitted for a single role in a three-class ideal society. There are hints that this may not be the whole story, but Plato's readers have usually chosen to ignore them. And there is a reason for this: the magic triads of self and social class have a clarity and distinctness totally lacking in the hyperbolic, and very ugly, image of the man encasing small man, larger lion, and giant hydra of Book IX! The nearly imbecilic simplicity of eugenics in Books IV and V is obviously preferable, on grounds of simplicity, to the many pheno-types that the Muses envisage in Book VIII. And the studies of Books VIII and IX could not have more empirical detail per line cited for confirmation if the most taciturn modern sociologist had composed them.

When we turn to the paired treatments of the "state" theme, theme D, in Books V and VIII, a similar relation holds. On this level of intellectual investigation, the appetitive part of the soul has been left behind. The pursuit of a clear ideal model, operating by divisions and distinctions, finally finds only the two highest classes on stage here. And these, in the limiting case of being nothing but essentially pure reason, can indeed give an operational model of virtue at work in which temperance is illustrated by abolishing private appetite, courage by exorcism of any possible fear, and wisdom by pure formal contem-plation. It is a fiction of sorts, and—as the tight cross references tying it to its companion treatment show—a fiction that is radically incom-plete. It is not "impossible" in the sense of involving logical contradic-tion; for it is our rational faculty which is alone immortal and the essential component of our humanity. But though it talks of becoming and change, the level from which the talking is done has ascended beyond them in its search for the principles of justice. The amusing thing is that the model city of rulers motivated by *no* self interest comes out in so many details identical with Aristophanes' town of free love and free lunches, set up on an exclusively greedy and self-seeking moti-vation. Aristotle is right on target when he points out that the appetites and the class of producers have been omitted in this section, but Plato has already made the point before him.

The problem of the decline of the state in Book VIII is now to deduce, as from a hypothesis, the new "patterns" that will result when ambition and appetite are once more added to pure rational existence, as the soul becomes attached to a body and embedded in a career in space and time. The frictionless model retains its relevance: it is still the norm from which we are measuring deviations.

This structure of the *Republic* accounts for many of its disturbing features. Did Plato believe in a reducibility of appearance to reality, semblance to form, without remainder? The first half of the work seems to support, the second half to contradict, this interpretation.

Does dialectic in its operation make for a pure rationalism, or can it be a method for empirical science? The first treatments of each theme could hardly be more anti-empirical, yet the second ones could hardly encompass more detailed data and observation. Did Plato think he himself was in a position to show how the vision of the good provided new criteria for ordering recalcitrant phenomena, or did he merely put this notion forward as a programmatic vision? Here the answer is not clear from either half of the *Republic*, but the first treatment rather supports the interpretation of the vision as an unrealized goal, recognized dimly by "divination," while the second treatments of each theme have about them an assurance—rather than a faith—that there is an order to be found when we use the light of the ideal to view the actual.

III

If we return now to a section early in the dialogue that embarrassingly escaped strict thematic pattern, the section containing the refutation of popular views of justice in Book I and the opening of Book II, we find that it seems to be a small-scale anticipatory demonstration of dialectic on its upward way, from myth and guess to generalized theory.

The comparison with the pediment design suggests that this interlude prefigures the grand sweep of themes from *eikasia* to *techne* to *dianoia*, ending with the good on the highest level, then descending again through the world of taxonomy to technique and on to poetry. In this sense, the *Republic* as a whole is an example of the method of dialectic that moves to principles and then must return from them, to focus applied metaphysics on the perplexing question of present existential choice.

These observations may have an air of evidence but vagueness about them, so that one wonders how far they really change any interpretation or relate to any controversy. To show the relevance of my analysis to explication, let me list nine new considerations and ideas that future interpretations must take into account.

1. The *Republic*, despite its title and history, is best described as a treatise on value theory and on theory construction in the social sciences, not as a political or psychological tract.
2. It makes a more impressive claim than has usually been thought, since it attempts to show the vision of the good in actual application, introducing order—both normative and

descriptive—into the complex phenomena of human nature and conduct.

3. There is some justification for the thesis that the portrait of the Utopian community is ironic. In any case, there is no adequate justification for taking this section, out of context, as the literal political doctrine of the *Republic*.

4. The discussion in the first half of the book is marked by sharp distinctions, simple classifications, and complete elimination of factors not directly relevant to the search for general principles. Each of these characteristics is reversed in the second half.

5. It is absurd to regard the *Republic* as anti-empirical; there is a fantastic range of empirical observations, but they are located toward the end of the work, not where a modern "empiricist" reader would expect them to come.

6. The complaint of unrealistic simplification, made by readers from Aristotle to John Dewey, overlooks the complex taxonomy of Books VIII–X. In general, the parallels between the *Republic* and the *Statesman* will now be seen to be much closer than has been previously thought.

7. While the state-individual analogy is a tight isomorphism in its first introduction, not all citizens are "typical" of their states in the second part.

8. The theory of forms is developed in a way that leaves room for "abstract entitles" which are "deviations" and "alternative roles we can choose"; and these, while atemporal, are not the "forms" in the strict sense. This point is important, because it answers the metaphysical objection of modern process philosophy that there can be no novelty in Plato's universe; so far as the *Republic* goes, all Platonism requires is invariant *criteria*, not an exhaustive set of forms causing and prefiguring all concrete decision or invention.

9. The concluding myth indicates how the *Republic* can, and how it cannot, be read as relevant to later cultural political situations. The "paradigms" offering possible choices in the "showcase of lives" will change constantly with history; but the criteria of excellence relevant to our selection will stay the same.

Plato's intuitive association of symmetry and beauty, his expectation of an audience familiar with his own aesthetic sense of drama and form, has been so little appreciated that—for all the impact it has had and admiration it has received—the *Republic* has never been wholly correctly edited or read. The lovely epilogue on balance in the cosmos became an enigma long before Proclus; the significance of shifts of speaker was thrown out of court as irrelevant as early as Aristotle; the resemblance of the structure to a pediment sculpture was never really taken seriously. But the fact remains that symmetry, truth, and beauty—three aspects of the good—are captured by the *Republic* in its drama, outline, and method. The fascination this work has exercised may be some evidence for the truth of Platonism, as well as a tribute to the author's artistry.

Note on the "Law of Nines"

The details of the "law of nines" can be found in J. Adam, *The Republic of Plato*, II, 473–479; Adam draws on J. Cook Wilson's article "Plato, *Republic* 616E", *Classical Review*, XXI (1902): 292–293. Some further suggestions will be found in my *Plato's Mathematical Imagination*, pp. 198–200. Detailed lists of the sizes, colors, and velocities of the "nested hemispheres" of this cosmic model are symmetrical with respect to the ordinal numbers which add up to nine. They are further balanced by having approximately equal sums for the two halves about a central axis of symmetry; and Cook Wilson points out a rule of "equable distribution" between paired sets such that "the order of magnitude of one pair is the reverse of that of the other" (for example, 7 1 8 2 is "more equable" in this sense than 7 8 2 1). For sizes we have:

COSMIC ORDER   1 2 3 4 | 5 6 7 8   (Sums of successive pairs—
SIZE OF RIM: 1 8 7 3 | 6 2 5 4   indicating "equable distribu-
                  = 19 | = 17   tion"—are 9, 10, 8 and 9).

For colors (I suggest that the metaphor of "balance" is extended to these because they indicate the degree to which the hemispheres have "more or less adamant in their mixture") the order of mention gives:

$$1\ 7\ 8\ 2\ |\ 5\ 3\ 4\ 6$$
$$= 18\ \ |\ \ = 18$$

And the velocities are:

$$1\ 8\ \ \ \ \ 7\ \ \ \ \ 432$$
$$= 9\ \ \ \ \ 6\ \ \ \ \ = 9$$
$$5$$
$$= 18$$

Further symmetries are found for the ordinal listing of size times color, and some for momenta (= size × color × velocity).

Chapter 2

Interpreting Book V when the Republic is Read as Dialectic

It is clear that a central question for discussion of Plato's theories of higher education is the nature of the science of "dialectic" which is to be the final theoretical course. It has been suggested that we are told just enough about it to show that the *Republic* itself counts as an illustration, and could indeed serve as one of the textbooks. We would, on that reading, expect the earlier Books to develop alternative "hypotheses" explanatory of human nature and conduct, alternatives which would be combined into an adequate account somewhere near the center of the work. My present discussion is designed to show how the utopian daydream of Socrates in *Republic* V fares in the context of this reading. The result is particularly interesting because, if it is correct, not only are Socrates' observations not to be taken literally, but he is not here identical with Plato, who does not endorse the rationalist utopia. The discussion must begin, however, with some remarks on the method of interpreting Platonic dialogue, and the relation in that literary form of the beliefs of the author and the main and subordinate characters in his casts.

My thesis is that, once we have discovered how to interpret the Platonic dialogue as a literary form, and have applied this discovery to interpreting the *Republic,* some traditional vexed questions about Plato's political and educational theories find easy answers, while others disappear.

I am particularly dubious about the assumption—first introduced by Aristotle in the lectures we now have as his *Politics* II—that Plato himself is responsible for every statement of his character, Socrates, in *Republic* V (not to mention some ideas Aristotle claims are put forward by "Socrates in Plato's *Laws,*" where, of course, Socrates does not appear).[1] How responsible is an author for his characters' opinions? A lecturer on "Shakespeare as Political Conservative" who gives us a pastiche of quotations from Hamlet's stepfather, Richard III, and Caliban as the author's true view would leave one remarkably unpersuaded; and I am left in that same condition by Aristotle's critical lecture.

The interpretation that I will defend rests on the following assumptions.

The Platonic dialogue is a way of presenting philosophy in which dramatic action and philosophic argument interact to form a genuine whole. This means that the widely current style of discussing only "philosophic argument" and setting aside "literary ornament" is bound to miss many important points.[2]

The dialogue form, as Plato develops it, is capable of two types of "self-instantiation." In the earlier dialogues, the cast and action give a concrete projection of the abstract argument. (Professor James Haden has called this device "existential re-entry," a phrase I rather like.)

The cast is chosen to instantiate the theme discussed; and the discussion leads in turn to changes in thought and feeling which have implications for the cast's action. The action gives concrete examples that illustrate, and sometimes contradict or modify, the propositions of the "philosophic argument." (It is interesting, and appropriate to Plato's Socratic heritage, that it is not always clear just what these modifications are: should we infer from the final "some other time, Socrates!" that Euthyphro has left without bringing his charge of homicide against his father?)[3] Once we recognize this interaction, it sometimes turns out that there are unexpected relevant relations. My own favorite illustration of this is the *Meno*. Meno opens the conversation by assuming that if virtue can be taught, such "teaching" must be by *precept* or *example*. Meno himself, student of the master rhetorician Gorgias, and an accomplished public speaker, is Plato's dramatic representative of the *precept* method. Anytus, admirer of the heroes of Athenian democracy, is the spokesman for the "example" alternative. Socrates uses yet a third method, a point emphasized when Meno, having watched Socrates experiment with the Slave Boy, agrees that the Boy has not been "taught" anything.[4] When the argument concludes that virtue is not taught, that conclusion still depends on Meno's tacit "precept or example" dilemma. We are left to ask whether Socratic method, which is neither of these, has or has not improved young Meno even during his brief encounter with Socrates.[5] But one need not be so exotic in looking at cast and theme: we can recognize at once in Critias and Charmides the two extremes of character which are opposite ways of missing the virtue of temperance; or in Hippothales and Ctesippus, a pair of opposite personalities who, gentle and spirited, fail to achieve friendship.[6]

If this is true, we should expect the two casts of characters in the *Republic* (the larger group of Book I, and the three main speakers of

Books II–X) to offer some similar dramatic instantiation of the theme of "justice"—both of popular opinions concerning it and its dialectical definition. When we recognize that Plato's context includes three important ethical ideals, which will match his psychological notion that there are three "parts of the soul," at least one reason for the selection of the casts becomes apparent. One of these ideas, Hesiod's ethical notion of the calculating middle class, is well described in J. M. Robinson's *Introduction to Early Greek Philosophy*; Eric Havelock, in his *Preface to Plato*, brings out the second ideal, of Homeric warrior as ethical model; Plato himself dramatizes yet a third ideal in the person of Socrates.

But in some of the later dialogues, and in *Epistle VII*, we find a different kind of self-instantiation. In these cases, where a *method* rather than a *virtue* is the subject of discussion, the dialogue itself *uses* the method it *discusses*. (Professor Haden calls this property "methodological re-entry.") That the methodological self-illustration in the later dialogues is intentional is made clear by the Stranger from Elea in the *Statesman*, when he tells Young Socrates that the true purpose of their discussion has been to illustrate "the great method of division."[7] That enterprise, as the *Sophist* and *Statesman* carry it out, is complex. (Various important insights are contained in the comments of L. Campbell, A. E. Taylor, Stenzel, and some others; and more recently, of V. Tejera.)[8] The same principle can be seen at work in a much smaller compass in the "philosophical digression" of *Epistle Seven*. Discussing the "means of gaining knowledge" (names, images, and definitions), and "knowledge and its object" which lie beyond them, Plato first *names* these five, then offers a general *formula* for each, then an exhaustive set of *"images."*[9] He goes on to criticize the "means" from the standpoint of "knowledge" and finds them all "unstable." Finally, from the nonperspective vantage point of "the thing itself," he offers a critique of Dionysius II's claim to have written a textbook of Platonic metaphysics.[10] Different contexts, in these later dialogues and letters, both show and talk about different methods, or moments of method. We find a "mental gymnastic" in the *Parmenides*; an "art of division" in the *Statesman*; "philosophical rhetoric" in the *Phaedrus*; and I will suggest that in the *Republic* we will discover the method of "dialectic."[11]

At least four organizing principles operate together in the *Republic*. On the level of drama, there is the challenge to Socrates to persuade Adeimantus and Glaucon of the *intrinsic* value of justice. Each of the main trio of characters speaks for one of the three "parts of the Soul," and the dramatic development moves from tension to harmony between them.[12]

The discussion itself has a balanced open-and-close bracket treatment of themes, which seems designed to guarantee *completeness* of treatment, and also to contribute an aesthetic symmetry. The themes can be briefly identified as justice as it figures in religion, in literature, in psychology, in social class structure, and in philosophy (where its relation to cosmology is also studied). The center of symmetry is the discussion of higher education and The Good; this is the only theme that does not receive double treatment.[13]

A third organizing principle accounts for the shift between the larger cast of Book I and the three-person cast of the remaining nine books. In the first book, we find spokesmen for "common sense," popular views of justice, based on various sorts of evidence. The first pair of speakers, Cephalus and Polemarchus, make this point clearly. The father is a spokesman for business ethics and for the myths of the poets who discuss religion. He is a representative of the appetitive part of the soul, of the middle-class tradition which is one part of the ethical heritage of Plato's time, and of the man who takes the poets as authorities.[14] The son is a spokesman for something more like an army officer's morality—do good to friends and evil to enemies—which makes him a representative of the spirited part of the soul. This is more a popular idea of justice in the Homeric tradition than in Cephalus's middle-class view.[15] But, like his father, Polemarchus bases his ideas on the authority of poets; Thrasymachus and Cleitophon represent a pair of "common-sense" views one level higher on Plato's divided line. Where the first two speakers appeal to poetry, Thrasymachus appeals instead to arts and crafts, to everyday experience, and to the operation of courts of law. His notion of justice as a successful capture and control of wealth and power depends, evidently, on the dominance of the spirited part of the soul, but this part acting on behalf of both itself and the appetitive.[16] This, then, carries forward Polemarchus's view, but restates it on the level of *pistis*, as opposed to *eikasia*. Cleitophon may be needed for symmetry—carrying Cephalus's orientation to the next level—but his identification of the "true interest" of the stronger with the "apparent interest" marks a very brief contribution. (Plato may have originally intended to give Cleitophon a larger role; the unfinished *Cleitophon* in the Academy's manuscripts could indicate what that role might have been.)[17] The crucial point here, however, is that Socrates catches Thrasymachus in a legal technicality, and so "out-quibbles" him. By appealing to the legal fiction of the flawless expert, Thrasymachus inadvertently turns his ruler into a benefactor, not an exploiter. The next move, when Glaucon and Adeimantus take over in Book II, is an ascent to the level of *dianoia* in the discussion. We go beyond empirical accounts, or poetic fantasies, to begin building general theories explanatory of human nature and conduct.[18] From this point on, we are working in a frame of reference which extends to the third level of the divided line.

First, the "aggressive man" view anticipated by Polemarchus and Thrasymachus is given a nice Hobbesian formulation by Glaucon.[19] Then, as an alternative, Adeimantus accepts from Socrates an "appetitively oriented" model which Cephalus would have recognized; in the limited sense that in it economic motives wholly determine human behavior, this is a Marxist rather than a Hobbesian model.[20] In short, the dialectical movement of Books I and II takes us from vague popular beliefs to focused technical discussion, by six stages, reflecting two aspects of human nature and three levels of the divided line.[21]

From Books II through X, there is a dialectical movement from becoming to being, then back to becoming, which combines a "vertical" pattern of progression with the "thematic" sequence already mentioned. Thus, a discussion of poetry is followed by one of psychology, psychology by politics, politics by education, as the argument approaches the science of dialectic and its subject-matter. One organizing principle is that of attempted consensus; another is that of presupposition. Thus, at each point, Socrates tries to find a place both for the views of Adeimantus and those of Glaucon (a state including both producers and protectors is one such attempted synthesis). The second principle is seen in the fact that poetry is evaluated by its psychological effect, psychology understood by an appeal to social order, and social order made to depend on sound direction of education and legislative policy.

The whole scheme hinges, finally, on proper education; and proper education culminates in the study of dialectic, following a rigorous course in the mathematical arts. What "dialectic" can be, however, is a much-debated point. Socrates in *Republic* VII is not of much help in response to Glaucon's question about "what parts and powers does dialectic have?"; he simply says Glaucon is too uneducated to understand![22]

Plato's readers have supplied their own ideas. These range from A. E. Taylor's Leibnizian notion that dialectic will deduce every detail of history and reality from the knowledge of the good, through F. S. C. Northrop's idea that the Good is an organizing structural property of the system of mathematical forms, to the Christian notion of The Good as a supreme being known by mystical encounter. It can also be seen as wishful thinking on Plato's part, the description of something not yet invented, but that he hoped the Academy could discover; or of something not yet invented by the dramatic date of the *Republic*, but developed in the Academy by the *Republic's* actual date of composition. It might even, it has been suggested, be a fiction, a mystification used to persuade his audience of Plato's claimed supernatural superiority; an unbased claim.

In cases such as this, a close look at the relevant text is surely not out of order. And the first thing that strikes me, at least, about this capstone of the argument is its supposed function in the total educational scheme. On the one hand, we have the preliminary study of mathematics as a "pure" model of logical precision in reasoning.[23] (The actual "ten years" I take to be hyperbole, exaggeration to underscore the rigor and purity of these studies.) On the other side, after this course, we find the graduate gaining practical experience in social and legal administration, policy making, and the like.[24] It seems obvious that this requires the function of "dialectic" to be the transfer of methods studied in mathematics to the subject-matters proper to political and social science. It raises major metaphysical questions when we ask whether and how such a transfer is possible; but the curriculum Plato outlines seems clearly to introduce dialectic as a study presupposing this possibility.

But in that case, it seems to follow that the focus of the course in dialectic, having to do with theory construction in social science, is exactly the theme of the *Republic* itself in its attempt at systematic explanation of human behavior.[25]

A first sign that this use of the principle of interpretation that I have called "methodological self-instantiation" is correct, is the isomorphism between the stages of the "divided line" and the levels of discussion both in Book I and in Books II–VII. Before working this out in parallel column, however, I would like to pause for a closer look at the line itself. For while Socrates does not spell out the study of dialectic, he does offer Glaucon *four* accounts of The Good, a set of four using the Line as ordering principle. Briefly, the Line as it is first introduced is a sort of taxonomic cabinet for kinds of "knowledge," ordered in terms of "clarity" and "certainty." In the Myth of the Cave, the Line receives a literary projection, and orders the stages of a story. In the ideal curriculum, the Line is a road map of stages of learning, a key to the *technique* of higher education. In relation to its own highest level, the vision of the Sun as causing and relating being and knowing, I believe we must think of the Line in its totality as a measure or criterion of completeness. The account of the Good Socrates gives Glaucon is a *good* account because it is, in this sense, a *complete* one. We find the Good on the level of fine art, of educational practice, of theoretical hypothetical-deductive explanation, and as an organizing principle holding these together.[26]

Now, there is no doubt in my mind that the Divided Line, which is an organization of inquiry as well as of static knowledge, is in fact the organizing principle of the contextual discussion. The movement of Book I and the early part of Book II from *eikasia* through *pistis* to *dianoia* is so direct, and its stages so neatly marked off, that it must be intentional. (Thus, even if Book I was originally a separate, inconclusive Socratic dialogue, it has surely been reorganized with this anticipation of *Republic* VI and VII in mind.) The becoming-to-being development of the discussion as it goes from poetry through psychology through society to philosophy is also organized along this route.

So far, then, as "dialectic" is a systematic inquiry designed to move from guesswork to science, the *Republic* is in fact an example of it.

But we are told a bit more than just this in Socrates' account of "dialectic" in *Republic* VII. It is preceded by a discovery of "what the mathematical sciences have in common." Earlier, I described this as an abstract subject-matter and a method of pure logical rigor. The order, however, involves something like a "principle of plenitude" instead of the "reductive" order that someone like Archytas would have preferred.[27] Keeping this fact in reserve, the next thing to notice is that dialectic "does away with" hypotheses, using them as steps for an ascent, rather than fixed starting points for a deduction.[28] Here the context helps clarify an obscure text. For it seems to me that both the men of Glaucon's and those of Adeimantus's states are "hypotheses" explanatory of human behavior. The peculiar problem of "dialectic" may result from the fact that, whereas the "principles" of mathematics seemed to classical thinkers to be a unique set, the "explanatory generalizations" available as principles of social science or value theory admitted alternatives. In these cases, the problem of exclusive but consistent and at least partially confirmable abstract schemata can be seen as a conflict of "hypotheses." If we are to end up with a sound theory, we must in some way overcome the apparent exclusiveness and partiality of these.

How this is to be done is indicated in two ways in Socrates' brief account. The "hypotheses" are to be transcended, by reference to some more general principle. And the result is to be tested by seeing whether the new account is "synoptic"—inclusive and complete. "Synopticity" and "synoptic vision" are the critical characteristics of dialectic and the dialectician.[29] (Consistency in deduction is the corresponding characteristic of mathematics and its practitioner.)

Given this much indication of what "dialectic" should do to move from guesswork to theory, from fact to value, let us look again at the view of human nature that is developed through *Republic* II–V. The interesting thing is that there seem to be *three* "hypotheses" presented in this discussion. We have seen the "aggressive" and "appetitive" aspects of human nature abstracted by Glaucon and Adeimantus, and projected by them into models of society. What about the rational part of the soul? It is presupposed by the provisions for education and social direction in Book IV; but what exactly would the "hypothesis" of human rationality lead to if it were treated as alternative to the social models constructed earlier? Socrates himself answers that question with his account of the purely rational society in Book V of the *Republic*.[30] A good final theory must combine, in a complete view of human nature, the three alternative "hypothetical-deductive" models of Socrates, Adeimantus, and Glaucon. To do that, the three should first be stated separately. When we note that in the dramatic development, the three main speakers tend to follow quite different lines of thought up to Book VI, and to act independently, we may take this as confirmation of our notion that their three distinct views need to be fused together.

The actual doctrine that lies behind the discussion here is that the human soul is *essentially* rational; if we want to see "its true nature," we look to this part alone.[31] But in human life, both spirit and appetite are—however logically expendable—existentially necessary.[32] The tripartite soul must form some sort of unity in any relevant ethical theory.

Thus Socrates' deductions follow well enough from the postulate that man is essentially and exclusively rational. The model *is* "possible" because there is in fact this aspect of rationality. But the three parts of Book V set up the Socratic utopia first by removing all appetite, then all possible negative effects of spirit, then all ignorance. The result is a projection of *one part* of the relevant data just as surely as the two earlier models were.

This suggestion is historically important. Since Book V has usually been taken as Plato's own utopian political model, and discussion has not centered on this point but on its feasibility, the suggestion quite changes traditional interpretation.[33] First, this state is *Socrates'* construction, not Plato's. Second, from its function in context, it is an *incomplete abstraction,* not a prudential blueprint. It is at the same time critically relevant—for man's reason will prove his most important capacity for social activity—and yet ironically incomplete. Socrates can at the same time put forward this community of saints as an ideal yet describe it as a daydream.[34]

Thus the men and women of Book V are part of an abstract model showing what society would be like if human beings were completely rational. Vanity, competition, and property have no place in such a scheme. But Socrates' utopia rests on the true but incomplete "hypothesis" of human rationality. That this is true, if incomplete, is also Plato's view. And it follows directly from the theory of forms that women have the same rights and responsibilities as men, since both participate in the common form of humanity. But it does not follow that they are indistinguishable as individuals or equally lovable. That is true because the human beings we are discussing are complexes—mind, soul, *and* body; spirit, appetite, *and* reason. And this complexity means that other qualifications must be added on to the pure form that is the starting point of the model society of Book VI.

The recognition of higher education as the key to a new and more comprehensive theory of justice, which follows in Books VI and VII, is largely Plato's own. And yet, having seen in Book V that Plato's Socrates has tendencies toward formalist exaggeration which his author does not share, we may want to allow for *some* lingering touch of this in his account of education. (He stresses the purity of the mathematical sciences at the expense of their ordering in successively greater comprehension; but it is the comprehensive extension that will be the clue to harmonious, systematic order.)[35]

What must be done is to explore this notion of a dialectical confrontation and synthesis of hypotheses by a rereading of the latter half of the *Republic*, to see whether the new synthesis serves to explain human nature and conduct, to define them, and to offer normative standards for their actualization throughout the different dimensions of appearance, becoming, and reality.[36]

At the same time, we should perhaps review the past interpretations both of Plato's political notions and of his Form of the Good. The political notions are less eccentric than is often supposed. The ideal is a society with functional classes, so organized that the claims alike of appetite, spirit, and reason are satisfied. Policy will be guided by reason, and education will equip legislators to formulate policy by the use of objective criteria of goodness. Where reasonableness and arbitrary custom conflict, the social order should move toward what is reasonable. (Equal rights and political duties for women is a case in point.) Where pure reason and impure human existence diverge—for example, when reason is incarnate in a self that also has appetite—harmony is the goal. (After all, Socrates stays in the Piraeus expecting to eat a dinner and watch a race as well as to engage in conversation.)[37]

There is no doubt, however, that Plato supposes questions of value—beauty, justice, and truth—to be objectively grounded, and rationally decidable. His science of dialectic aims at exactly such a method of discussion and decision.[38]

Chapter 3

Republic *VI: The Divided Line*

I. Introduction

By the fourth century B.C., philosophic writing stabilized in two main genera: dialogue and didactic exposition. The choice of form reflects two different ideas of what philosophy is, and how it can be taught. If philosophy is an objective, demonstrative enterprise, on the model of physics or mathematics, then there are problems and solutions which can best be presented in uninterrupted lecture or treatise form. But if philosophy is essentially, not accidentally, a shared inquiry—an inquiry in which it is pointless to offer answers until the reader has become completely engaged in the questions that they answer—then it is best communicated in some species of the dialogue form. There are three main genera of philosophic dialogue: the Socratic, the Ciceronian, and the didactic. In the Ciceronian dialogue, an underlying Academic skepticism is expressed in a balanced comparison of opinions regarding ultimate questions that have no final answers; there may be engagement, but there is not a metaphysical or logical sense of direction. In the didactic dialogue—for example, in Augustine's *De Magistro*—the master knows the answers and the respondent merely agrees and asks for passing points of clarification; there is, we might say, direction (as there is also in the formal lecture) but no real engagement. In Platonic dialogue, engagement and direction combine.

But how do they combine? First, through an intrinsic relation of the drama and the dialectical theme. The meaning of an idea is given us by the actions of the characters who accept it, as well as by what they assert. The characters in each drama actually undergo some development as the discussions move on. The dialogue as a whole may present us with a case of self-instantiation which adds to or qualifies the ostensible "conclusion" of its argument. Philosophy in this mode is radically reflexive; and its presentation, consequently, self-referential. Unlike the omniscient lecturer, the Platonic character—or reader— cannot step outside of his human situation to appraise or counter an isolated philosophic argument.

In the late dialogues, we find a different structure: here the self-reference is methodological far more than existential. By this I mean that the statement of a method takes place in a context where the method in question is employed and illustrated in leading up to the formulation of it. In the middle dialogues, both of these types of self-instantiation are employed simultaneously.

But Plato does not stop here in his attempt to secure engagement; the reader is led to identify himself with characters in the drama, and to shift that identification as the development goes on.

My present theme is the element of *direction*. Shared inquiry takes place in the context of a metaphysical scheme, where we all share some divination, however dim sometimes, of the existence and nature of the form of the good. The result is that if investigation progresses, it finds us moving from one sort of thinking and evidence to another in our pursuit of a good account; and, if we are sincere, the stages of approach are the same regardless of differences in starting-point. The existence, attractive power, and epistemological location of the good are constantly shown by the direction of shared inquiry. The road map that gives us an abstract view of this orientation is the divided line in Book VI of the *Republic*. This offers us a key to the direction of discussion in the Platonic dialogues in general. In addition, however, I hold that this diagram in context represents a sound direction for our contemporary inquiries, once the line is understood.

How are we to "understand" it? The answer is, by seeing it from each of its own four levels of cognition: it functions differently for every one, and a synoptic view of the four should be as adequate an explication as we can give. This is using the property of self-instantiation to explicate a single geometrical image in a dialectical context, a project that the reader may well think unpromising.

Before we are done, however, I hope to have shown that the line functions on the level of *eikasia* as a concrete picture that provokes inquiry into the relations it represents; on the level of *pistis*, the line is a map of stages of inquiry, an ordered method of learning; on the level of *dianoia*, the line is an epistemological (and by implication an ontological) taxonomic table, allocating kinds of object and knowledge to classes; on the level of *noesis*, the line is a criterion of completeness, by using which we can evaluate inquiries, sciences, images, and systems. The figure in fact functions in all four of these ways in the *Republic* itself, as I intend to show.

II. Eikasia

The most technically difficult part of this interpretation is the one that seems least important, the recovery of the actual picture of the diagram. But I think it worth some effort at reconstruction, since the picture itself should give us an intuitive preview of the relations to be treated more abstractly later, and should offer provocation to inquire further.

The actual *picture* of the line should not be as vague and detached from all context as later reconstructions have made it appear to be. A suggestion here is that Plato still presupposed a feeling for mathematical metaphor and symbol which dissipated by the Hellenistic period, so that the original directions, in context, carried both more specificity of design and more suggestiveness of contextual relation than has been recognized.

1. *Actual later designs.* These vary in respect to whether the orientation is vertical or horizontal; vary in whether the segments are represented as equal or unequal (or whether the segments are represented at all, rather than being replaced by an array of ordered terms); vary in which type of cognition is represented by the longer segment, when the segments are unequal; sometimes redesign the figure as a tree or set of arcs; seem to have no definite principle of relative length when an unequal segment figure is present. (As a sample, I have taken the *scholia vetera;* Bessarion's *scholion;* Adam's diagram; Cornford's diagram; Iamblichus's reported diagram.)

2. *Orientation.* The purpose of this design is to help Glaucon visualize two things: the distance that separates the knowledge of the philosophic ruler from that of the political technician; and the location, in the "logical space" of the forms, of the form of the good. This relates directly to the pervasive metaphors of height, ascent, and descent in the context of the dialogue. The metaphor of altitude seems to be the key to the vertical organization of the progress of discussion from becoming to being then back into becoming, as a thematic balance provides the horizontal order of topics and accounts for changes in speaker. However typographically inconvenient, it should be clear that the line is *vertical*, not horizontal, in its orientation. (A horizontal line suggests either a temporal order of progress or a taxonomy of entities on the same level of reality. The first suggestion is not incorrect, but it is not the relevant point in the present measurement of distance of degrees of reality; the second suggestion is entirely misleading, and would transform Plato's scheme into a diagram more suitable for illustration of Kant or Aristotle).

3. *A line means a line.* To serve its function as a measure of vertical (being-becoming) distance, the line must be a line. Suggestions (e.g., Robinson's),[1] that any set of four distinct regions, kinds, or compartments will serve as well misses the relations—in addition to difference—of continuity and altitude which the image of a line provides. It is a more extreme extension of the notion that the line can be drawn horizontally, which we suggested disconnects it from the contextual metaphors that give it an ontological dimension. The notion that the line could just as well—or better—be a tree, or set of connecting class-inclusion arcs, on the other hand, does away with the sharp differences in kind between levels, by suggesting that the lower are included in the higher, where the moral of the scheme is rather that they are transcended by it.

4. *The segments are unequal.* This is clearly the right text; the notion that *anisa* is an incorrect gloss on the direction to cut it in two, since such cutting means bisection in ordinary use, simply points out why *anisa* is needed to make the directions explicit. It is true that this will run into incompatible mathematical metaphors presently; but to equate the segments loses the whole metaphor of increasing unclarity as the distance between the knower and the object of cognition grows greater. (Compare the many references in Plato to opinion and conjecture as dreamlike states, in which the object of thought cannot be clearly seen, as though it were at a distance. In the *Republic* itself, the comparisons of the search for justice to a hunt stress the need for a *clear view* as the quarry is approached.)

But this use of "inequality" implies that the longer segment is not the better; quite the contrary. A similar equation of larger distance with greater ontological distance from the real and the good figures in the tyrant's number, where the interval of 729 states separate the just man from the tyrant. This result fits well with the Pythagorean preference for arithmetical *simplicity;* the smaller numbers are somehow clearer and better. (Plato may sacrifice this inequality, however, when he wants to use the line as a component in constructing other figures, where a different geometrical function will serve the same purpose of representing ontological distance.)

The opposite view has in its favor the increasing extension (hence, perhaps *synopticity*) of the ascending types of knowledge. Against this, however, we must notice that what is involved is greater *certainty* and awareness of the role played by the good, and that neither of these properties is a necessary consequence of increased extension leading to greater generality. In fact, if we were to follow out *this* way of interpreting our picture, we might well find general knowledge empty, and merely potential as compared with knowledge that is more specific—a line of thought Aristotle uses in his ethical and metaphysical critiques of Platonism.

The picture, then, is vertical, with the segments unequal, decreasing in length as they go from the one representing *eikasia* at the bottom to that representing *noesis* (and the point representing the good?) at the top.[2]

4. *The line is only one of a gallery of pictures in the* Republic. This involves a kind of mathematical imagination wholly foreign to us, lending a felt ethical and political relevance to the design.

The *Republic* uses mathematical images for purposes of illustration a number of times. The branches of mathematics from which they are drawn run from arithmetic through one-dimensional geometry to plane geometry to solid geometry to astronomy—with uses of harmonics bracketing the sequence from the one-dimension static to three-dimensional dynamic images at either end. (I do not, of course, mean that "analogy" and "harmony" are relevant only to the initial musical scale and the state comparison, and the final "music of the spheres"; as a matter of fact, whenever the *proportions* of the geometric figures are relevant, there is an internal relation).

The images in question may be worth tabulating.

1. A number and its factors—Book I.
2. A scale and temperance—Book III.
3. A line and levels of knowledge—Book VI.
4. A triangle, elaborated into a solid, as stages in the "decline of the state"—Book VIII.
5. A solid constructed from a plane base by squaring and cubing—Book IX.
6. An astronomical model, with balanced properties as sensible evidence of "cosmic justice"—Book X. (In this last model, Sirens stand upon the moving hemispheres, and "sing in harmony.")

(The "cycle" (*kuklos*) in Book V is an instance of "technological-mechanical" rather than "mathematical" imagery, I think.)

Between 3 and 4, we are introduced to a mathematical curriculum, in which the rigorous method of mathematics is extended to relational systems of increasing complexity. The sequence of its studies matches the sequence of mathematical images we have just noted.

The point of this note is that a modified projection of the line (in which its vertical orientation and four segments are retained, but the inequality of segments is unspecified) figures both in the initial right triangle of the nuptial number and in the underlying matrix of the tyrant's number. The line should thus be pictured as part of a pattern of increasing complexity, functioning as a principle of order in the realms of political and psychological study in Books VIII and IX of the *Republic*. Conversely, overtones of symbolic significance reflect back on the line in this context, when we locate it among the other pictures. The main importance of this is the *eikastic* suggestion that our diagram is not to be thought of as isolated from that wider context; and that in that wider context, it has symbolic overtones that are not immediately evident.

5. *The segments of the line are incommensurable.* This follows if my suggestion is correct that "in the same ratio" refers to the "mean and extreme ratio" section. In this case, the line as Glaucon (and the reader with wax tablets) is first directed to envisage it relates directly to the class of mathematical images of incommensurability used by Plato throughout the dialogues as a symbol of the difference between knowledge and opinion. (The two references to incommensurables—roots and surds, and rational and irrational diagonals—in the next image of the *Republic* set bears out this notion that there is an intersection here with this other class of symbolic designs.) The segments cannot be understood separately, if we try to measure the whole by any one of them; yet they add together to produce a unit line. This reminder of the *Meno* and *Theaetetus* constructions and the problems they symbolize adds another dimension of significance and "provocative interest" to the drawn figure. (I find no scholiast who has actually pictured the line with segments in this relation; but that does not change my conjecture that this should be done.)

6. *In other contexts, not all of the properties of this picture remain invariant.* What does remain, in the subsequent diagrams, is the vertical orientation, the continuity, and the division into four main segments. But this seems legitimate for a symbolic design, functioning on the level of myth and conjecture.

III. Pistis

Although Plato puts the line forward as a timeless scheme of taxonomy, it proves useful in other contexts as a device for locating and ordering temporal stages of inquiry. In that role, it offers a technique of investigation, at once a key to the historical evolution of Greek philosophy and to the stages that must come in sequence in any philosophical investigation. (It is particularly suggestive to the modern philosopher to notice that these stages exactly match Whitehead's sequential moments in his "rhythm of education," and those, in turn, match his account of the "phases of concrescence" in his metaphysical theory.) This temporal functioning of the line at once indicates the importance of *continuity* in the diagram we draw, and the possibility that concept formation cannot begin on the more abstract levels without preliminary concrete experience.

The first book of the *Republic,* and the opening of the second, must do three things. First, they must establish the real relevance of this discussion: the motif of a choice of life for Adeimantus and Glaucon helps to do that. Second, they must move the discussion beyond the confusions of common sense notions and uncritical popular opinions to an analysis of the nature of justice in its own right. Third, if one reading of the dialogue is correct, they must illustrate the method of "dialectic," as a way of anticipating and giving some content to the cryptic description of this "science" in the ideal curriculum of *Republic* VII. At the same time, these sections may help us to understand the kinds of knowing and objects known that the four levels of the line set up statically.

I think the point can be made quite clear with a simple paraphrase, keeping interpretation to a minimum, of the cast and conversation given in the text itself.

The theme of justice is first introduced by Cephalus. A retired wealthy manufacturer of shields, living quietly in the Piraeus, he first is described as a sort of picture of the old age of a just man. With his sons about him, garlanded, seated on a throne, he is a striking figure. At the outset, however, Cephalus is less concerned with justice than with the journey of the soul from life to death. As an old man, he takes more seriously the stories told by religion, and is thankful that his good fortune has made it possible for him to pass through life with all just debts paid, both to men and to the gods. This opening theme is balanced by the account of the return of the soul from death to life in the Myth of Er that concludes Book X of the *Republic.* Socrates notes that Cephalus's notion of "the right thing to do" is simply an uncritical acceptance of business ethics. No doubt this "keeping the ledger balanced" is what passes for justice among the retired businessmen of his generation whom Cephalus knows. This is the kind of proverb that cannot go very far as an adequate definition; but Cephalus is satisfied with it. He has no desire to examine his ideals but leaves the argument to his son, Polemarchus, and goes to sacrifice. Now, what kind of "knowledge" does Cephalus have? He appeals to religious myth and to business practice; he does not follow the standard practice of citing poets as authorities, nor has he learned through experience what the consequences of justice and injustice are. He is not a theorist nor a lawyer but a respectable aged man. (It may be an unkind suggestion, but we may see Cephalus as the prototype of the soul in *Republic* X who never was unjust because he was never tempted to be, and who chose the life of a tyrant from the samples offered.)

Father and son, two generations, together offer us spokesmen for knowledge based on convention and conjecture. Polemarchus cites the poets as his authorities, and interprets them in the manner of a young army officer or a Mycenean hero. Justice seems to him the military virtue of "helping friends and harming enemies"; he pictures himself in the role of a character in epic poetry. It takes only a brief question from Socrates to point out that in real life, as opposed to poetry, friends and enemies are not so simply distinguished—in life, unlike television Westerns, not all the good guys ride white horses, not all the bad ride black! He is equally simple-minded in his concept of "harm" and in his notion of justice as "a useful craft." Simonides' saying "to each his due" sounds wonderfully persuasive; but his young admirer cannot interpret the inspired saying. (Polemarchus, like the father of the oligarchic man in Book VIII, is about to be dashed against the rulers of the state. His assassination by The Thirty is perhaps foreshadowed here by his concern with gallantry and war. In any event, the kind of knowledge he displays can count at best for *eikasia;* he has apparently chosen a role from poetry and begun to play it without even reading the part carefully.)

So much for the first two popular notions of justice, resting on myth, proverb, and poetry. Thrasymachus is posing as a political realist, as he interrupts to advance the argument to another level. The things that stand out in Thrasymachus's encounter with Socrates are three. First, he is a legal technician: Shorey's notes indicate his use of "accuracy" as technical terminology from contract law, and in his later characterization of the stronger as error-proof he introduces the "legal expert" as a fiction to evade a line of questioning he wants to avoid. Second, his arguments are appeals to experience—to what we actually see happening to just men, unjust men, ruler and subject. Experience has convinced him that the king as "shepherd of the people" accepts this role because he is looking forward to fleecing and barbecuing the sheep. (Incidentally, this is an analogy Socrates had used to characterize the rule of The Thirty). Third, Thrasymachus practices what he preaches: he tries to overpower Socrates in argument, sets aside his own beliefs in the interest of a contest of debating strength, loses his temper.

My main point is that Thrasymachus is not, either in disinterested standpoint or in actual doctrine, a political theorist; he is rather the empiricist who knows how things happen, and the technician able to argue powerfully. It is because his thesis is an advance beyond mere hearsay, to a level of experience and art, that his case is generally recognized by readers as wholly different in strength from the notions of the first two speakers. But it is because of failure to recognize the difference between a sardonic technician and a genuine theorist that the same readers feel that Thrasymachus is treated unjustly. In fact, he seems to get exactly what is his due: he is tripped up by his own legal technicalities, and outmanoeuvered by Socrates. The "strong man" who, by hypothesis, has the art of rule and, therefore, never mistakes his interest, is introduced on the pattern of the legal "expert" in medicine or navigation; and when *that* analogy is pressed, Thrasymachus has lost his case.

His ideas, however, are taken up by Glaucon and Adeimantus as the second book opens. Glaucon comes forward with assumptions about human nature which are general and which lead deductively to a "social contract" theory of the state.

Here we need careful reading to identify what is happening. In the first place, Glaucon, unlike Thrasymachus, is talking about what justice is, and is offering a general account. His brother, Adeimantus, less a theoretician and more practical, offers concrete confirmation by his observation that what priests and parents really praise is *apparent* justice, not the *reality*. (From this point on, the brothers stay in character: it is Glaucon who follows the more technical and abstract discussion as respondent, while Adeimantus comes onstage to offer objections that an ordinary man might make, to work out details of application, to check Socrates' accounts of inferior states and errors in content of pure poetry.) Now the case against justice as intrinsically good or as profitable has been made stronger by being generalized and put on a deductive basis. The brothers are genuinely engaged in the inquiry, unlike Thrasymachus, and Socrates can no longer do his work simply by citing empirical counterexamples or by refutations resting on technicalities.

If the topic under discussion were geometry or chemistry, it would be clear that a shift has been made here from experience to hypothesis, *pistis* to *dianoia*. Given Plato's project, revealed in Book VII, of taking mathematics as the preliminary model for "dialectic," which is to reason about ethical and political problems, it seems fair to describe the present development in the same way.

But who is Glaucon talking about? Not about actual tyrants, law courts, or clients; not about characters in poetry (though he does open with the myth of Gyges); but about "anyone" who had Gyges' power to commit injustice, and "anyone" else judging him. In short, he has set up a theoretical construct of "human nature" as aggressive and greedy.

In chemistry or geometry, the inquiry might stop for a time at this point. Given a periodic table or a Euclidean set of principles, a considerable genius for inquiry and a considerable period of history might be necessary before anyone asked *why* the table was organized as it is, or *why* these axioms were suited to the theorems of geometry (how they function, for example, as special cases of "harmonics," the general theory of quantitative relational patterns.) But in dealing with society, it is immediately clear that there are *alternative* abstract explanatory constructs that account for human behavior. Socrates and Adeimantus promptly offer one of these—in the form, later to become standard for Western political theorists, of a fictitious account of "the origin of the state." If Glaucon's natural man sounds like Hobbes, the new greedy consumers and producers are much closer to Marx or Locke. "Anyone" will recognize that his *needs* are best satisfied by peaceable economic cooperation; by an extension, the same rule holds for the satisfaction of his *wants* as well.

The clash of hypotheses now requires some third model, and the three-class state, with isomorphic three-part soul, will be put forward as the needed hypothetical construction. The explication of the presuppositions of this scheme, the outlines of the roles its citizens play, and the testing of theory against historical and psychological fact will occupy the remainder of the *Republic*. We must be sure that this third account is consistent and comprehensive; that it is a good one.

For my present purpose, however, I can stop in Book II. For it seems clear that the organizing principle of the discussion has been the Divided Line. A diagram brings this out.

CEPHALUS: EIKASIA, AND
POLEMARCHUS: EIKASIA::
THRASYMACHUS: PISTIS, TECHNE::
GLAUCON: DIANOIA, HYPOTHESIS::
SOCRATES, ADEIMANTUS: DIANOIA, ALTERNATIVE
                                         HYPOTHESIS::
SOCRATES: ATTEMPT AT SYNTHESIS INTO A THEORY

We move from hearsay to a discussion which tries to criticize, compare, and transcend "hypotheses," not being content with deducing the consequences of each of them. This will be exactly the function of the art or science of "dialectic" when we meet it in the ideal curriculum of Book VII of the *Republic*.

IV. Dianoia

It is easier to recognize the difference between "knowing" that is mere conjecture and "genuine science" than it is to explain in detail how the objects of each differ in status and stability. We can take a simple example—a chemistry student will do—and run through the kinds of knowing that he achieves as his education goes on. But when we try to classify and supply the entities he "knows" at each stage, we find ourselves faced with intrinsic metaphysical difficulties, complicated by apparent ambiguities in Plato's own account.

I have used the example of the chemist before, because I have some personal feeling for the first three stages, and because it lies nicely in between the nonexperimental but purely formal world of logic and mathematics and the radically vague but concrete world of politics and ethics. Imagine a young boy who has just been given a chemistry set. It is romance unlimited; he has no time to read the labels or the manual, but must handle each small bottle in turn—open it, smell it, look at its color when he dissolves it or pours it into a test tube. He will invent his own stories about the reagents; perhaps some are hostile and other friendly; or some light, others heavy; or some pretty, others ugly. Having seen movies and TV commercials featuring scientists, he strikes the pose of a laboratory research worker as he mixes things in the dramatically held test tube. His uninitiate young friends may mistake him for a real chemist: he has the equipment and the right professional air. His father, however, if he has any sense, will start the two of them reading the manual and working out some standard experiments together.

After a while, having read the manual, the young scientist emerges as a chemical technician. That is, he knows as a matter of past experience what mixtures will produce interesting results; what changes of litmus paper color test for acids and bases; how to produce hydrogen sulphide and Chinese gunpowder, or invisible ink and glycerine soap. *Why* any of this works as it does remains a mystery; but *that* it works, he has discovered; mix so many parts of this with so many of that.

The high school chemistry course, in which the periodic table figures, comes as a new revelation. Now the student knows why the reactions proceed as they do. Taking account of valence and the balancing of equations, he can calculate and predict reactions without having to try them out. The taxonomic table with predictive value represents a crucial step beyond funded experience, into a new level of generalization.

In fact, however, one more question needs to be asked: Why does the periodic table work? After all, there could be any number of classificatory tables. Here we move to the level of basic chemical theory— into atomic structure, equations of energy level, principles that the successful table presupposes, but does not define.

It takes no great imagination to see mathematics as analogous to chemistry in this sequence of kinds of knowing (though the final step, when for example we look for the principles of the multiplication table, is much subtler, since we don't usually envisage *alternative* possible tables of multiplication). Nor is it hard to see how the analogy might suggest a program for ethics and politics: the classifications of kinds of personality and audience in the *Phaedrus*, for example, as well as Glaucon's notion of the natural man who finds justice a necessary evil, look something like the mathematician's tables of factors or initial definitions of figures.

The problem begins when we try to say what it is that the knower on each level has as object of his thought. The account of *eikasia* in the myth of the Cave seems to involve two contradictory properties in its objects. "Shadows or reflections in water," the natural phenomena that a released prisoner is first able to recognize, are a pair that involve an appearance-reality distinction; but the two types of derivative relation are opposite in kind. The *shadow* is a sharp quantitative projection, but wholly deficient in catching any inner qualitative detail. The *reflection*, particularly in water, is qualitatively like the thing reflected, but wavering and deformed in outline. We get no help on this point by closer scrutiny of the apparatus of the puppet-show in the cave, nor by a more inclusive perspective of the context.

The puppets casting shadows would suggest at once translucent colored outlines. But we are also told that they are "made of wood and stone and other materials." Perhaps one reason for this is that the solid puppets were the only type controlled by strings or inner wind-up devices that would *seem* to give them a motion of their own. Certainly another reason is the desire to use a metaphor of three- versus two-dimensionality to bring out the lower degree of reality of the projection. The vagueness and variability of outline which holds for the later reflections in water may be contributed here by the dimness and flickering of the fire which is the machinery of shadow-projection. The guessing games played by the prisoners, who confuse temporal contiguity with causality, underscore the total independence of each shadow-item as they perceive it. Yet behind the wall there are the concealed masters of the puppets; showmen, who make the shadowy parades enact stories of adventure, of processions and battles, of peace and war. It would be a mistake to overlook them; but their contribution is to supply a context in which some "and after that, this" aesthetic principle does relate the shadows on the screen.

In context, we seem to confront the shadows on either side of *Republic* VII. In the final Myth, they are the "paradigms of lives" from which souls choose their next incarnations. In the third book, they are the heroes held up for admiration by popular authors of poetry. (In the first book, they are the criteria by which Polemarchus is inclined to decide what constitutes just and unjust behavior.) Like the shadows, these roles are two-dimensional; in the third book, at least, their adventures are paratactic. In our age of television, it is hard to appreciate how beautifully Plato projected the oral tradition of his time into isomorphic *visual* imagery.

But what is the status of these projections? They surely are not the "forms" we hear about in the middle books of the *Republic!* They are individual and idiosyncratic, useless as class definitions or general normative criteria, even too unstable to be the fixed meanings of names that communication requires. They are, however, atemporal—through a lack, not a positive reality. This suggests the following metaphysical comments.

1. *Eikasia* has as its object either of two things: roles as written parts—as it were—and roles as observed performances that we may imitate. (The boy imitating the scientist on the TV commercial, who is himself as actor following out the commercial writer's script, illustrates this point.)
2. The two terms, *eidos* and *paradeigma*, in *Republic* VI and *Republic* X *do not* coincide in extension; *paradeigmata* include *whatever* ideals, conventions, or fictions can be taken as objects of technological or ethical imitation; *eidē* are at the least general natural classes or types; at the best, ideals that can serve as criteria. Consequently, atemporality alone is not a sufficient condition for something to qualify as a "Platonic form."
3. *Eikastic* objects become opaque if we detach them from their context; like textbooks, the lines of each character keep making the same speeches to us; there is no conversation, no encounter with a soul. They give an illusion of coherence and causal sequence within their aesthetic context—this is why one must

beware of the enchantment of Homer. They project genuine types and ideals with such mad and wide indexes of deviation—the distortion of reflecting rivers, of brightening and dimming firelight—that only someone blessed with a gift of divination can discern the realities and ideals they imitate and resemble.

I have often thought—and once briefly suggested in a short paper—that Whitehead's "eternal objects," construed as novel possibilities for ingression, are like and overlap the eikastic paradigms of Plato's Myth of Er. The roles in the set of sample lives—unlike the eternal forms—vary with history, and admit of constant novelty. No Mycenean could have chosen to incarnate the form of courage by choosing the part of an astronaut; no tyrant could have dabbled in nuclear demolition. The conjunctions of simple qualities and structures that Whitehead sometimes identifies with his complex eternal objects sound very like the conjunctions of properties in the sample lives that Socrates enumerates in his final advice to Glaucon: "We must observe which combinations, of wealth and poverty. . . ." In short, the mistaken identifying of an *eidos*, known only on the level of *noesis*, with the evanescent and deviant *paradeigmata* that outline projections on the level of *eikasia*, has led to needless anti-Platonic criticism in process philosophy. We may still not want the really stable *eide*; but we need not reject them from a claustrophobic notion that there is an eternal fixity of roles which rules out all ontological status for historical creativity or novelty.

What sort of things are related to our guesses and conjectures as the puppets in the cave are to their shadows? The answer is the public objects in the physical and social world, connected by causal relations which make *techne*—production, prediction, and control—possible. The contrast between a craftsman who makes a real bed and the painter who makes an image of it is offered as a key to this distinction. Poetry and conjecture deal with perspectives or refractions from the things in the technician's domain.

The main defect in this kind of knowledge is the dependence of its object on time and other contexts; a second defect is an intrinsic ambiguity in the object itself. (This is particularly clear when we look at customs and laws, which I am including here as types of "object.") A technique does not understand the causes that account for its success, and, therefore, when it is uncritically repeated, runs the risk of misfiring because some crucial factor has been left out of account. Open lamps attached to miners' hats are technologically suited to give light in a coal mine—so long as there is not an explosive concentration of gas there. Naval power is the key to security and empire—until air power displaces it. And so on—funded experience gives only probable results, a commonsense that can be outrun, an unconscious assumption that "other things will be equal," when in fact they seldom are.

One of the key topics of classical rhetoric was the dependence of values on context. This proves fatal to the attempt to reduce ethics, for instance, to a series of objective rules which are situation-independent. "Gold is the beautiful," says Hippias to Socrates, replacing the general answer the latter wanted by a concrete specific instance. But he quickly takes this back when asked whether he would prefer a golden mistress to a living one! Lying is usually bad—but surely not *always* so, as the "technological" approach might suggest.

Plato has a reputation for deprecating arts and crafts, and for shortchanging physical reality and empirical encounters with it. But as a matter of fact, he seems to do neither in his actual philosophic practice. He is short on what we might call pragmatic theory in his metaphysical discussions largely because it seems to him that this is an area of agreement, well enough understood by everyone, about which there is nothing mysterious to be said. What *does* need saying is the unsuitability of substituting common sense for more abstract theoretical explanation and study. But—confirming what was said before about the Divided Line as road map for a technique of inquiry—at every point we pass through the findings of ordinary language, common sense, and special craft as a stage in investigation more stable then individual random imaginations.

To collect a full anthology of relevant references in Plato's text would not be worthwhile for the present discussion. But what *is* worthwhile is to point out the context in which the "deprecation" of arts and crafts occurs. We tend to forget, because history has preserved only scant allusions, that one Sophistic project was to displace the "useless" liberal arts with "knowledge" that was good for something. Thus we have, on the constructive side of the project, Protagoras's pamphlets on various techniques—for example, wrestling; Hippias's essays towards works of reference and his achievements as a weaver, ringmaker, and cobbler; and Prodicus's greater lectures on correct use of language. As critical moments, there are still on record Gorgias's demolition of the pretensions of philosophy and cosmology, and Protagoras's critique of pure mathematics as inapplicable to real phenomena. Naturally enough, the counterattack blasts the limitations of arts and crafts— sometimes rather more snobbishly than a good American would wish— but against a background that presupposes the exaggerated claim made for them.

A further point that may well figure in this controversy is the role of convention and invention in ethics and politics. There had been a great upsurge of ingenuity—and optimism—over the operational devices by which technology could ensure fair pricing, impartial jury-trial, equal opportunity for office holding, scrutiny of judges, and so on. It would be a temptation, and one the Sophists succumbed to, to identify the conventional character of the operational definitions with the nature of the concepts so defined. And so we find a hesitation on Plato's part, which A. E. Taylor emphasized, to talk about an "art" of justice or an "art" of living well. In the historic context, such an "art" might seem on a par with a new way of cornering the market or loading the ballot box.

But, on the other side of the ledger, Socrates' constant counter to the relativism of the Sophists is the difference between the amateur and the skilled artisan. This line of argument is common to early, middle, and late dialogues. And Plato's own references to the arts and crafts, whenever he wants to move discussion from individual idea to a more stable basis of universal experience, are ubiquitous and encyclopedic. (In this connection, it is interesting to notice that the preparation for mathematical studies in the *Laws* is handling activity of a technological kind. It is as if the student could not appreciate pure formal concepts without the previous challenge of operational experiment and puzzle.)

The objects of *pistis* are a mixture of being and non-being. They have relatively persistent identities in space, in time, in language, and in practise, which the phantoms of *eikasia* have not. They have a status in a public world which goes with this stability; their credibility, as it were, can summon many witnesses in its support. And yet, this identity does change both with place and with time; and pure conservatism will always prove fatal as it is outrun by history. In the *Cratylus*, we get a reflection of this analysis in the notion that names have been given by poets, by legislators, and by mathematicians; but for correctness of naming, the dialectician should be the authority. In the *Statesman*, we find that the translation of ideals into actualities requires *art* as the middle term in the procedure. In the *Timaeus*, natural science rests on the efficiency and intelligibility of the work we should expect from a divine *craftsman*.

As a final footnote, it is instructive to look at the references to arts and crafts, and their functions, in the *Republic* itself. In searching for types and regularities in phenomena that offer a key to generalization, art and craft, knowing how to get results, funded experience, lead the way.

One could wish for more analysis on Plato's part of the sensible, public world which he takes as obvious. In the *Parmenides*, for example, the notion that a physical thing can be analyzed into contrary properties is dismissed as too familiar to be puzzling; in the *Philebus*, the "mixed class" is explained through being fractionated into the components of the mixture; in the *Timaeus*, the cause of individuation comes out of a matrix difficult to discover and even harder to describe.

But clearly the referents of *pistis* are the familiar items of our experience, and in Plato's view these present no special problems for the interpretation of his figure of the line as a scheme of ontological-epistemological taxonomy.

The entities that are referents of the kind of "knowing" that lies on the third level of the line are the ones that cause considerable trouble. There are five reasons that, conjointly, account for much of this troublemaking power.

1. Although what we are concerned with as philosophers is the ontological status *in general* of the objects of *dianoia*, what we are given in most of Plato's discussion is the special case of mathematical knowing. This leaves us in exactly the position of the student in the ideal curriculum who has worked with mathematics as a preparatory study, and is now left, in his course in dialectic, to perform the generalization and transfer to other subject-matters as a further step. This may be consistent on Plato's part, but it creates difficulties on ours.

2. The difficulties are compounded by what at first seems a helpful supplement: the explication of Plato's notion of "intermediates" by his prize student, Aristotle. Aristotle, too, is inclined to argue the case from mathematical examples; though he does, from time to time, indicate the more general applicability of his paraphrases and criticisms. But Aristotle had committed himself to a view of the foundations and nature of mathematics radically different from Plato's and his paraphrase is refracted through the lenses of that alternative standpoint. (Or at least, the view he attributes to Plato is different from the dialogues which seem clearly to be alluded to in Aristotle's restatement.)

3. As has been noted, the history of ideas has brought about shifting concepts of what it is to be a Platonic "form"; and, even without Plato's restriction of his examples to mathematical examples and Aristotle's obscuring of the issue by his injection of a divergent view of mathematics, this shifting context brings complications. It becomes almost impossible, if "forms" are re-

construed as realistic "universals" or empiricist "ideas" or Kantian "concepts," to recognize what on earth a distinctive set of
"objects of *dianoia*" could be.

4. We are impatient with the precise uses of analogy Plato sets out
   in explaining the proportions connecting the two subdivisions
   of each segment of his diagram. We know that the *key* structure
   is the being: becoming continued proportion that relates all
   four; and we can see that an interference of two spatial metaphors makes it impossible to incorporate this proportion *and*
   the notion of "unequal segments" into a single figure. But,
   given so much, we are inclined not to persist in wondering why
   Plato himself holds fast to his metaphor of proportion so firmly
   in his comparisons of the relation of the first and second segments to the third and fourth. Yet there could be a sound dialectical reason for directing our attention to a limited relational
   pattern which lacks the full scope we eventually hope for. Half
   of that reason may well be negative: the attempt to take an
   incomplete account too literally is corrected by a built-in mathematical impossibility. But that should be only half; the simile
   of the sun is "demonic hyperbole," yet illuminating!

5. We have probably lost the key to much of the "mathematics"
   that Plato's student is supposed to bring with him when he
   confronts the mathematical projection of the metaphysical
   scheme.

Beginning with the fourth difficulty, let us see whether our exploration of the line thus far helps toward a solution. What about the
insistence that the relation of *noesis* to *dianoia* is the same as that of
pistis to *eikasia?* Whatever the analogy is, it must not involve time,
since although the shadows, reflections, laws, and objects of the world
of "opinion" are temporal, those of the upper two segments emphati-
cally are not. But can it involve "projection"? That was the crucial
relation in the myth between substance and shadow. If it does, one
would expect dianoetic objects to have the sort of thin context independence, with sharp edges, that the shapely shadows on the screen pos-
sessed. One would expect a hidden dimension of causal connection to
be visible from the level of *noesis* which is not so on that of *dianoia*.
One would expect the same multiplicity of perspectives to relate one
"form" to its many associated "hypothetical projections" that relates
one three-dimensional "puppet" to its projected shadows. And the
young scientist who is satisfied that he knows the causes of things because his taxonomic table predicts their combinations and operations

should be told that he must still look for the justification of his table on a higher theoretical level.

In the second place, if "the same relation" is supplied for the two others, we would expect some counterpart to the "reflections" of the myth as well as to the "shadows." The shadow has sharp structural outline but not internal qualitative similarity to the projected object; the reflection has a vague, wavering structure, though qualitative resemblance remains. So the dianoetic entities that project a form should have a plurality about them, a range in some field of logical space where we recognize them as forming a family, but where we have difficulty in a precise delimitation of their boundaries.

If we press the *eikastic* analogy still further, we may want to transfer another relation as well. The rigidity of the puppets is responsible for the identifiable, sharp, but isolated outlines of the shadows they cast, and in some cases for appearances that are taken as causal connection. (If the horse-puppet with a wavy mane is in fact a rigid part of a horse-followed-by-chariot-puppet, for example, we can safely bet that the chariot-shadow will come next after the wavy-maned horse-shadow.) The difficulty in precise identification is a result of the machinery of projection: the firelight wavers, and the outlines sometimes blur. The annoying variability in the order of the parade is a result of the different stories the masters of the puppets invent and act out. (These stories, in turn, are selected aspects of adventures in a real world, and may vary in their truth or falsity.)

I am suggesting the following: (1) If we disregard the fire and background wall, and focus on each shadow, it is sharp but thin; externally related to the other shadows, but readily identifiable in each occurrence. (2) If we pay attention to the wall and fire, the individual shadows look less sharp, and it is not so clear where "one" begins and ends relative to "another one." *But* we can pay attention to this aspect only when we are far enough on our way out of the cave to see the shadows in the context of puppets, firelight, and wall. As long as we are chained in our places, we have only the view of the brittle patterns to go on. (3) It will only be after leaving the cave that we can look back and recognize the puppeteers, and see that they are playing out stories and roles based on a world of nature which lies outside. Their various purposes and persuasions unify the multiple fables and allegories that dictate alternative sequences. This is the suggestion we are given when we try to picture objects of *dianoia*.

Suppose we move to the next step, and ask how these objects are related to the technique of inquiry, to the level of *pistis*. My conviction is that once we go beyond guess and sheer historic fact the dianoetic objects are what we are talking about. In other words, when the *Republic* examines the consequences and predictive value of alternative general assertions concerning human nature and conduct, those assertions are dianoetic "hypotheses" to be confirmed by deduction and prediction and to be transcended by combination, rejection, or generalization. This assumes the earlier explication of dialectic as inquiry, and *Republic* I and II as examples of it. The comparison with mathematical postulates is as misleading in one way as it is illuminating in another here. The illuminating thing is the arbitrary character and one-directional functioning of the "postulates" of the mathematician. He asserts the existence, exactly as defined, of his calculator's units, arithmetician's odd and even number classes, geometer's lines and three kinds of angle. He gives no further account of those, but works out deductive proofs and applications of their consequences. His starting-points are incorrigible; if you try to chop up the computer's units, he simply multiplies (preventing "fractions" from messing up his system; they can get in only as restated in the form of ratios.) In this sense, the "natural man" of Glaucon or of Adeimantus or of Socrates is like the deductive system framed by any of these "postulates"; the postulate is incorrigible.

The comparison is not illuminating—at least not to us—because Plato's world of mathematics does not seem to provide for alternative possible systems of arithmetic or geometry. What is the relation between two different explanatory "postulates" in this formal scheme? Logically, as abstract postulates, it seems to me that all we can say about them is that they are *different* and, usually, *inconsistent* because of that difference. But, going back to the fifth difficulty above, it is not certain that Plato saw the world of mathematics as quite so clear, closed to alternatives, and free of tension as we think he did. Aristotle, at any rate, devotes two baffled lectures to distinguishing the existential status of the entities postulated for computation (sets "having multiplicity") and those postulated for number-theory ("numbers" which don't seem to be identical with aggregates of units).

The conclusion that one draws from this is that the domain of dianoetic entities on the third level is very close to our modern realm of "hypothetical constructs"—sharply defined, nontemporal entities derived by selective abstraction or generalization. Staying within mathematics for the moment, these are neither forms nor objects but intermediate schematic instances of forms, selective abstractions from objects. Metaphysically, they present an interesting problem. If we take each instance of "triangularity" separately, we have a multiplicity of distinct, separate abstract types of triangle—just as we had sharp separate shadows in the cave. If, however, we take a different view, and try to define the projection of triangularity into a mathematical space that admits of shape, of great and small, the total set of triangles adds up to the undifferentiated field of projection itself. The unity of a given mathematical triangle thus involves something more than the unique form of triangularity, and also something less than the comprehensive field within which the many instances of triangle are superimposed as they are projected.

By an analogical extension, the dialectician can say the same things about the other "hypotheses" and "forms" he is studying.

I think that starting with my fourth difficulty has helped to resolve all five; and, in particular, to justify my notion that "hypothetical constructs" is a good modern translation for the third-level entities that are the objects of *dianoia*.

The proper conclusion to this moment of exploration is to draw up a taxonomic table of atemporal entities, corresponding to the different kinds of knowing.

EIKASIA: "Roles"; "notions" derived from poetry and myth.

PISTIS: Physical objects, actual or imagined; techniques; customs and laws representing public consensus.

DIANOIA: Abstract descriptions of classes; formal models; the objects of "hypotheses" in mathematics, and by extension, in inquiry generally; taxonomic classificatory tables.

NOESIS: "Systems"; forms in context; criteria for evaluation; explanations of the reasons for the conjunctions of abstract properties that make up an effective taxonomic classification.

All four of these entity types are "atemporal"; all four, in one context or another, are referred to in the *Republic* as paradeigmata. All four, also, are considered as *eide* by Aristotle, *if* atemporality is taken as a condition for something to count as "a Platonic form." The *first* group—concrete sensible snapshots—are the "ideas" of British empiricism, which historically have suggested one interpretation of "forms" in the history of Platonism. The third set are the "universals" of Aristotelian and Medieval logic, which have suggested an alternative (equally unsatisfactory) interpretation. (In particular, the language of self-predication will lead squarely into paradox if "forms" are construed in this way.) Perhaps the Marburg School interpretation of these forms as concepts, and of concepts as rules for schema construction, counts as a second-level identification. The forms as fourth level are none of these, clearly; but it is less clear what they *are*.

V. Noesis

I have said that the line, looked at from the standpoint of its own fourth level, serves as a criterion of completeness, by which we can distinguish a good from an inadequate image, inquiry, or scientific explanation. My case here rests on three points. First, this function is suggested by the picture of the line as we reconstructed it above. Second, this function corresponds with the actual scope of Plato's inquiries. Third, this way of looking at the line is philosophically suggestive in the twentieth century. But for my present discussion, this fourth moment must be presented only in outline; its explication in detail, if that is possible in discursive form, would evidently be coextensive with presenting a complete systematic philosophy.

That the diagram is meant to be a complete picture is surely indicated by the location at the top of the figure of the form of the good, a form beyond which dialectic cannot go. That it is a picture in which the good is responsible for rational order of the relation of the lower segments is suggested by either of two pictorial properties. On the one hand, if we accept my suggestion that "unequal and cut again in the same ratio" would suggest a mean-and-extreme ratio construction to Plato's reader, the segments that add up to a single unit are incommensurable with one another—with the (accidental?) exception of the middle pair. But if this is doubted, and doubted partly on the ground that irrational versus rational magnitudes are usually represented by a side and a diagonal in Plato's imagery, there is a second suggestion. In the Nuptial number, the initial figure, from which the rest is developed, is a 3-4-5 triangle; the side of 4 is one of the two sides that yield the hypotenuse as a *resultant* diagonal, though in this figure the diagonal and sides are commensurable.

Without engaging in undue phantasy, note that the relation of incommensurable lines—diagonal and side—figures in the mathematical imagery of two passages in contexts where the relation of knowledge and opinion is central. The problem is to relate and transform the measure of one into that of the other, by adding a new dimension. But the background suggests that the sides jointly *produce* the diagonal as their resultant or offspring. There are thus two problems: (1) How are the pair of unit sides "productive of" the square root of two irrational diagonals; (2) How is this perverse offspring to be named and assigned a *logos* within the geometry established by the "unit lengths" of its ancestry?

The line, with two pairs of incommensurables added together to produce a final unit line, looks like the completed solution of a geometric puzzle. If we have all four pieces and arrange them vertically, the scheme comes out a rational whole even in one dimension. If we go back to the two-dimensional construction, we see how the lengths are related, and why this arrangement ends up rational and complete. But without the key of the construction, no rational fraction of the total line, taken as a unit, will exactly measure the two-times-square-root-of-five sections; and the solution presupposes seeing the line as single whole.

How far this echo of the root-and-surd symbolism is deliberate, and how far it is persuasive to a modern reader, I am not sure. But I am sure that the picture of the line presents a synthesis in which the elusive irrationals have found a place, and have been combined in a pattern where their sum is rational.

Along the same line of interpretation, the inquiry into justice of the *Republic* follows a thematic pattern that is complete only when it has moved from the vague but vivid world of myth and poetry to a high point of abstract focus, then back to poetry and myth again. The structure of inquiry, I have argued, is a double one: horizontally, there is a thematic balance; vertically, a becoming-to-being symmetry. The horizontal "themes" are religion; myth and poetry; the soul, its parts and virtues; the state; and in the symmetrical center, the good. These recur, after the good, in reverse, close-bracket order. It is only within the final myth, and its account of the return of the soul from death to life, that the initial questions of Cephalus and Adeimantus find an answer, the choice of life-styles of Glaucon and Adeimantus finds justification, and the inquiry finds its conclusion. The vertical movement—after its ascent from guess and trust to rational hypothetical-deductive method in Books I and II—is a straightforward ascent and descent of the levels of the line. The ascending moments look constantly for form—for what is single and essential, lying beyond the multiplicity of phenomena; the descending moments use the central principles as explanatory, and, by adding logically inessential but existentially unavoidable properties and deviations, try to reconstruct the complex phenomena in a more ordered range. The symmetry is atypical of Platonic dialectic, but the sequence is not. The progress of discussion from personal notions to the more stable foundation of expert opinion, then beyond this to the greater clarity of a scientific definition and deduction, is a standard Platonic pattern of inquiry, from the earliest dialogues to the latest.

On the level of *dianoia*, the line is a criterion of completeness in another, logical, role. Suppose that we construct "world hypotheses," based upon the various sections of the line all with atemporal entities proffering "explanations" of phenomena. Is there any reason to choose Plato's version out of the set; is there not, on the contrary, good reason to choose, as more simple, any of the alternatives that involve less ontological commitment? Since what we are concerned with is philosophic *knowledge*, the ontological question can be restated and tested epistemologically. If we try to construct a unified philosophy from any isolated segment or incomplete set of segments of the four-part taxonomy of "knowing and its cognate objects" set up by the line, what will happen? Looking back again at our picture, we would expect that there would be real difficulty in finding a logos for knowledge or reality, because such a *logos* would presuppose a rational *measure*. Or, put another way, we would expect all such attempts either to generate systems that were radically open because they involved regress, or radically incomplete because they concealed the actuality of kinds of knowing or of being that were not constructible from the elements they had postulated. I was led to suspect that this is in fact an organizing philosophic principle of a central group of later dialogues from my adventures with the *Parmenides*. Take the whole scheme of the *Republic* except for *noesis* and the good, and try to give a coherent account of unity and plurality—properties basic to definition or intelligibility. What is the result? A maze of antinomies in which open regresses haunt the logician. What about a scheme that proposes the reduction of "knowledge" to "opinion"? This was a Sophistic proposal, but the *Theaetetus* shows its inadequacy by proving opinion and knowledge "incommensurable": we cannot generate the latter from the former, yet we must give some account of it. Still, the *Theaetetus* recognizes a distinction—after Socrates has persuaded the ghost of Protagoras— between eikasia and pistis, expert and inexpert "opinion." Perhaps a true dialectical hero—a Megarian or Eleatic—could reject even *that* concession, and put his ontology entirely on a single plane of timeless phantasms, *eikastic* entities? If so, his attack would have to be purely logical; for if he began on the level of common sense, that would commit him to the existence of a kind of knowledge irreducible to opinion. But in the *Sophist*, Plato explores just such a radical reduction. The Sophist rejects any talk of "degrees of reality" as meaningless, since it involves an apparent reference to non-being, and instead he presents us with a frozen world as a totality of externally related fact, in which "totality" is not to be construed as an "entity" of another order. The trouble with *this* project is that it does not account for the necessary stability of significant discourse, which requires both etymology (terms having fixed public meanings) and syntax (categories of relation by means of which combinations of terms into assertions are possible). Non-being gets back in—first as logical otherness, then as truth-functional otherness, then as existential otherness—and once back in, sets the stage for a new analysis which would retrace the *Theaetetus-Parmenides-Republic* hierarchy. (Rather as if one should go from Wittgenstein through Dewey through Russell—in his more realistic phases—to Whitehead).

The *Statesman* concludes the dianoetic voyage of exploration with a qualified return to the *Republic* once more. Practical decision can neither be wholly guided by an abstract vision, nor wholly unguided under power of forces of cosmic history: it presupposes normative measure, as an art. This art sounds like "dialectic" under another name, and its introduction sets the stage for posing a final alternative to the "man as measure" thesis of Protagoras that was central in the *Theaetetus*. Whether Plato planned a final *dianoetic* counterpart to the *Parmenides* that would spell out this presupposition, or thought he had provided it either in the *Philebus* or the *Laws*, or decided it could not be provided after the failure of his lecture on the good, we do not know.

But the line as criterion of completeness, on the level of *dianoia*—of the logical and epistemological coherence and completeness of a system of entities—seems to be the background frame of construction for the "logical" series of "later" dialogues that follow the middle period.

What about the line as criterion of completeness, viewed from its own highest level? Clearly, this should give us a way of telling whether or not the account of "the good" is a good account, at least "good" in the sense of being complete. "Complete" here would mean *inclusive* of all the entities that figured in the dianoetic taxonomic survey, and *explanatory* of the cross-level causal relations that hold them together. In other words, if Plato were using his line in the self-referential four-level pattern that has been suggested, the account of the form of the good, in *Republic* VI and VII, would have to present its vision from each of the four levels. It would make philosophy and education easier if one could start at the top, with a direct intuitive vision of the good—"beyond knowing and being, yet the cause of both"—in itself. But, without a substructure of formal science, practical experience, and personal engagement, such direct presentation is dazzling and unclear. The simile of the sun, which is as close as Socrates can come to such a direct description, provokes Glaucon into his response: "By Apollo! What demonic hyperbole!" Well, one might try to show Glaucon where the good resides by a dianoetic table, of a taxonomic kind, locating it in an ontological space in relation to the cognate objects of "knowledge" of various kinds. And just that is the function of the diagram of the Divided Line: to give an abstract, dianoetic projection to the dazzling direct vision. But how do simile and schematism relate to *us?* Where are we as individuals; in the sunlight, or in the cold atemporal diagram? Only a poem or myth can describe the existential relevance of the good, in its story of "prisoners like ourselves," by a projection "downward" two levels of reality of the distinctions of the line, so that our immediate perceptions are of shadows of statues of individuals which are instances of the structures that schematize forms! One thing is needed to complete the account: a *technique* by which we can move toward a recognition of the good, a key to the cave's allegory. And that is exactly what we are given by the ideal curriculum of *Republic* VII. There, we work through the successively more comprehensive formal postulates of abstract mathematical science, until we are ready to pursue "dialectic." That pursuit will begin by seeing "how the branches of formal science are akin"; it must proceed, if it functions as it is assumed it will, to transfer this insight from mathematical to other, social, ethical, and ontological, subject-matters. And when the transfer is completed, we will have found an adequate instantiation in the *Republic* itself. The four accounts of the good add together to emphasize a causal connectedness which was no less apparent in the nondynamic diagram of the line. The power of the good reveals itself in the mutual relevance of each level to the others.

As a postscript, let me add that a look at current discussions of educational theory seems to confirm the intrinsic philosophic soundness of the suggestion that the "criterion of completeness" function of the line is its proper *noetic* philosophic role. Sometime ago, the N.E.A. worked out a taxonomy of current positions in educational philosophy. These were existentialism, with a stress on creativity and individual authenticity; pragmatism, with a stress on social effectiveness and technical efficiency; and liberal arts humanism, with a stress on mental discipline and recognition of form. Not mentioned was a ghost of "Idealism" which came back to life to haunt commencement speeches, but offered only an ideal, not a position or program. Each position could argue, and—as I recall the controversy—did argue, that *without* its distinctive emphasis, an educational program would lose something important. Each tended to go on and claim that therefore, *with* its distinctive emphasis accounted for, a program would be a good one. Each, that is, except "Platonic idealism": that was limited to pointing toward a dazzling goal of human betterment, attractive but not easy to view steadily. However, if we can persuade the idealist that his goal connects with us, our social world, and our intellectual power, as the stages toward its concrete approach, he suddenly can see that the three positions were not, as they seemed, incommensurable, but that they add together to produce a single unified temporal, or taxonomic, or aesthetic, line.

First published in the Philosophical Forum, Vol. 2, Number 2, 1970–71. Reprinted by permission.

Chapter 4

Republic *VII: The Ideal Curriculum and Education*

This chapter has two main parts. In the first, I will reconstruct Plato's proposed ideal curriculum from the *Republic*. Some relatively recent new interpretations of the dialogue add sharpness to this reconstruction. I will argue that the plan seemed to Plato a "realistic" one insofar as the educational project matched his analysis of the levels of reality and their connection. In particular, the figure of the Divided Line functions both as a metaphysical summary and as an educational guideline. In the second part, I will suggest that our contemporary educational philosophy, and philosophy in general, have lost touch with Platonism and the Platonic tradition. But in spite of this, the twentieth century schools and discussion fall into a general grand pattern that the reader of *Republic* VI–VII finds completely familiar. As examples, I first take the *N.E.A. Yearbook* on Philosophy of Education (1954); then Morton White's anthology of twentieth-century thought, *The Age of Analysis* (N.Y., 1964). The *educational* positions of Existentialism, Pragmatism, and Liberal Arts Humanism recognized by the N.E.A. exactly match Plato's *eikasia, pistis,* and *dianoia*. But the N.E.A. treats these as *practically*—and implicitly, I think, as *logically*—incompatible. A survey of the contents of a decade of issues of *Educational Theory* finds that this same general attitude and three-way classification remains operative in educational philosophy. White's set up of three main contemporary tendencies, Existentialism, Pragmatism, and "Analysis" (a very mixed bag as he illustrates it), is similarly isomorphic with Plato's Divided Line.[1]

These same families continue to be the major positions, and to engage in mutual debate, from 1954 to about 1984. A content survey I did found the three positions and their differences dominant in the *Philosophy of Education Society Proceedings* for the period 1960–1975. Nathaniel Lawrence and I found the classification a useful and relevant one for our *Philosophical Themes in Modern Education* in 1974. And I was able to use it again to help locate and develop a process philosophy educational theory in my *Whitehead, Process Philosophy, and Educa-tion*, published in 1982. A book by Brian Hendley studies the practical work of educational theorists. His selection for detailed study consists of one representative each of analytic philosophy (Russell), pragmatism (Dewey), and process thought (Whitehead). Russell's stress on logical discipline aligns him with the educational theory group of liberal arts humanists (however strongly they differ as to the possibility of disci-plined treatment of ethics and aesthetics); Whitehead's emphasis on "Concreteness" and "depth of individuality" shows his close relation to the educational theory group of existentialists (though, again, there is a difference in the extent to which process and existentialism view hu-man existence as "absurd").

After 1974 or thereabout, there is a tendency in both educational and general philosophy to focus on increasingly smaller specific prob-lems, and a new crosscurrent of debate in the education field over the proper balance of the disciplines of *philosophy* and *education* in "phi-losophy of education" (or "educational philosophy").

White is convinced that speculative system building, of a Platonic sort, is futile. His editorial remarks also suggest that decision criteria *among* these three families of philosophy depend on *taste*—for ex-ample, on tolerance of vagueness as a price of generality. (Although his selections somewhat hide the opposition between Pragmatism and Positivism, the addition of Russell's chapter on Dewey from the for-mer's *History of Western Philosophy* would certainly bring this out.)[2]

Yet once in a while, even today, a stray glimmer of Platonic ideal-ism still appears. Plato's Cave, for example, figured in a recent wel-come to Yale's freshman class. But the idealism seems to be reserved for ceremonial occasions, such as graduations and perhaps fund-raising appeals.

I think that Plato had excellent general ideas both about the dif-ferent dimensions of reality and about the possibility of a realistic phi-losophy of education, which would see these levels "synoptically" in a coherent relation. And I think we ought to look at these ideas again. (A first step toward such a second look is my *Whitehead, Process Philoso-phy, and Education*, Albany, 1982.)

I have focused on the N.E.A. Yearbook and White's anthology because they illustrate the point I want to develop particularly clearly. (And when we are dealing with a twenty-five hundred year sweep through time in our history of ideas, two or three decades seem much more a part of the *present* than of the *past*.)

Plato had already mapped out, in the *Republic*, an ideal curricu-lum.[3] It took account of the multiplicity of *aims* an educational system must have in order to serve a complex society which depends on special-ization of functions. At the same time, this curriculum took account of the complex nature of "reality"; and if, in the end, the prizes for being "most real" went to the world of forms, the road to that domain passed through the theater, the market, and the Academy. For although the Platonic forms defined the types into which things fell, and offered attractive ideals, still the physical world of space and time had its own characteristics, and could not be reduced to forms without remainder.[4] If the form of cat was timeless and without weight or color, still each existent cat was orange, black, or some other color, with a definite weight, size, and age. And cats required food, which the ideal of cat-ness did not.

Furthermore, the forms were still more pluralized, temporalized, and modified by perspective as they appeared in the world of creativity, or fine art. For fine art was limited neither by the deductions of science nor the efficiency of crafts. The playwright and painter used imagina-tion to construct intense and exciting adventures in a realm of pure possibility. (It is here that the cat Garfield, hero of cartoon books and comic strips, belongs.) The range and order of *possible* worlds included much more variety, and in some cases much more of some types of unity, than did everyday life. The forms were still recognizable, per-haps, but only by someone able to adjust and synthesize an almost unlimited diversity of refractions.[5]

Now, while it would be foolish to accept imagination as equivalent to actual observation or scientific deduction, its products could have a special beauty that was not only *attractive* but educationally impor-tant. In fact, life would not be complete or civilized without music, painting, drama, and poetry. Plato further thought of dances, cho-ruses, processions as participatory forms of fine art. (Athletics, too, had its aesthetic quality, but its competitive character put it in a different category.) Just as the world of space-time *fact* was not reducible to pure form with no remainder, so the world of phantasy was not reducible to the world of fact. The fine artists "imitated" natural things, and used natural materials as media. But the creative power of imagination ranged far beyond the bounds of history; "imitation" of human beings was not mirror-like representation but more akin to new creation. One might then argue, as Plato did, that the fine artist's appearances are doubly removed from the *actual, unchanging, logically structured* do-main of forms. Yet justice, and temperance, and wisdom share the quality of beauty which fine art presents; and aesthetic sensitivity, de-veloped young, is crucial to later social effectiveness and engaged indi-vidual existence.[6]

But the world of form itself could be looked at in several ways. The discovery of this world took place originally in mathematics and physics, by the intellectual method of generalization, deduction, extension, and confirmation. In Aristotle's logic and Euclid's geometry, we will find a clear account of these structures in the world of form. Given definitions, postulates (= "hypotheses") and axioms, logical deduction could develop proofs by "if . . . then" reasoning. The valuable things about these formal systems were taken to be their *generality* and their *consistency.* Mathematical right triangles did not vary with the material they were made of, did not warp in a wet climate, or spoil a tiling because of an inexact fit. The *mental discipline* by which premises and conclusions were linked seemed a mode of thought that would guarantee avoidance of mistakes wherever that method could be applied. (Obviously, this could not be said of the method of imagination of the poet, or the technician's habit of the craftsman.)

This hypothetical-deductive approach can evidently be extended beyond the domain of mathematics and natural science. For example, if we could discover and agree upon a general definition of *human excellence,* or, if we could isolate what is essential to human behavior, we could *deduce* what would and would not lead to human betterment. (Compare Dewey's title, *Human Nature and Conduct,* which suggests the project though the book itself doesn't carry it out.) The abstractions we start with may be of many kinds; one might, for example, want to work out the behavior of an "economic man," a hypothetical ever-prudent consumer and seller.[7]

There are two evident defects in this kind of formal knowledge, however; and when one tries to build a social science on the model of mathematics, they are immediately evident. The *first* is that some phenomena admit alternative and exclusive "hypotheses." If Plato was mistakenly sure that there was only one meaning that applied to "all triangles are . . . ," he was correctly sure that "all men by nature are . . ." admitted more than one plausible meaning. So some further step was necessary to choose among or synthesize alternative consistent and (at least partially) confirmable generalizations. But the other thing about this deductive "knowledge," typical of professionalization, was its limited attention to anything outside of its assumptions. A modern chemist assigned the job of exterminating boll weevils might, for all that his chemistry cared, destroy the population of Mississippi. But in fact things—the forms included—do not exist in isolated specialized packages but in larger interconnected *systems.* And the forms that structure these systems are more like forms of *value* than forms of *fact.* (Completeness, compossibility, aesthetic contrast, mathematical simplicity, some types of symmetry. . . .) To go beyond the limitations of exclusive plurality and absentminded single focus requires some other method, of the same kind for both corrections.

The reader will be pleased to learn that this final study of the total system of the forms, which Plato calls *dialectic*, concludes the ways of knowing, and the inventory of things to know, and so would conclude and complete an ideal curriculum as well. Plato suggests that dialectic discovers "The Form of the Good" which is the organizing principle of the world of forms.[8] Presumably, Truth, Symmetry, Efficiency, Justice, and Beauty are reflections of this form on different levels of the appearance-reality scale.[9] From the place it occupies in the *Republic*, and what is said about it there, we can draw several conclusions about this elusively presented domain and discipline. One is that the Good is *comprehensive*: a person able to see things *together* ("synoptically") can become a dialectician, but others cannot.[10] A second conclusion is that dialectic will be concerned with *value*, not simply *fact* or *formal consistency*. A third conclusion (this one is inferential, but still seems to me certain) is that "dialectic" will include a transfer of the methods that have been successful in the natural sciences to the study of the more complex phenomena of what today we call the "social sciences," and to ethics as well.[11]

This introduction of The Form of the Good emphasizes something important in Platonism. This is that the forms are not simply classes and structures, but often are ideals as well. (Perhaps we see this most easily in the concept of "good form" in figure skating, diving, gymnastics; and in the concept of "good conformation" in dog, cat, and horse shows. Our ordinary language has some such idea built in: "he's a *real* shortstop.")

In the drama of Plato's dialogues, more perhaps than in their explicit statements, it is clear that the ideal acts causally on the actual. Thus the *Republic* reflects the conviction that the proper function of "political science" is to design an *ideal* state. The whole dramatic direction of the *Phaedo* is given by Socrates' pursuit of an ethical ideal. The *Philebus* presupposes that ethics is not meant to be a mere description of what is in fact the case, but rather that it should define "the good for human life." And finally an enlightened legislator will have an ability to choose among alternative combinations of statutes and policies.

Since this is the structure of reality, Plato can set out a *realistic* curriculum which is at the same time an *ideal* in its matching of increasing insight and increasing reality. His system has three institutions with separate admissions criteria and curricula, but sharing common aims of individual and general welfare. (One level, that of common sense and technology, does not find a *special* course or institution projected for it in the *Republic*. The *Laws*, later, suggests that this would be in order as an addition.)[12]

All citizens attend the public, first-level, school. There they pick up some basic skills—reading, writing, computation—which are more or less taken for granted. The main content, however, is "music and gymnastics." "Music" includes the whole range of literature, as well as song and instrumental music, and part of the study of literature is by *acting out* episodes and roles. "Gymnastics" includes dancing, and the idea of "grace" which is part of athletic training. (Compare the vase painting of young athletes practicing to music, Metropolitan Museum of New York, *Greek Athletic Games*, picture 1.)[13] The fundamental *aim* of this education can be described as "aesthetic appreciation." The theory is that children, "growing up with beauty and with grace," will recognize and prize these qualities later. This will lead to "temperance" or "moderation"—an avoidance of out-of-balance excess, and a friendliness between citizens with different vocations (for example, producers and soldiers). But finding suitable materials is not an easy thing to do. In the first place, we do not want ugly or trivial things to be presented as beautiful. In the second place, we do not want *socially undesirable* ideas (which Plato equates with *false* ideas) to be presented as fact. (A hero, for example, can't—by definition—have hysterics; so we must modify the story of Achilles.) In the third place, we want *aesthetic forms* which can lead on to a vision of timeless ideal patterns, rather than art that stops thought on the level of picture thinking and free association. Further, the students in this curriculum must participate; this is not passive; and they must do so without coercion; it is not slavish, either. (Advocates of "discipline" have never thought this last idea a good one; compare Kant's view that children should go to elementary school mainly in order to learn to sit still.) The whole society will share aesthetic awareness; even the furniture, and of course the architecture, must be beautiful. And the individual will act, appreciate, and respond with full engagement. (When and how far individual preference and taste will appear, however, is left unclear. It does show up constantly in Plato's myths, but tends to drop out in the abstract arguments).

A selected group of students will go on to the institutions of secondary education.[14] This is the training for future soldiers and civil servants with executive responsibilities. And this is to be a stage of discipline, first physical, then mental. The physical side will be taken care of by military training; the mental by mathematics and logic. (Grammar was not formally developed enough to include at this time.)

But before we move on to the selected secondary school students, we must recall that Plato's vision of reality includes a world of nature, arts, and crafts, between the realms of poetry and pure precision. He seems to assume *first*, that most citizens will have vocational training; *second*, that everyone will have a sound "common sense" familiarity with the everyday space-time domain; and just possibly, *third*, that young intellectuals must be indoctrinated against the colorful, competitive, world of the market and the local fair. (How far one *can* take adequate common sense familiarity with this level of reality for granted clearly depends on the complexity and scope of the relevant social structure. Every young Greek had seen goats milked and sheep grazing; most young Americans have not. A small mill-wheel is one thing, but, I think, a hydrodynamic electric dynamo is quite another.) That this level of his world needed more attention than he first thought dawned on Plato progressively as he wrote his works that come after the *Republic*.[15]

The two things that stand out in the secondary educational level are the constant demand for precision and the curricular order of increasing formal comprehension. On the one hand, the students are not to be concerned with the *application* of their studies. At the same time, however, the studies themselves increase in complexity and comprehension, moving from simple numbers to formal systems that can treat movements of planets and stars, and patterns of melody and harmony. From arithmetic to harmonics, each new discipline adds a new "dimension"—classes, lines and planes, solids, velocities and vibration ratios.[16] A retrospective course for students who go to the third educational level explores "how all these mathematical studies are akin."[17] The kinship rests, clearly, on their shared deductive method of proof and their rigorous logical consistency. Plato assumes that *some* of this precision will transfer to other contexts. I suspect this is the point in having Glaucon keep pointing out that these courses are useful for soldiers. For, in fact, the executive officials of the state must be precise in their deductions of those operations that will carry out given legislated policy. (There is something fanciful about this part of the account, and I suspect Plato's Socrates of exaggerating his point to shock and impress the intended readers. "Ten years" is too long; "no applications," impossibly sterile, and probably fatal to any intended transfer; and one would have liked some *verbal* precision running parallel to the mathematical.)

The third level, "higher" education, is concerned with questions of value. The students have by now learned how to think consistently. The next problem involves thinking comprehensively. As the questions discussed range over ethics, politics, and economics, the limits of the hypothetical-deductive method must become clear. The awkward fact seems to be, here, that *precision* is usually bought at a price of *incompleteness*, and that alternative plausible views must be accommodated. I think one part of this dialectical method is well illustrated in the *Republic* itself.[18] Seeking a definition of human nature, Glaucon offers a model of man as aggressive, Adeimantus of man as acquisitive, Socrates of man as speculative. The fact is that all three views must be combined, and once they are, the tangled mixtures of political history and diverse individual personality should lend themselves to ordered explanation. We are not told here how the higher educational institution will explore and define the good and its associated forms. But clearly this clarification of criteria and ideals will be the primary aim. Here Plato's metaphysics goes beyond our current notions of higher education. But the ideas that things must be seen in their interconnection, that shared inquiry can deepen appreciation, and that values are akin, are still viable as guides for college education.

In looking back over the plan, with its progression from feeling to form and from appearance to reality, it becomes clear that Plato has oversimplified his account. In the interest of stressing the differences between his levels of schooling and the standard practice of the day, he has unduly emphasized the separation of stages. But in fact the scheme will fail if the secondary school cadets never see tragedy, march in singing processions, and admire works of architecture. Nor may the university crowd burn their mathematics texts on entry and move into a humanistic scene filled with verbal elegance but set free of the rigors of logic. This point needs to be added, and its addition qualifies the singleminded correlation of each institutional level with just one educational aim; the correlation which makes the schematic statement so clear. Somehow, we must use dialectic and try to fit these alternative directions into a single, comprehensive, new idea of "education" and "excellence."

The way in which these different dimensions interact seems to me to be illustrated by the method of explanation which Plato uses in the *Republic* itself. There is an alternating pattern of common sense observation, abstract mathematical schematization, and concrete mythical illustration that runs through the dialogue. (If one mistakenly thinks that the *Republic* advocates the banishment of all mythology, it must seem odd that the dialogue uses it so consistently, and that it ends with a myth.)

This is what I take Plato's plan for education to be and to involve: it must have multiple aims, to be effective; it must have different levels and methods to be "realistic," because of the metaphysical structure of reality. There is a natural sequence of learning, running from fine art to philosophy, which parallels human development of mental power and intellectual maturity. What relevance does all of this have for educational discussion in the twentieth century?

Dewey, who is surprisingly sympathetic to Plato and the Greeks, points out two defects that must be remedied before we can appraise Platonism in a modern context. First, we must correct for the fact that Plato—here agreeing with both the poetic and scientific traditions—holds that aptitudes are strictly hereditary. The practical implications are quite clear. Only *some* people will have the inherited talent needed to take advantage of secondary and higher education, or, eventually, to decide questions of public policy wisely. A drastic correction is needed here to undo this error of fact. The second defect Dewey finds is that Plato's notion that society involves *only three* functional classes, each requiring different training, is a disastrous oversimplification. Here, I am sure Plato would agree that this is oversimplified: in other contexts he gives plenty of attention to the plurality of arts and crafts, and one interpretation of a passage in *Republic* VIII supposes that there are 24,300 different types of personality if we take account of their development with age. The danger with Dewey's view is that it may easily lead to a loss of the distinction between *specific skills* and *general principles of crafts*. When this happens, vocational education becomes overspecialized too early, and technological advance quickly makes the specific tactics out of date. (How often will *you* use your slide rule next year?).

Whitehead, process philosopher and Platonist, offers two main contributions to current discussion of educational theory. His first point is that education, in addition to teaching skill with abstractions, must also teach appreciation of individual things as concrete.[19] This goes beyond Dewey in one important way. Whitehead agrees with Dewey that attention to *classification* as opposed to *use* is a mistake. But he implies that looking at things *as tools* is also a kind of classification—the kind that sees a slender bamboo as a fishing pole.[20] It may seem strange that Whitehead's emphasis on the concrete occurs in the Platonic tradition, with its traditional stress on abstract form. And yet, this concrete realm is where Plato's educational scheme begins, with effects which we assume will continue. The Greek problem which Plato faced was not too little attention to the concrete but too little general familiarity with new levels of abstraction. Dewey points out appreciatively that the Greeks were too vital ever to become dependent on bookish authority; the Romans, he thinks, started that. Whitehead is like Plato in the latter's practical planning role in his desire that the different dimensions of education coexist and carry forward. If all aesthetic excitement is lost in a dry four years of pure discipline, it will not be recovered.

Whitehead's second contribution was his notion of "the rhythm of education."[21] All learning that is significant takes place in three successive phases. First, there must be a stage of romance, which provides the impulse and motivation that are needed for learning to start. This looks over a wide territory as a scene for exploration and adventure, but the details are not clearly seen nor discriminated. The second stage is that of discipline; Whitehead calls it the stage of precision. It is here that analysis and skills build up the clear view and the control of exact details that make up the means and ends, parts and wholes, of the romantically surveyed terrain. Here we need words and numbers; classifying tables and paradigms; concentration on sentence structure, or painting style, or equations. All of this is fine so long as the original impulse to learn is carried forward. The third stage is one of satisfaction: the student can now, looking back, see both the precise parts and their articulation into a whole. The lines of *Beowulf* bring fine detail of meter and alliteration to combine into the telling of the powerful epic story. (In his early work on teaching mathematics, Whitehead remarked that in a given course the student should accomplish something definite and should know that he or she had accomplished it. Today our teaching, at least of elementary and high school science, tends to do just the opposite; we tell our students that they won't really have mastered anything until college courses, if then. Recall that Plato had some intuition rather like Whitehead's in mind when he planned to end the study of several mathematical sciences with a retrospective study of their relation to each other.) The three stages we have enumerated, Whitehead argues, are all essential and their sequence is not variable. The reasons for this are metaphysical, along a rather different line from Plato's middle dialogues. Yet the suggestion is quite Platonic: it seems simply to apply the large scale patterns of the ideal curriculum and the Divided Line to smaller scale "learning" situations.

Two other twentieth-century books suggest a continuing relevance of Plato's grand philosophic road map, though both give that map a different interpretation and appraisal from its author's intention.

The first of these is the 1954 *N.E.A. Yearbook*, devoted to philosophy of education. The American scene, as reported here, finds an ongoing debate between three "types" or "schools" of educational theory. The three are called "existentialism," "pragmatism," and "liberal arts humanism." The third label refers particularly to the Aristotelianism of the 1930s and 1940s at the University of Chicago, and the courses and programs stressing the "Great Books." The three groups can be compared by looking at the different objectives put forward as criteria of effective education. The existentialists were particularly concerned with "individual authenticity." This meant self-realization without enforced conformity to any arbitrary or authoritarian "system." It represented a continuing reaction both against totalitarianism and against the "role playing" enforced by modern industrial society. (Sixteen years later came the protest movements by college students in exactly this direction.) There clearly was some truth—a good deal—in the idea that no one else can have students' experiences for them; and that learning about experience via text and lecture is not equivalent to having it at first hand. (For example, from a traveler's description of Greece, no one can taste the distinctive flavors of grilled octopus and cold retsina.) Ordinary notions of efficiency seem to the existentialist to dictate *standardized* practise which has exactly the wrong educational effect.

Pragmatism, the second philosophy, has as its aim social effectiveness. It holds an instrumentalist theory of meaning: that the meaning of something is given by its implications for action. Intelligence is interpreted as instrumental as well; it has evolved as a tool for solving problems by directing interaction of the organism and its environment. Logic, in this tradition, becomes a theory of inquiry. Learning, this view has it, takes place by way of social activities with shared objectives. Now, it seems quite clear *in theory* that social effectiveness need not mean social conformity. And yet all of the methods and materials that this theory suggests for school use do in fact presuppose shared goals and definite criteria governing cooperation.

The third position, liberal arts humanism, may perhaps best be characterized as aiming at *appreciation of form*. This holds for the forms found in mathematics, in literature, in scientific theory. Education is conceived as intellectual development, a development aided by the disciplined study of classical examples, classical languages, and mathematics. The view of intelligence involved here is quite different from those of the other two schools. It may be true that mind evolved by way of efforts to modify the physical environment; but it has now reached a point where it can contemplate and appreciate the nonmaterial realm of form. That realm is fixed and objective, and it includes a common ideal of human nature—exactly what the existentialist, who believes each of us is free to *choose* what our natures will be, denies at the outset. (This denial is the famous slogan that "existence precedes essence.") The social activities that concern the pragmatist, the social or antisocial adventures in lifestyle that engage the existentialist, seem only needless distraction to the engaged Aristotelian administrator. An ironic conjunction in place, though not in spirit, had occurred in Chicago earlier, where Dewey's Laboratory School was on the eastern border of the university that Robert Hutchins was redesigning along "liberal arts humanist" lines.

The discussion between these positions, by and large, opened with each group claiming that *its* aims were necessary for education. As debate went on, this tended to change to the view that each distinctive set of principal aims was not only necessary but sufficient—or at least entitled to exclusive immediate first priority. At that point, the alternative hypothetical-deductive models were seen as excluding one another.

Relatively unnoticed were some remnants of Platonic idealism, which continued to appear in commencement speeches and the statements of institutional aims that opened secondary school evaluation reports and college catalogues. Basically, the message of this position should have been a double one. First, according to the Platonist, since all of the proposed aims are good, they must share a common form which must make them logically compatible, not exclusive. But on the other hand, the stratified four-level complexity of the world may well require different strategies for realizing diverse kinds of value in different orders of reality.

The Platonists should have gone back to the *Republic* and noted that each of the three "positions" treated by the N.E.A. matches one—and only one—of the three bottom segments of Plato's Divided Line.

(THE GOOD)

REASON	:	WHOLES, IDEALS, VALUES
UNDERSTANDING	:	HYPOTHETICAL-DEDUCTIVE STRUCTURES
EXPERIENCE	:	ARTS AND CRAFTS; LAWS AND TRADITIONS
IMAGINATION	:	FINE ART; LITERATURE; CREATIVITY
	:	

Figure 1: The Divided Line

REASON
UNDERSTANDING   LIBERAL ARTS HUMANISM
EXPERIENCE   PRAGMATISM
IMAGINATION   EXISTENTIALISM

Figure 2: Three Philosophies of Education

Looking again at the argument of the first half of the *Republic*, we find a similar pattern to that of the N.E.A. scheme holding between three proposed alternative *definitions* of what "human beings" really are. The *Republic*, having set up three consistent but apparently exclusive models, proceeds to combine them in a more complex and better definition, which insists on the tripartite character of every human soul.

In the present case, if Plato's general view is right, the different parts of reality are not likely to be mastered by any single skill or method. Creativity and pursuit of the aesthetically interesting may be best in one dimension, precision in mathematical and logical deduction in another. Machines can teach some kinds of skills and items of information, but used too widely their company seems antisocial and becomes boring. The aims of education must, says the Platonist, be fourfold. Education aims at realizing in each individual aesthetic sensitivity, social effectiveness, mental discipline with logic and mathematics as key tools, and a philosophic view which sees the three "synoptically." (Whitehead's three stages of learning, his "rhythm of education," match the first, third, and fourth of these Platonic levels.) With some Whiteheadian modifications, I think Platonic idealism offers a genuine contemporary educational philosophy, and perhaps a genuine metaphysics as well.[22]

Bearing on this latter point, let me cite Morton White's tracing in *The Age of Analysis*, of Western philosophy, particularly American, from about 1900 to 1964. During that period, he finds three distinct and parallel trends. One may not want to call them "schools"—perhaps "styles" would be better—but each of the three groups shared enough of aims and methods to constitute a distinct family type. The three are existentialism, pragmatism, and "analytic philosophy" (here including positivism and logical empiricism). The positivists shared, much more restrictedly, the concern for form—formalization, logical deduction, confirmation—of the liberal arts humanists; but they did not believe that their disciplined methods could apply to ethics, politics, or fine art. The existentialists and pragmatists are exactly the same groups we have already encountered in the *N.E.A. Yearbook*. It looks, then, as though the discussions of education and educational philosophy mirror the wider, general philosophic scene. So, if Plato's Line helps to locate and understand education, it should work for modern metaphysics as well.

First published in *Educational Theory*, 37, no. 2 (Spring 1987): 169–77. Reprinted by permission of the Office of Patents and Copyrights of the University of Illinois and the Editorial Office of *Educational Theory*.

Chapter 5

Republic VIII-IX: On Mathematical Imagery

We have said that the symmetrical structure of the *Republic* results in a return, in Books VIII-IX, to the topics debated in Books II-IV. But it now returns with two insights that make more explanatory organizations of political phenomena possible. One of these is the presence and interaction of three parts of the soul and classes in the state. The three *taken together* give an account that goes beyond the "hypotheses" of the earlier Books and is an adequate "synoptic" vision. The second insight is the role of The Good as a principle of explanation. If all animate things desire the Good, we can understand their behavior by seeing what each believes this goal to be for which it feels the desire. For most creatures, The Good is attractive in the guise of pleasure. For human beings, however, wealth, honor, and wisdom are other goals that may be thought to be its realization. What life a person chooses to live is a function of intelligence and character—the extent to which reason is present, and the "part of the soul" that is dominant. What structure a society has depends on the good that the ruling class pursues—perhaps the wealth of the nation, perhaps its honor and military power, perhaps the general welfare.

The resulting organization of types of state, types of personality, and choices of life are illustrated by mathematical imagery in the last three books of the *Republic*. We have lost the key to the fine details of much of this, but still, I think, can see the basic outlines and function of Plato's diagrams. At any rate, the figures match the text and aid, rather than hinder, the teaching of the *Republic*.

It seems to me that Plato's "mathematical" passages in the *Republic*, which have baffled most later readers, were meant to describe diagrams (to be drawn, from their description, by the reader) illustrating key relations in the context. The first such figure, the Divided Line that ends Book VI, is a model of a *helpful* summarizing diagram. Its schematization of kinds of knowledge in terms of degree of clarity and reality of its objects is one of the most copied figures in the history of philosophy.

THE GOOD

REASON	:	PHILOSOPHY
BEING	:	KNOWLEDGE
UNDERSTANDING	:	SCIENCE
SKILL	:	ARTS AND CRAFTS
BECOMING	:	OPINION
IMAGINATION	:	POETRY AND FINE ART

The Divided Line, *Republic* VI

The second such passage, *Republic* 546A, opens with a reference to a 3-4-5 triangle which is the key to an explanation of the classification of kinds of state and of individual psychology to be treated in Books VIII and IX. (That it is the key is attested by Aristotle, who cites the passage.) Since the classification is determined by the respective *motivation* and *intelligence* of leaders of states and of individuals, a suggested reconstruction of this second diagram is the following:

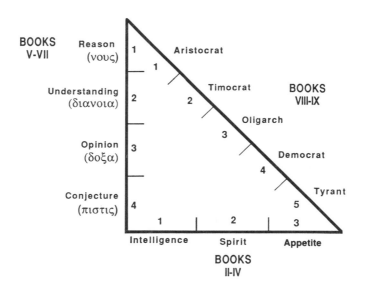

The imagery has gone from a line to a triangle (then elaborated into a three-dimensional set of some sort).[1] If the images follow the order of mathematical studies in the curriculum, we would expect the next topic, the relative pleasure of the types of human life, to use the resources of solid geometry. It does do this, but with a modification of the *five* types of the triangular second image to *nine*. This is the significance of the way the distance between the just man and the tyrant is described in the text: it is three stages from aristocrat to oligarch, and three again from oligarch to tyrant, hence equaling nine. Since human characters are determined by intelligence and relative dominant part of the soul, they offer nine possibilities (assuming that no one remains entirely in the hallucinations of *eikasia*.) The list of nine occurs in the *Phaedrus* as part of the list of typical occupations souls find in reincarnations. The square underlying this would be:

Strength of Intelligence —   N   1   2   3

                             D   4   5   6

                             P   7   8   9

                             R   S   A   —— Dominant Part of Soul

The left-hand column characterizes the three classes (rulers, protectors, producers) of the ideal state. All three are "reasonable" in character, but differ in intellectual ability. The tyrant is located in position 9, the lower right-hand corner. The hypotenuse of the triangular diagram we have just seen runs through positions 1-4-7-8-9.

The *Phaedrus* passage on reincarnation lists lifestyles which are also organized by intelligence and character (character this time defined by love of mind and soul, or love of the body, or love of property). It runs:

intelligence

	1 Philosopher	Gymnast	Artisan
	2 General	Prophet	Sophist
	3 Merchant	Poet	Tyrant
lover of	——(soul)	(body)	(property or power)

In each case the "distance" from philosopher to tyrant is 1:9. But Plato's next diagram will be designed to show three respects in which the life of the philosopher is more pleasant than any other, particularly that of the tyrant. These respects are: correctness in choice of ends, skill in selection of means to ends chosen, and opportunities for putting chosen means-end plans into operation. In each of these respects, we want to show that the 1:9 distance applies; but to do this and still keep the two-dimensional representation of types of character would require more than three dimensions.

But since geometry is limited to three dimensions, and Plato wants to represent three factors for each of his nine lives, for his next diagram he reorders this 3 × 3 matrix as a line of length 9. This becomes the side of the figure measuring the tyrant's relative pleasure in Book IX, as shown below. (Note that Glaucon seems not to be baffled by the transformation of five characters to nine, nor by the "squaring and cubing," but rather by the arithmetical difficulty of the computation of 9 cubed.)

The number of the tyrant's pleasure in Book IX sets up the relation in excellence of aristocrat to tyrant as one to nine. But *three* "dimensions" are all relevant to relative pleasure—the reality of ends, efficiency of means, and opportunity for action. In each of these respects the 1:9 distance of aristocrat and tyrant holds. The suggested intended figure is therefore probably the following:

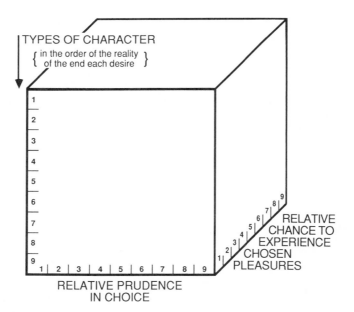

Since the philosopher is located at the upper left hand corner of this solid figure, the tyrant at the lower right hand corner, the distance between them is $9 \times 9 \times 9 = 729$. Each constituent cube of the figure represents a possible combination of opportunity, prudence and wisdom, which, in their combinations, determine the relative pleasure of the lives their possessors will lead. Each axis of 9 represents the same 9 types of character distinguished above in the discussion of character types.

The final imagery goes to astronomy and harmonics to compare the structures of individual human lives. There are so many more of these even than the types of life in the preceding figure, that Plato can't enumerate them. What he does instead is to show each soul a paradigm of a *good* life's structure, in the form of a cosmic model. In that model, balance is built in, and is preserved by each part keeping in its own place and moving with its own proper speed relative to the others. This is the lesson of the stars, as Socrates later tells Glaucon when he summarizes the point of his Myth. What we must discover, he says, is which combination of qualities will balance to give a life of happiness, and this is the one we must choose. The model, like the ideal city, is in the heavens.

The arithmetical details that intrude in the Myth of Er seem designed to show that Justice holds in the heavens. This is revealed in the *symmetrical balance* of the sizes, colors, and speeds within the system. (The metaphor of Justice as balance—holding a scale—goes back to the pre-Greek Egyptian Book of the Dead.) These figures use a symbolism of the *balance* of numbers (ordinal numbers) and their sums, a Pythagorean-inspired notion that ceased to be used or appreciated after Plato. Four of these figures of balance are given below. (The Figures were drawn by Mr. Christopher Dustin.)

This final imagery is introduced as part of a myth in which souls are allowed to choose their next lives from a large sample set. As part of the procedure, in order to ensure fairness, Plato gives every soul an opportunity to see the working of cosmic justice in the heavens before it chooses its next human life. This power is represented by a model of the cosmos in cross-section, held and moved by Necessity and her daughters. The lesson is embodied in the *balanced symmetry* which relates the eight nested hemispheres representing the orbits of planets and the stars. This *balance* is underscored by a detailed numerical-mechanical description injected into the poetic flow of the myth. That description, however, seems put there for the benefit of the *reader*, not for that of the soul about to choose a life—the latter either does or does not recognize the moral of the model by a direct aesthetic intuition. The idea of "balance" or lack of it among ordinal numbers is hard for the modern reader to respond to sensitively, though it is squarely in the tradition of Pythagorean mathematical metaphor that Plato draws on for his imagery.

1 2 3 4 5 6 7 8

1 8 7 3 6 2 5 4

Figure I: Balance of the Hemispheres

The top row of numbers gives the ordinal position of each hemisphere, from inner (1) to outer (8). The second row gives their *relative sizes*. The symmetrical pairs that balance by adding to nine are shown by connecting arcs.

1 2 3 4 5 6 7 8

1 7 8 2 5 3 4 6

Figure II: Balance of the Colors of the Hemispheres

The top row of numbers gives the ordinal position of each hemisphere, from inner (1) to outer (8). The second row gives their colors, indicating density, in order of mention. The symmetrical pairs that balance by adding to nine are shown by connecting arcs.

1　2　3　4　5　6　7　8

1　8　7*　6*　5*　4　3　2

Figure III: Balance of Velocities

The top row again is an ordinal listing of positions. The relative velocities, adding to nines, are again shown by connecting arcs. This time, however, the starred hemispheres (7*, 6*, 5*) have the same velocity, so that the balanced sets have 9 at either end, about a center of 18.

1 2 3 4 5 6 7 8

8 1 2 6 3 7 5 4

Figure IV: Balance of Momenta

The top row is again an ordinal listing of positions. The second row shows relative ordinal values of momentum (Volume from Figure I times Velocity from Figure III).

Thus, as these images suggest, a dialectician can find order in the complex phenomena of the world of becoming, a world that ranges from individual human beings through their societies to the unending cosmic justice of the stars.

Perhaps there is no way of finally proving my case, but it does make sense of otherwise *very* obscure passages. (For further detail, see the end note and my *Plato's Mathematical Imagination*, Bloomington, Indiana, 1954.)

Reprinted, with some additions, from *Teaching Philosophy* 3 (1980): 331–36: 7 (1984): 223–27, by permission of the Editor and *Teaching Philosophy*.

Part II

On Some Platonic Questions

Chapter 6

Doctrine and Dramatic Dates in Plato's Later Dialogues

My purpose in this discussion is to raise—without expecting to finally resolve—the question of the doctrinal significance of the several internal cross-references in Plato's dialogues, and particularly his indications of a proper sequence for the reader. In the background, I will assume an order of *dates of composition* that, at least by groups of dialogues, is generally accepted. And part of my discussion will aim to establish a match between this chronology and the author's several strategic purposes, as the works reflect them.

There are two reasons for this exploration, one metaphysical, one largely technical. The *technical* reason is that those of us who insist on the inseparability of "literary" and "argument" dimensions of Plato's work have not done very well in articulating the *larger* literary questions of sequence as functions of the central drama of ideas. The *metaphysical* reason is that there is a necessary problem of perspective inherent in the Platonic theory of forms, anticipated in Plato's own statements and destined to haunt and divide the Platonic tradition into a neo-Platonic "formalist" view and a "process" view.

Platonic metaphysics does not lend itself to literal, didactic presentation. Part, at least, of the reason is that the metaphysician must address us from a definite standpoint in his reporting. If that standpoint looks to the forms as future alternative goals or values, its prospective report will differ from the purely descriptive accounts of the forms as classes or universals that look to them in a nontemporal eternal present.

In short, the different functions of the forms involve different refractions through becoming, and no one account can do justice to the theory.

But there are other problems of perspective. One of these is the relation of the knower to what is known. Here we are confronted with the simultaneous ideas of philosophy as final vision, and philosophy as unending inquiry. This may, again, be a question of temporal stance:

$7 + 5 = x$ is a problem, a theme for inquiry, until x is "seen"; but then, retrospectively, $7 + 5 = 12$ is an analytic insight.

Another is the puzzling problem of participation. Whitehead suggested that this relation is different from the standard relations of mathematics and technology in that it is asymmetrical in respect to its "internal" or "external" character.[1] That is, if A is a form, and a is an instance, the participation relation $P(A,a)$ is *external* from the standpoint of A, but *internal* from the standpoint of a. Whether $a = A$ or $A = a$ depends on whether we stand with the form (by itself, just what it is) or the participant (owing its name and its identity to the form it grasps). It is disquieting to have to accept such pairs of alternative accounts that seem at first glance exclusive. For example, in the *Parmenides* we find Parmenides saying that if, indeed, the forms are independent of our world, they will be unknowable by us; but if they enter into relations with us so that they interact with our knowing, they will become partly mind-dependent. The difficulty is not eased by the fact that between the "forms" taken in their immanent qualitative presentation, there are intermediate stages of formal determination—paradigms, types, roles, type specimens—each of which presents the same asymmetry of internal-external relatedness to the entities above it and below it in the formal hierarchy.

Very early in his career, as soon as he tried to develop his defense of Socrates into a systematic philosophic vision, Plato discovered this difficulty. Having written the *Phaedo*, in which Socrates has attained "blessedness" by realization of the form of justice, Plato felt compelled to complete the picture with the contrasting *Symposium*. Where the *Phaedo* gives forms that are perfect, pure, and attainable, the *Symposium* gives forms that lie at the end of an impossible quest, a demonic pursuit of creativity.[2] If for an instant the *Symposium* allows a glimpse of the Beautiful, that glimpse is followed by a return to time in which the philosopher again functions as a *daimon*. The two dialogues, by every test of style, structure, and historical reference, were written almost at the same date. They are internally linked by parallel detail that relate them as a comedy to a tragedy (as an initial point of relatedness in contrast here, we note that the patron of the *Symposium* is *Dionysus*, the patron of the *Phaedo* is *Apollo*).

This attempt to get the portrait of Socrates and his thought properly done, by doing it in two contrasting lights and styles, addresses a problem that is reflected throughout the Platonic tradition. Within that tradition, there tends to be a polarization between interpretations that follow the *Phaedo* in a stress on the purity and remoteness of the real world—this is the orientation of neo-Platonism—and interpretations more appreciative of the role of Eros, of the forms as creative powers—this is the orientation, today, of process philosophy; earlier, Renaissance admirers of the *Symposium* shared the view. The neo-Platonic tradition tends to take the mythology of the *Phaedo* literally and to treat the forms as remote and separate and as completely determinate particulars; this rules out any rational account of participation. The process view, reducing the forms to relevant possibilities, makes their actuality dependent on choices and minds, and loses the objectivity of ethical value standards that was the most important original impetus to the theory.

The theme of my present discussion is that Plato's indications of the interrelations of various dialogues represent his attempt to indicate relatively complete perspectival accounts of his philosophy. How optimistic he was about the final success of a great projected sequence of eight successive Socratic discourses to provide a complete, perspective-including picture we are not sure. But the final judgment of *Epistle VII*, Plato's or not (and I am certain that it *is* his own), is surely right: Platonic philosophy does not lend itself, as other topics do, to literal, textbook forms of statement.[3]

It is generally assumed by twentieth-century readers that the doctrines of the "later dialogues" and of the middle ones, particularly the *Phaedo*, are incompatible. The explanation usually given is that Plato discovered that the "middle dialogue" theory of forms had two defects: first, it was not needed to explain the phenomena of knowledge and communication that it had been invoked to account for; second, it was not coherent in the face of rigorous logical analysis. It is also generally assumed in the twentieth century that a satisfactory but metaphysically far more modest theory is found in the "logical" later dialogues. A further assumption—and this is one that goes back to the earliest neo-Platonists—is that the theory of forms in the middle-dialogue version is given a *literal* statement by Plato's Socrates in the final section of the *Phaedo*.

What I propose to do is, first, to organize the dialogues in groups related by common internal cross-reference or common strategy; second, to show how this illuminates the interrelation of the "logical" later series; third, to reconstruct the location and method of the *Philosopher* as part of this projected set; fourth, to show that if the *Phaedo* is correctly read, it can appropriately come *after* the *Philosopher* in a dialectical order. If this is convincing, I will have shown that the open alternatives for understanding Plato remain, as they have always been, a neo-Platonic stress on transcendence or a process philosophy stress on immanence and emergence; and that the contemporary attempts to read Plato as an analytic or linguistic philosopher completely miss the intended strategy of the texts usually taken as central in this Megarian enterprise.

Literary form, internal indications of rhetorical intention, and (with increasing relevance for the later work) stylometric data, fit together consistently in a grouping of dialogues that approximately matches their supposed dates of composition.[4]

After the death of Socrates, young Plato—presumably in Megara—began writing dialogues in defense of his older friend and hero. The *Euthyphro, Apology*, and *Crito* certainly belong here. Of these, the first defends Socrates against the charge of impiety by contrasting his attitude toward religion and the gods with that of the fundamentalist, Euthyphro. The second, a recreation of Socrates' speech at his trial, at once makes it clear what the real basis of the charges against him were, namely, his persistent inquiry, and brings out his seriousness. (Xenophon's *Apology* is evidence that many Athenians saw Socrates as a kind of eccentric crank.) The third defends Socrates against the charge of bad citizenship, implied in the phrasing of both counts of the indictment. The form is highly dramatic, brief, and without much metaphysics or positive doctrine. A next set of dialogues is the *Lysis—Laches—Charmides*, which defend Socrates against the charge of corrupting the youth, by showing him in action. The case studies are designed to show his concern and the good effect of his method on young audiences—if not on elderly generals. Again, the form is highly dramatic, the conversations brief (an Aristotelian critic would say that Plato deliberately uses a form that has a beginning and middle but no end), the emphasis ethical, metaphysics relatively lacking. Another, though implicit, charge that Plato felt a need to answer was the notion—central to Aristophanes' *Clouds*, and persisting in the public mind—that Socrates was just another sophist. In fact, as Plato saw it, the whole project of Socratic inquiry presupposed a nonrelativistic possibility for rational treatment of value questions that was at the opposite pole from the sophisticated intellectuals of the "sophist" persuasion. In presenting this second line of defense, Plato has Socrates encounter the leading intellectuals of the day. These dialogues are longer; the casts are larger, the action more dramatically complex. An element of contest enters, more strongly than before, with Socrates the winner. Plato's Socrates, in these discussions, now introduces myths to illustrate his points and begins to use mathematical examples. The theory that knowledge is recollection becomes explicit in the *Meno*, one of the later dialogues in this set.

In his middle dialogues, Plato tries to carry out the project of systematizing the philosophic vision of Socrates and of offering a final justification for Socrates' behavior. M. Fox drew attention some years ago to the way in which Socrates describes his final conversation as a "trial" in which he defends his way of life before a jury of philosophers: if Ionian naturalism were the final philosophic answer, Socrates' idealism would indeed have been unrealistic.[5] The *Phaedo* is a presentation of Socrates' thoughts on the subject of immortality; it is a continuation of the *Euthyphro-Apology-Crito*, but both form and content indicate a later date of writing, with the Socrates-versus-sophists set, ending with the *Meno*, in between. But at about the same time, the *Symposium* gives an alternative portrait of an engaged Socrates, a *daimon*, in pursuit of immortality by his creativity. These two dialogues fit closely together by every criterion—style, relative length, explicit systematic extension of Socrates' insights—and parallel details stress their intended complementary character. But "the" Platonic philosophy they present offers a strong temptation to take one *or* the other. It is important to notice Plato's careful parallel construction, designed to force his reader to accept both accounts, rather than to reject one in favor of the other.

The middle dialogues continue with the great philosophic vision of the *Republic*, developed by dialectic; and the account of philosophic rhetoric in the *Phaedrus*, where Phaedrus's character forces Socrates to persuade him by myth and cosmological argument of doctrines Plato proves by something more like ontological or teleological arguments elsewhere. In these dialogues, we are dealing with a full-scale philosophic vision; myth and mathematics alternate in importance; the method depends heavily on analogy and metaphor. The outcome is a picture of the sort of world in which Socrates' conduct is justified, his vision confirmed, and systematic metaphysics established. In particular, the "Divided Line" of the *Republic* summarizes a new epistemology and projects a new plan of education, consistent with a Socratic inquiry that hopes to find constructive solutions.

These middle dialogues have interesting structural properties. The drama instantiates the argument—that is, the characters with their problems and notions offer concrete examples of what the discussion is about. (Thus the cast of *Republic* II–X has a spokesman for each of the three "parts of the soul.") At the same time, when a method is an important topic of discussion, that method is illustrated by the contextual dialogue (so "dialectic" is illustrated by the *Republic*, "philosophical rhetoric" by the *Phaedrus*).

So far, except for readers who wonder about the compatibility of the types of immortality offered by the *Symposium* and *Phaedo*, or about the compatibility of the method of division of the *Phaedrus* and the speculative dialectic of the *Republic*, this is a classification with which there is pretty general agreement. But note that in the conclusion of the *Phaedo* Socrates presents his project for a philosophic-scientific system as just that: a vision, a hope, a project. And in describing Plato's middle dialogues as "vision," we try to do justice to an evident emphasis on speculative coherence that sets aside precision and sharp refutation.

This leaves Plato, after the middle dialogues, with three lines of investigation to follow. The first is *logical:* Can the four-level theory of knowledge of the *Republic* establish itself against critics who argue that the forms are (a) not intelligible, or (b) not necessary, or (c) not as extended a domain as the *Republic* makes them? The second line of investigation is *cosmological* or *physical:* Does the mythical faith that nature and history are ordered with regard for value find confirmation in empirical science and in historical plausibility? The third line is *ethical:* If this philosophy is true, it should be possible to take it back to the marketplace from the Academy, and to show that, indeed, far from being "idle talking" (Isocrates' description of Plato's work in the Academy) it is a practical tool for human betterment.

Quite clearly, the second of these purposes motivated the projected *Republic-Timaeus-Critias-Hermocrates* tetralogy. Bracketing the more metaphysical portions of Socrates' account of his city in the skies, Timaeus concentrates on the empirical details of natural science,[6] ending with medicine. In the next dialogue, Critias, in turn, moves from cosmology to mythical history, with his "true" story of a small but virtuous state (ancient Athens) triumphing over Atlantis, a large but bad one. Hermocrates, in turn, could be expected to give an account of the fate of a later Athens that had lost the excellence of the ancient city in Critias's story. (This theme of Greek history, from mythical to contemporary, was transferred by Plato to the *Laws,* leaving the *Hermocrates* unwritten and the *Critias* unfinished, though perhaps for another reason.) The thrust of the *Timaeus* throughout is that natural phenomena can be explained by models and laws that embody aesthetic properties of beauty, simplicity, and precision. The implications of this were stated earlier in the myths that conclude the *Republic* ad the *Phaedo.*

The third strategic target of Plato's later writing is clearly the motivation of the *Philebus* and the *Laws.* The *Philebus,* both by theme ("not the good itself, but the good for human life") and the cast (young men who are not very philosophical), centers on the practical application of philosophy; the *Laws* offers a concrete sample demonstration of the philosophic legislator in action, establishing "right measure."

In the *first* set of post-*Republic* dialogues, Plato shows why we need the forms by showing what happens if the philosopher, or scientist, or craftsman tries to do without them. In fact, not much is left. If, for example, we give up the highest level of Plato's scheme, with forms which are ideals and criteria of value, we may still have abstract hypotheses, but no way to choose between them. A dialogue that puts all forms on this hypothetical level will end with alternative consistent abstract philosophies but no criteria for preferring one to another. A dialogue that allows forms to exist and be referred to only on this level will end in an antinomy. Even less satisfactory results follow if the forms are limited to rules governing processes in becoming, or to associations of symbols in imagination. A later dialogue explores each of these possibilities. In general, this set of dialogues is more technical than Plato's other work and seems designed for a more specific Academic audience. They are sometimes read as successive changes of mind on the author's part, but it is hard to see why he would discard the theory of the *Republic* for alternatives that all turn out unsatisfactorily. But, though technical, something of the methods and doctrines of these writings were well enough known to the general public to be the target of jokes in comedy.

The *first* of the strategic sequels to the middle dialogues opens with the *Parmenides*, a dialogue with a double strategic purpose. The first point this dialogue aims to establish is that neither the Megarian nor the Eudoxian interpretation of the Socratic theory of forms is tenable. Both are consistent, but the former has no room for sensible things, and the latter makes its forms immanent in process, and so, in effect, sensibles. If we take these two positions—Megarian formalism and Eudoxian process—as exclusive and exhaustive world-hypotheses, we have a real antinomy. But are the forms necessary at all? Yes, Plato argues that they are. But it follows from the *Parmenides* deductions that a theory of forms must do more than explore *hypotheses;* on the level of *dianoia*, there are many logically consistent alternatives that are nonetheless philosophically incomplete. Thus, when Parmenides decides to demonstrate what happens to the theory of forms on the level of *dianoia*, the result is an indirect proof that forms on the *noetic* level are necessary. (We were prepared for this when these forms—the beautiful, the right, and the good—came early into the discussion with Parmenides before the dazzling hypotheses.)[7]

We have thus a model of a *reductio* proof that the forms are necessary; that this must include the noetic "value" forms is shown by the incoherence of an account of "unity" that tries to do without them. The divided line cannot be simplified, then, simply by dismissing the top level. Monsignor Diès caught this point clearly in his remark that "the word *nous* and its derivatives are absent in this dialogue, with the exception of the rejection of conceptualism. . . ."[8]

What would happen, however, if someone with a pragmatic temperament suggested that "forms" are philosophically redundant, whether we treat them as *dianoetic* classes or as *noetic* systematic patterns? The answer is that it would be impossible to explain the possibility of knowledge that nevertheless we actually have. For mere memory and experience can never give us the necessity or universality of mathematics and ethics. The *Theaetetus* is an indirect proof of this. Note that the cast has a spokesman for each of the four kinds of knowledge distinguished on the Divided Line.[9] It turns out that Theaetetus' adventures with physical-physiological models, models that become the standard paradigms of later Western psychology and epistemology, cannot explain mathematics or Socratic ethics. (And we are given examples in context—Theodorus's and Theaetetus's incommensurability theorems, and Socrates' "digression" on the life of the philosopher—which show that mathematical and philosophical knowledge must indeed be possible, since both are actual.) The intention on Plato's part to have this strategic line of inquiry intersect the ethical-biographical earlier dialogues is shown, not simply in the explicit reference to the indictment at the end of the discussion, but throughout in the attention to trials, law, legal imagery (which would, without this explanation, seem puzzling intrusions, needing the sort of external explanation that Gilbert Ryle proposed).[10]

Cornford catches the point tersely, as Diès had for the *Parmenides*. "The forms do not appear," he writes, for the reason that Plato wants to show the futility of an attempt to do without them.[11] If we claim to have other entities, such as "concepts," "dispositions," or "ideas in our minds," serve as alternative to the "forms," this is not because Plato endorses the substitution!

The *Theaetetus* still recognizes the existence of arts and crafts. These depend on some sort of paradigms for construction, enumeration, operation. If there are no forms of a systematic, *noetic* sort, there is no philosophy; if there are none of a universal, *dianoetic* type, no mathematics or philosophy; but what if a critic of the theory rejects even the common sense world of paradigms and copies of the *Theaetetus*, and insists on a total identification of *episteme* with *eikasia*? Would anyone try this? Yes, a thoroughgoing sophist well might. But the price he must pay for this is to give up the art of communication—of refutation, or persuasion, or deception—and this deprives him of his income and function. The forms are still presupposed here, but only in the very weakened role that they play as public "meanings" that make discourse possible, and as the "syntactical relational frames," connecting isolated meanings into assertions. A demonstration is given of a "method of division" that at first seems able to handle the relations of "forms" without reference to systems, wholes, and so on; it does not turn out until the end of the next dialogue in the series that the method in fact presupposes more elaborate logical and metaphysical distinctions. But with the final capture of the Sophist, at the end of the hunt, this most radical proposal for dispensing with "forms" seems to be laid to rest.

What one would now expect is a rehabilitation of the theory, arguing from the existence of arts and crafts to the fact that these presuppose forms as types and measures, then from the existence of formal systems of measures and types to the fact that these connections presuppose normative forms of system, the value forms.

This return is begun in the *Statesman*, where the forms are presupposed by the arts of statesmanship as the criterion for "right amount" that separates the "too great" from the "too small"; and since there are arts, there "must be such measures." We are tentatively promised a "later" discussion of the nature of "normative measure."

As the project is set up, the Eleatic Stranger has served his turn: he has handled the levels of *eikasia* and *doxa* admirably with his critical logic, but now Socrates and his namesake, Young Socrates, should carry on the conversation in the *Philosopher*. That conversation should, in terms of the symmetry of the dialogue set, argue to a systematic logical order among the forms—not necessarily to the total normative system of the middle dialogues, but to the sort of coherence that is presupposed by the deductions of the *Parmenides*, the definitions of the *Sophist*, the operational accounts of the *Statesman* and the *Theaetetus*. The result would be something like the theory of forms that Socrates describes himself as devising in the *Phaedo*, before his encounter with the book of Anaxagoras set him off on a further line of speculation.[12] In effect, this stage of the theory rests on the axiom that logic is relevant to physics and ethics because the systematic relations of the forms are causally projected and binding on their participants. But this does not yet tell us *why* the formal system is organized as it is, nor whether there are normative functions for the forms that require that they be more than simple "classes," "types," or "Universals."

Why Plato never wrote *The Philosopher* admits no final answer. But our discussion of the grouping of casts and topics does suggest what it was destined to say had it been written. We can show this in a tabular form.

NOESIS	(*Republic*)			(????????)
DIANOIA	PARMENIDES			PHILOSOPHER
PISTIS		THEAETETUS	STATESMAN	
EIKASIA			SOPHIST	

Should one go back, from the *Statesman* to the *Parmenides*, where Young Socrates is the respondent, and imagine Old Socrates now speaking the lines of the great Parmenides, as the *Philosopher?* Should one assume that this part of the project inspired the Lecture on the Good, which "was highly mathematical," and aimed at a proof of the unity of the system of forms? Might we go off in another direction, and say, as Klein suggested (but only half-seriously), that perhaps the *Apology* is really also the *Philosopher?*[13]

In any case, the sequence of these logical later dialogues has an announced theme and a proposed structure of questioners and respondents that is related symmetrically to the metaphysics of the *Republic* via a symmetrical descent and ascent of the levels of the Divided Line. We are clearly entitled to locate the *Republic* where we have: Adeimantus and Glaucon are put into the cast of the *Parmenides* for that cross-reference, and the four-person cast of the *Theaetetus* is clearly meant to be a projection of the four levels of cognition.

Notice also that the theme of justice and law that is built into the *Theaetetus*—partly via "digression"—is also central in the *Sophist* and, as an art of justice, central to the *Statesman*. (An earlier political overtone was the selection of young Aristoteles, "who later became one of the Thirty," as the second respondent in the *Parmenides*.)

The crucial point is that the last word of Plato's Socrates is still the *Phaedo*, going beyond the technical, projected *Philosopher*. There have been intervening discoveries in cosmology, logic, and law incorporated by way of qualifying remarks in dramatically earlier conversations, anticipating changes and objections chronologically later, but Plato refers us back to the *Phaedo* to bring the story to its close. Once more, he offers us side-by-side presentations of positions that later readers prefer to think of as exclusive. The Megarian type of analysis of the *reductio* defense of forms contrasts to the visionary Myth of the True Earth as precise analytic philosophy does to exuberant mysticism.

There are, however, two comments in order here. The *Phaedo* must be correctly read. In particular, one must not miss the point of the final myth. Socrates, having given up natural science, recounts his next adventures in two stages. First, he develops a new and powerful logical method, hypothetical-deductive, but from constantly strengthened "hypotheses"; and this leads to the proof that soul is indestructible.[14] (It does not prove personal immortality, however, which is the main interest of the audience). Then, inspired by Anaxagoras, he forms a notion of a still better method of explanation: this would be to relate the order of all things, forms and cosmos alike, to the Good as a first principle.[15] If this can be done, philosophy will be able, perhaps, to establish the existence of Cosmic Justice, written in the stars. In a world ordered in that way, the fact that Socrates *ought* to have personal immortality would lead to the conclusion that he does have it. But this is only a story, a hope; it is a project bequeathed by Socrates and pursued throughout his career by Plato.

The Myth of the True Earth has two important properties. First, it expresses Socrates' faith that the insight into the Good as ordering principle is sound. It is a myth inspired by Apollo. And in the story, something a modern reader may not immediately recognize, the findings of scientific geology—the work of the impious atheists who "pry into things beneath the earth"—exactly match and confirm the Orphic stories of a subterranean purgatory.[16] The problem of the shape and stability of the earth is solved by an appeal to what is best, and the mix of eschatology and geology proceeds on the same line. When Aristotle cites two causal explanations of thunder, fire quenched by cloud and a noise to frighten prisoners in Tartarus, the notion that both may apply exactly echoes this mythical application of the search for what is best.

The second property of the story is that, as myth should, the account transforms abstractions into personifications and reifications. Thus the True Earth has showcases of precious stones and living gods who greet visitors to their temples face to face. The invariability of an atemporal logical domain is represented by the beauty of the museum of perfect instantiation. Such projections are as philosophically misleading, when their proper status is not recognized, as they are aesthetically and religiously effective. One can hardly resist comparing this great Myth to Kant's account, in his Third Critique, of religious vision as an aesthetically coherent presentation of "what we may hope." Like Socrates, Kant had his own conjectures—of the way in which the various planets are used for education of our souls and their purification. (But a number of editors and translators have omitted this unscientific final section from their editions of the *Universal Natural History of the Heavens*.)[17]

By the time of his farewell to Socrates, before the *Laws*, Plato had developed his philosophy systematically. As he wrote successive conversations, he managed to correct—by anticipations if one follows the dramatic dates, by newer findings if we follow the topical and chronological grouping—misinterpretations and to take account of new findings. In the end, he saw that Socrates' faith in a total moral and aesthetic order, and in philosophy as contemplation of that ideal, remained not only a central hope but one of the central insights of Platonism. But Socrates' last word was a message of purification and escape; and it did not do justice to the Socrates who challenged his fellow

Athenians, bringing philosophy into the everyday arguments of the Agora. For that, a further extension was in order; an extension that would once more find its expression in a pair of aspects that modern readers at first glance find antithetical.

The second part of that contrapuntal final portrait is the "process-oriented" doctrine of the Athenian Stranger in the *Laws*. The Athenian Stranger is, like Socrates in the *Phaedo*, an old man. He has had wide political experience but has only lately encountered higher mathematics and cosmology. His arguments are empirical and cosmological. Nevertheless those arguments carry him to certainties strong enough to be the basis of law, proofs of the rightness of Anaxagoras's conjecture well beyond the knowledge available to Socrates at the time of the *Phaedo*.[18] And the two traditions of Platonism—the ascetic moment of the *Phaedo*, where we see the whole earth from remote space, and the engaged creativity of the *Laws*, where we regulate and survey all of the fields and rivers in our own section of the earth—are once more presented together in the final strategy of Plato's philosophic presentation.

An appendix to the *Laws* seems also to have been drafted by Plato, though it is doubtful how far our extant text represents his own execution, or, if it is his, how completely it carries through his intention. But the *Epinomis*, a sequel to the *Laws*, is an astronomical myth parallel in location, similar in theme, and probably intended to be similar in its moral, to the Myth of Er at the conclusion of the *Republic*. And both of these myths seem to draw their inspiration, ultimately, from the Myth of the True Earth at the end of the *Phaedo*.

Chapter 7

Diction and Dialectic:
A Note on the Sophist

An interesting effect of Eric Havelock's discussion has been the constant reminder of the location of Plato at the end of a dominant oral tradition, without which there might be the temptation to take Platonic dialogue as a discontinuous leap into literacy, thus leading a modern reader to misread the texts. For example, we easily assume, because we have not thought about it, that reading was done silently in Plato's time; that there were equivalents of our copyrights and publishers; even—in some cases—an axiom that "mature" thought must be expressed in clear, monochrome treatise. All of this helps misunderstand the dialogue form.

As Plato writes, we are *overhearing* conversation between people with different personalities, professions, and life styles. Their creator may not agree with his characters—in fact, he often seems to agree partially with each of a set, rather than having one as his spokesman against the rest. In the *Republic*, as a case in point, Glaucon and Adeimantus constantly contribute needed reminders that the human self as we know it, existing in space and time, is composite, not pure reason alone.

The purpose of my present comments is to relate this framework to the interpretation of Plato's *Sophist*, with a passing glance at the *Statesman*. In particular, I want to follow up a suggestion I made earlier, that the principal speaker, the Eleatic Stranger, is an imported bounty-hunter, brought in to shoot the Sophist down (or, more exactly in the absence of the rifle, to catch him in a net).[1] The "weapons" are, perhaps, new (or old) techniques of method and language. (For this simile, compare Socrates' remark in the *Philebus* that he will now require "weapons of a different kind" to resolve a shifted point under debate.)[2]

This is a rather difficult point to establish, and I can only suggest it in outline for the present. The style and dramatic structure of the *Sophist* are a terrain that literary critics and connoisseurs of style have left unexplored. This dialogue and its companion piece, the *Statesman*, have never been described as particularly poetic or romantic—indeed, for almost a century many scholars doubted whether anything so pedestrian could be authentic.[3] Once their title to authenticity was recognized, however, the general tendency was not only to regard them as the work of Plato, but to identify the audience with a group of students in the Academy, with the preliminary training required to follow this intricate pair of analytic lectures, centering on semantics. (This is a particularly congenial notion to some of our contemporary analytic philosophers who, given the chance, would have delivered just such presidential addresses to the graduate scholars of ancient Athens. Of course, this congeniality does not prove that the interpretation is wrong.)

Two studies, an article by V. Tejera and a book by Mitchell Miller, find more drama and character in the *Statesman* than had been previously recognized.[4] And an article by Frederick Oscanyan actually develops the notion that the first set of definitions-by-division in the *Sophist* displays a sense of humor on the Stranger's part.[5] If he is right, perhaps even here, in what the nineteenth century found arid treatises, we are more in the spirit of the genuine dialogue and the oral tradition than one at first believes.

The Stranger is certainly a guest professor with an odd, pedantic sense of humor. (Noted by Jacob Klein in his asides to the effect that the Stranger is "smiling, perhaps," in his *Plato's Trilogy*.)[6] For example, he thinks it a "good joke" when he points out that quadrupeds walk as the power of human diagonals—this has provided later readers with only slight laughter.[7] (This is the case even if they avail themselves of the relevant picture, sketched by a scholiast in the margins of Vienna W.)[8] Actually he is more amusing as he insults various well-known Sophists by his first set of "definitions," which take the form of discreditable genealogies.[9] Professor Oscanyan shows how these "definitions" match Plato's sardonic characterizations of Sophists in the earlier dialogues: manufacturers, exporters, and retailers of food for the soul; debaters with a likeness to a wolf; paid hunters of rich young men. To put this in the form of genealogies locates them in a standard classical and modern Near Eastern genre of literary insult, the fictitious ancestry. (Note also that this theme of genealogy was apparently much more of a living metaphor in Plato than it seems to us today.)

The Stranger is also a logician, and brings with him what he represents as a relatively unfamiliar logic. He is addicted to his "great method of division," a method that, just from the name, sounds as though it might be the "art of division" praised by Plato's Socrates at the end of the *Phaedrus*.[10] But the fondness is not uncritical: the method left to itself can go astray. In the *Statesman*, a first try at definition locates man as a featherless biped; a rerun finds him a two-footed pig. To explain this misfiring, there are variations on a theme first proposed by Lewis Campbell: we are shown how to use the method correctly by successive corrections of defective use, commented on as such. A. E. Taylor follows this line of interpretation; so does Mitchell Miller; so, I think, does Jacob Klein as he points out that some of the apparatus of division is not to be taken too seriously. It certainly is the case that points that we, as readers of the *Phaedrus*, had thought obvious, emerge only with much elaboration. In fact, if we did not have the *Statesman* with its continuation of the lessons on method from the *Sophist*, most of the needed qualifications would not emerge at all. For example, the stress on dichotomous division in the *Sophist*—which is certainly a rule of safety when one is hunting with a net—is finally modified late in the *Statesman* to the alternative rule that divisions should match the number of different coordinate kinds there are in the large class being divided. Perhaps in part to emphasize the break with the earlier technique that this involves, the example chosen divides into an arithmetically unlikely set of *seven* as the total of coordinate "kinds."[11]

Although there has been a tendency to identify this visitor with Plato himself, there have been some other suggestions. We might make him a Sophist (Tejera); a formal logician (A. E. Taylor, Mitchell Miller); a surrogate Socrates (Diès, if I understand him); or something of a traveling pedant (Hamilton and Cairns suggest this, without actually saying it; some of my undergraduates at Yale say it).[12] Whatever we decide about character, I want to suggest a closer look at the Stranger's *diction*. He brings his own philosophic dialect with him, I think. This seems to be a language not yet sharpened and made technical by the Megarians, by Socrates, even by Prodicus. This may be the point underscored by the fact that while the narrator of this conversation, Euclides, and his auditor, Terpsion, are Megarians, the Stranger shares with them only a more distant ancestry; he is from Elea. (One is reminded of Cephalus, narrator of the *Parmenides*, who also invokes a more remote philosophic past by his opening statement that he and his philosophic companions are from Clazomenae.)[13]

The Stranger uses the terms "form" (*eidos*) and "being" (*to on*), with a sort of pretechnical and simple signification, something he would not have done if he had come from, and represented, contemporary Athens or Megara. The equation of being with "power" is variously regarded by later metaphysicians; in context, it is at least a sort of neutral device to get the opposing gods and giants to communicate with one another.[14] And the adventures of *eidos*, which includes such "forms" as gluttony and impiety on the same level as the rest, has a similar wide extension and at best only semitechnical sense.[15] (The shops of Athens today amaze the passing Platonist by their continuation of this ordinary use of *eidos*, as they seem to advertise ELECTRIC FORMS, ELASTIC FORMS, even ALL OF THE FORMS.) While the Stranger would be understood in the Academy, it would be by an audience that believed they had a technical language that was philosophically better. As early as the *Phaedo*, when Socrates talks about *eide* "that everybody recognizes," it is Platonic forms with Pythagorean affinities, not nondescript natural abstractions, that he is discussing.[16]

A similar thing seems to me to hold for the Stranger's use of *nomos* in the *Statesman*. The true Statesman, he insists, is "beyond the law."[17] But the remark holds because here "law" is used in one ordinary sense, that of "written statute." The true statesman, having an art, is not merely the custodian and enforcer of rules engraved on stone. We may safely assume, I think, that some of Plato's intended readers would have thought of the "statesman" as bound by established statute, and not have had the conception of a "Political art," the norms of which would of course be binding. (In this connection, there is an interesting stylistic point: when the Stranger mentions "law," the immediate context usually also contains the expressions "writing" or "written law." Later, Aristotle uses a similar device to keep clear one technical sense of *eidos* by associating it, in context, with the term *schēma*.) But for the present, I will return to the Stranger in his role as Sophist-hunter.

If this visitor were really speaking for Plato, there would have been a critical change in the doctrines of Platonism from the middle dialogues to this later stage in the Academy. Interestingly enough, it seems to be a weakening of the earlier metaphysical position in two directions. The sharp break between being and becoming is moderated by the new equation of being with power. This is a metaphysical qualification that A. N. Whitehead admired and saw as a change in Plato's thought toward process philosophy. The identification of the forms with meanings seems to be a new development; as early as *Republic* V, it was clear that all meanings can be forms, but the conversion by which all forms count as meanings is a modification in the direction of language analysis and analytical philosophy. The method of collection and division that is praised in the *Phaedrus* is projected into a mechanical logic of descriptive dichotomous classification, a long way, apparently, from any theory of recollection as an account of our recognition of form. The *Statesman*, however, if we take the idea of the ruler as "beyond all law" in the sense which that phrase would have had in the *Republic* or the *Laws*, marks the sharpest break with the middle dialogues. The ideal ruler of the *Republic* is the maker of statutes, but he makes them as imitations of the objective form of political excellence—sketching and painting as he *imitates*. Far from being beyond law, he is bound by his vision to conformity with an ideal, and so are the legislators of the *Laws*.[18]

But if Plato is *not* here speaking for himself, why should he reach back into an ancestral past and create this personage with high intelligence but pretechnical diction? There are two considerations that may offer an answer.

The first is a philosophic reason for the modifications Plato has the Stranger make in Plato's own theory. Some pairs of philosophic positions cannot communicate with each other directly; they seem to be mutually unintelligible.[19] Platonism stands in this relation to the various types of atomic theories, with whatever kinds of atom. And the Sophist who figures in the present dialogue has developed an atomism of isolated appearances as his philosophic view.[20]

Atomism *can* be argued with (and the arguer can claim it has been refuted) from either an Aristotelian or an Anaxagorean philosophic orientation. Both of these can communicate with Platonism: the former because it shares a formalist explanatory direction, the latter because it shares a synthetic "dialectical" method.[21] Since Plato's overall intention is to defend the theory of forms, he turns over the critique of the Sophist to an expert who is much more of an Aristotelian than Plato (rather than to an Anaxagorean).

The Stranger is able to mediate the two positions involved. Thus he introduces notions of "being" which include the views of both the "gods" and the "giants." He uses a barely disguised lecture method: only two or three moments of genuine dialogue brighten his conversations. He is able, as Aristotle was later, to disconnect problems of semantics and syntax from questions of ethics, or physics, or metaphysics. His gradual refinement of a technique of definition or division moves in the direction of Aristotelian genus and species classification. And he is able to argue, on the basis of premises the Sophist will admit, the thesis that some sort of formalism must be presupposed even by Sophistry.

The second consideration is the overall strategy that structures the dialogues later than the *Republic* and the *Phaedrus*. Plato treats three themes, having to do with three extensions and applications of the vision of the middle dialogues: the three can be roughly characterized as logic, physics, and ethics. The logical extension, with which we are most immediately concerned, may have been designed as the set

Parmenides-Theaetetus-Sophist-Statesman-Philosopher, though the last of these was never written.[22] The theme seems to be a defense of the theory of forms by showing that it is presupposed by scientific deduction, by arts and crafts, and even by meaningful use of language. It is not the theory in its full metaphysical development that is shown presupposed in each case, but only the partial version adequate to the immediate point. (The arts, for example, presuppose craftsmen's *criteria;* the relation of these to a larger architectonic need not be developed to make this point.)[23]

The second set of later dialogues deals with the relation of Plato's vision to the findings of empirical science and the relation of value to history. The program for this called for a tetralogy: the *Republic-Timaeus-Critias-Hermocrates;* of this set, the *Hermocrates* was never written, and the *Critias* was left incomplete. Plato's *first* point here, made by the *Timaeus,* was to show that the theoretical structure of the *Republic* actually matched detailed models and measurements in the world of scientific fact.[24] Since Timaeus is a Pythagorean, *his* way of thinking and talking about *forms,* about *being* and *becoming,* about *classifying formulae,* is like that of the *Phaedo,* where the two main respondents also are Pythagorean.[25] The discrepancy between Timaeus and the Stranger from Elea can in this way be explained by the difference in Plato's purpose in the dialogues in question. And this relation holds regardless of the relative chronological dating of the *Timaeus* and the *Sophist.*[26]

The third direction of application and extension in the post-middle dialogues, in the direction of ethics and politics, is presented by the *Philebus* (the latest Socratic dialogue) and the *Laws* and *Epinomis.* The grand philosophic vision is applied to practical ends in these latest writings: to outlining—for an audience not expert in technical philosophy—"the good for human life," and to writing out a model legal code, in as full detail as if it were about to be adopted for actual implementation.

Guest experts take the conversational lead in parts of each of these three enterprises. Timaeus is, as we have seen, a Pythagorean scientist from South Italy. An Athenian Stranger is the main speaker in the *Laws* and its appendix, the *Epinomis.* Parmenides, the great logician from Elea, is the historical figure who introduces the "logical" sequence. And the *Sophist* and *Statesman,* later in that series, have as the leader of their conversations the Stranger from Elea.

We will turn now to the strategy of the *Parmenides-Theatetus-Sophist-Statesman* series. The first three of these occupy successively lower levels of the schematism of the divided line in the *Republic.* In

the *Parmenides,* it seems that the "method of hypothesis," while necessary mental training, cannot decide between alternative "hypotheses"
without appeal to forms of a normative kind. In the *Theaetetus,* the
attempt to define knowledge on the level of physical process, of *technē,*
with models of the mind as tablet and aviary, fails to account for the
certainty and universality that mark knowledge of forms—as opposed
to particular sensibles. This looks like the beginning of a *reductio* proof
that the theory, in its full four-level *Republic* version, is indispensable.
(It is worth noting that later systems of Western philosophy do in fact
advocate schemes that are like Plato's, but with less apparatus in the
form of levels of reality. Pragmatism, for example, operates at the level
of the *Theaetetus;* logical positivism, with its relegation of "framework" questions to pragmatic concerns, admits three levels but not the
top, fourth. Existentialism in some guises, beginning with Sartre's order of precedence for existence over essence, looks like an attempted
reduction to a supremely individual one-level order.) The objection to
the reduction of the line to three levels, in the *Parmenides,* is that then
we can have no philosophy; the objection to the reduction to two levels
in the *Theaetetus* is that then we can have no mathematics (an ironic
result since Theaetetus himself is a mathematician), and no dialectic of
a Socratic sort, either. What is the comparable objection to a reduction
of knowledge to a single level of words and semblances? It seems to me
the point must be that unless we introduce something like a distinction
of levels between kinds of symbol and referent, meaningful communication cannot be shown to be possible. This need not require the full
theory of forms; the *Theaetetus* inquiry would have worked as well in
the absence of the third level of the line, without invoking the fourth.
But what must be shown is that the domain of meanings is objective
and immune to the challenges of neo-Eleatic notions of lack of meaning
for terms supposedly without any reference. *If* the Sophist admits selective "combinations" of forms as meaningful and not meaningful, the
presuppositions of that admission are capable of being shown inconsistent with his nihilistic division of statements into truth and nonsense.
Since the Sophist depends on communication for his livelihood, he cannot afford to hold a view that implies that meaningful discourse is
impossible. But there is a problem here: the Sophist keeps moving to
questions of metaphysics (questions with an Eleatic ancestry) to evade
issues of semantics.[27] Socrates and Plato have developed a technical, or
semitechnical language of their own. (Or at the very least, have selected certain types of use from the rather diffuse ordinary language
that is discussed in the *Cratylus.*)[28] It presupposes certain possibilities
for discourse: there is a theory of reference which involves meanings;

these in turn relate to forms in an abstract, descriptive domain; while the latter are given relevance and order through their relation to forms of systematic scope and normative type.[29] It is important to distinguish designation from denotation in this theory; a meaningful term or statement must designate some combination of meanings, but it need not denote any sensibly existent facts or instances.[30] The Sophists, by doing two things, can obscure the issues. They can insist on an identity of designating and denoting; and they can then appeal to Eleatic metaphysics to argue that negative and false terms and expressions have nothing to denote. Thus when Socrates, discussing virtue with Euthydemus and his brother, tries to show them that their view is false, they rejoin that falsehood is impossible. Plato's final word on the matter, in *Epistle* VII, is that when someone tries to explain the forms themselves, anyone who wants to can upset his argument, because of the weaknesses inherent in language.[31] In that case, it would not be good strategy to introduce considerations of the forms themselves into a debate with the Sophist in the dialogue named for him. One topic after another, from sense to reference, could be rejected by way of a critique of the language used.[32] Thus the appropriate character for the confrontation with the Sophist is not Socrates himself—his interest is primarily ethical; nor would it be Plato himself, for his interest remains primarily metaphysical; but some guest expert whose orientation is logical, and who can't be accused, even by the Sophist, of smuggling in Platonic logic or vocabulary. That is why the Stranger uses a logic of classification which is a simple descriptive net: no invidious value judgments are built into it. He uses a vocabulary which is deliberately "neutral" in its definitions of key terms—neutral as between gods and giants in the notion of "being," neutral as between Platonic, ordinary, and Sophistic uses of "form."

Thus I see the Stranger as carrying on the major project of a defense of Platonism in an "ordinary" language, non-Platonic enough so that even the Sophist cannot object that he does not accept or understand its technicalities. When the Sophist wants to appeal to Eleatic metaphysics, the Stranger overrules him: Parmenides is not to be invoked as authority in this cause.[33] (It is not as rude a criticism as Aristotle's exasperated remark that a true denier of the possibility of contradiction would be "no better than a vegetable," but I think it makes the same point.) As the programmed series of later dialogues goes on, we expect that the theory of forms will emerge, level by level, each as presupposed by the one below it.[34] But for the present level, we need an expert semanticist, introducing, for the sake of this argument, a weaker theory than Plato or his Socrates would like to defend. Socrates would want to *improve* the Sophist ethically; Plato, if he put himself onstage, would want to educate him metaphysically; but the Stranger from Elea is content to entangle him in a net semantically. It is indeed interesting that the Stranger's analysis can be detached from the background of the Socratic-Platonic theory, even though, if I have understood Plato's strategy, it will be shown to presuppose that theory as we move beyond meaning to being. It is a remarkable view of Plato's skill as an analyst to see him work out this position.[35] But this need not be, and in fact is not, a new doctrinal version of Platonism.

I like this guest professor, with his professorial sense of humor. I am even glad that he came from the ancient, but now provincial, intellectual center of Elea, rather than the more flashy recent sites of Athens, or Megara, or Cyrene. He can do things that Plato's Socrates, his younger namesake, Young Socrates, and his image, Theaetetus, cannot. The reason is that while he sympathizes with their metaphysics, he does not wholly share their language, their logic, nor even Socrates' ironic sense of humor.

At any rate, I prefer my notion to the alternative idea that Plato himself has suddenly changed his philosophical position. He cannot carry on a dialogue with the Sophist in his own proper person and vocabulary; but he can invent a guest logician able to refute the Sophist from a position mediate between Sophistry and the Academy. That Plato himself sees his forms functioning as "meanings" on occasion is clear from such dialogues as the *Cratylus*, and from Book V of the *Republic*. But to assume that meanings and forms are identical is quite a different thing.[36] In the research of the Academy, and the philosophy of Plato, the forms are objective entities studied by set theory, logic, mathematics, and normative ethics; and the distinction holds firm between being and becoming.

We need some of Havelock's sensitivity to language to be secure in the distinction of treatise and dialogue in Plato's post-*Republic* logical disquisitions. But it seems clear that the *Sophist* is in fact a conversation, and the usages of the Stranger from Elea, while functional enough, by no means represent a retraction or reformulation in Plato's own vocabulary of forms or philosophy. Perhaps the strongest evidence for this claim is the contrast between the present protagonist and Timaeus of Locri, another guest speaker in another post-*Republic* technical dialogue, who is Pythagorean not Eleatic in his intellectual ancestry.

Reprinted with a new final paragraph, with permission from *Language and Thought in Early Greek Philosophy*, Ed. Kevin Robb, copyright 1983 The Hegeler Institute, La Salle, Illinois, 61301, publishers of the Monist Library of Philosophy.

Chapter 8

Plato's Atlantis: Myth or History?

Atlantis is back in the news again, this time identified with the violent eruption of the volcanic Aegean island of Thera in the fifteenth century B.C. I have always been fascinated by the legend of the lost continent, with its lush vegetation and technological megalomania, but I am quite sure that archaeologists will never find its sunken capital or traces of the elephant-inhabited mountains. On the other hand, some adventures I have had on the Aegean island of Ikaria make me think the archaeologists are right in tracing the inspiration of the part of the story that deals with the overnight destruction of Atlantean civilization back to the Thera catastrophe. Like many problems in the humanities, the historical basis of the Atlantis myth admits no simple answer and requires measuring of probabilities based on literary criticism, mathematical symbolism, and archaeology.

The single original source of the whole story is to be found in two dialogues written by Plato, *Timaeus* and *Critias*. In the *Timaeus*, a visiting expert on astronomy prefaces a lecture to Socrates with a summary of the history of a great war that took place nine thousand years earlier, between a good state—ancient Athens—and a hostile aggressive power—Atlantis. The Atlanteans were defeated, and then, in a single night and day, the whole continent of Atlantis sank beneath the sea, and floods destroyed the records and civilization of the Athenians, leaving only a group of survivors in the mountains. In the *Critias*, we are given an account in great detail of the lost continent: its geography, government, army, and agriculture. But the text breaks off just as the Atlanteans are about to launch their war on Europe, and it seems that Plato himself left the story in this incomplete form. All later references to Atlantis trace back to these two literary works as their source. Accordingly, before starting on expeditions, it may pay to look at Plato's story from the standpoint of the literary critic and the historian of philosophy.

As an undergraduate, I remember that I expected Atlantis to be discovered either by digs or by undersea exploration. I read with interest the many accounts that seemed to confirm Plato's story, such as cities or geographical features under the Atlantic or evidence of cultural diffusion in Central America. Circular cities with walls and harbors that more or less fit the specifications of the main city of Atlantis were identified, locating it in Tarshish on the coast of the Spain; in a dried Libyan lake; in Egypt, at Memphis; in Cornwall; just off the coast of the North Sea island of Helgoland; and a dozen more. Authors who took the story more literally pointed to the peculiarities of the Atlantic ocean floor near the Canary Islands, where our maps show the high ridges of the "Plato Seamounts" and "Atlantis Seamounts." A catalogue of real and fancied identities of Minoan and Mayan styles in architecture, in ornamental motif, and in fine art made the case for joint cultural diffusion from a central continent to Europe and America attractive.

But all this literature presupposed that Plato was telling the truth when he said the details of his account traced back to "Egyptian inscriptions" which the priests had obligingly translated for Solon.

I specialized in ancient Greek philosophy, and just before World War II wrote a thesis on the place that mathematics played in Plato. A mathematical analysis of the numbers Plato mentioned in his account of Atlantis shows a pattern that indicates they are his own invention and not historical report.

It seems likely that Plato's history is for the most part an invention with a moral. Plato was familiar with the arts and crafts, gave them a place in his scheme of "kinds of knowledge," and constantly cited them in his dialogues. But it is interesting to see, in his account of Atlantis, that he had almost by precognition a vision of the disorder and damage that would follow if an "almost superhuman" technology were left to its own direction. The Atlanteans had just such an unrestrained technological power, and in the end the disorder to which it contributed figured in their downfall.

Perhaps the most striking contrast between Atlantis and ancient Athens is that where the latter centers around an institution of higher education, the former has only technological training. The reader coming from the numbers of the carefully tuned world-soul in the *Timaeus* and the prescribed course in number-theory of the *Republic* is particularly struck by the fact that the Atlantean rulers met alternately every fifth and every sixth year, "paying equal honor to the odd and even." (In *Gorgias* 451b, we learn that arithmetic is a study of odd and even for numbers of any size: in *Laws* 717A, there is careful specification of which sacrifices should be made in odd, which in even, numbers.) Now, if we take this confused equivalence of odd and even as a symbol of lack of education, the numbers 5 (3 + 2) and 6 (3 × 2) are the ones that best express it, being the sum and product of the first odd and first even numbers. After the *Timaeus* harmonies (featuring 1,2,3,4,9,8,27), a system of 5s and 6s is just as much in contrast as are the circular canals of the capital city to the moving circles of the world-soul.

Let us take a look at the numerical detail which Plato so liberally gives us. Poseidon has *five* pairs of twin sons. His statue shows him driving *six* horses. His engineering constructs *five* circles of water surrounding a central island of *five* stades diameter. The total widths of the circles of sea and land are in the ratio of 6:5. The plain which his descendants irrigated was *six* million square stades in area. The outermost canal of their irrigation network had its breadth related to its depth in a ratio of 6:1. The total length of this encompassing ditch, ten thousand stades, seems an exception until we note that it is generated by adding (3 + 2) to (3 + 2) stades. In the same vein, the dimensions of the temple, in a ratio of 2 stades to 1, are given in *plethra* instead, so that their ratio is expressed as 6:3. No king may be sentenced to death without the concurrence of 6 princes. There are sixty thousand military districts, and the total army is sixty times that of the forces of ancient Athens. Each allotment supplies one-sixth of a chariot.

It is hard to believe that these figures are in any way historical. Their purpose, in this context, is to show the confusion of odd and even which marks a lack of education that proves fatal when combined with powerful technology. At the same time, of course, the profusion of numerical detail furthers the illusion that we are listening to a genuine history, translated from ancient inscriptions.

There were other, possibly stronger, indications that calculated fancy, not "Egyptian inscriptions," was the real source of the Atlantis legend. In discussing his "ancient Athens," Plato suggests to his reader that it was well-ordered, rather like the ideal city that figured in the earlier *Republic*, and that therefore he need not give an item-by-item description. But the few details he does give us are matched by their exact opposites in the Atlantis account. For example, the soldiers of the good state are all-around "athletes of war"; the Atlantean army is made up of units of specialists—archers, light-armed infantry, bowmen, slingers, chariot-borne light infantry, heavy armored infantry, charioteers. (Probably this helps set the stage for a projected account of the defeat of this outsized expedition in the mountain passes along the northern frontier of ancient Athenian territory.) The soldiers in the good state lived together on a central acropolis, surrounded by a simple wooden fence, and had one spring of temperate water which served them in summer and winter. The soldiers of Atlantis were dispersed in garrisons throughout the town, with only the most trusted mercenaries on its central island; there were both hot and cold springs, and separate baths for men, women, and horses. A simple diet sufficed for the ancient Athenians; Atlantean production provided a menu of spectacular variety and quantity, including a course of fruits "of the sort that bring relief from over-eating." The Athenians had an army of 2,000; the Atlantean army, once one works it out from conscription districts and specialist units, is 1,200,000 men strong. And so the contrasts go.

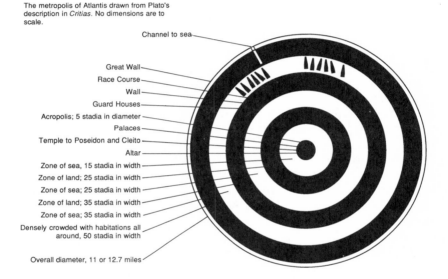

The metropolis of Atlantis drawn from Plato's description in *Critias*. No dimensions are to scale.

Channel to sea

Great Wall
Race Course
Wall
Guard Houses
Acropolis; 5 stadia in diameter
Palaces
Temple to Poseidon and Cleito
Altar
Zone of sea, 15 stadia in width
Zone of land; 25 stadia in width
Zone of sea; 25 stadia in width
Zone of land; 35 stadia in width
Zone of sea; 35 stadia in width
Densely crowded with habitations all around, 50 stadia in width

Overall diameter, 11 or 12.7 miles

Although many scholars disagree entirely about this, it seems clear that Plato meant his Atlantis to be a blueprint of a bad society, eventually corrupted by prosperity, disorganization, and lack of education, just as surely as he meant his other cities in the *Republic* and *Laws* to be models of good order. Atlantis is almost a prevision of contemporary Manhattan, though some scholars seem to believe that this must mean Plato thought it a good thing.

But where did all the other details come from? Well, if one were writing a negative utopia today, where would he go for apt detail? Obviously, to current places and practices that fit his intention. Plato apparently did the same.

For example, it has been suggested that the idea of a king living in a palace on a fortified central island was inspired by Syracuse, where Dionysius II lived on the fortified island of Ortygia, which was connected to the city by a causeway. (Readers of Mary Renault's *Mask of Apollo* will recall her description of this fortress and its mercenary guard.) But Plato has moved the island to the center of the city for symmetrical contrast with the Acropolis of his ancient Athens. The list of edible crops on Atlantis is food for a Syracusan banquet menu (if we had any doubt, the inclusion of a kind of fruit "which we serve to relieve overeating" among Atlantean farm products should resolve it). Plato elsewhere goes on record against both the quantity and variety of the Syracusan court banquets. The list of foodstuffs ties in well with the characterization of the elephants who roam the mountains as "that most voracious of all beasts." The outsized, gluttonous elephant is included almost as a symbol of Atlantis itself; if Plato were to design coinage, with the animal associated with the city on the reverse (as Athenian coins had the owl, Aeginetan the turtle, Milesian the lion, and Tarentine the dolphin), the elephant would no doubt be his selection for Atlantis. He had heard of elephants from Carthage, but he does not put them to military use in the Atlantean army—though the Carthaginians did—because that army is based on a different historical model. The complex conscript army of Atlantis, with its multiple specialized units, is an obvious echo of the Persian army, as its defeat was no doubt inspired by the Persian War. The location of Atlantis "outside of the Pillars of Hercules" almost certainly does not refer to a minor interisland strait within the Mediterranean, but is jointly inspired by Homer's location of Ogygia (Calypso's island) and by the mystery the western Mediterranean held for the Greeks of Plato's time after the Carthaginians had excluded their ships from it. The choice of Poseidon as patron goes back to the legendary rivalry of Poseidon and Athena.

For other central motifs, we need look no further than Plato's contemporary Athens itself. Its seaport, Piraeus, with new wall and tower fortifications, looks like the model for the noisy harbor, towers, and walls of Atlantis. The extensive public works program initiated by Pericles had drawn disapproval from Socrates and Plato. So presumably Atlantean fondness for buildings and technology comes from that origin.

There are some details, however, that remain unaccounted for. One, which I will only mention, is the significance of the list of names of Poseidon's five pairs of twin sons. Plato makes such a point of these names, which were turned into Greek names from the original Atlantean by the Egyptians, that there must be some still undiscovered importance to them.

Details of the worship, hunting, and sacrifice of bulls are evidently a memory of Minoan civilization, inspired by such legends as the Theseus saga. And the sudden catastrophe that destroyed Atlantis in a single day seems equally rooted in legend. I thought, in 1953 when I was untangling these strands, that some story of the sudden fall of Knossos on Crete must have been part of the current folklore that attracted Plato's literary imagination. The two strands—Minoan bull worship and natural catastrophe—do run back into some legendary past, that really did exist in history. Possibly the catastrophe theme is part of the same strand; if so, it should intersect somewhere the network of Minoan memories. And at least this much of the Atlantis material might be the kind of history that archaeologists can check, after all.

In fact, I am sure it is the kind of thing that archaeologists can check, as I think back to my visits to Ikaria in 1963. This rugged island, northeast of Crete and Thera, once had another name, but it was changed to Ikaria after Ikaros (Icarus) fell into the sea just off the southern shore. It still has an active oral tradition and the fall of Ikaros had all the air of an historical event to the islanders. (After I had told my Greek friend Sideris something about Schliemann and Troy, he told me, "I am surprised, Kyrie Bomby; I always knew that Ikaros was history, but I thought the Trojan War was just a story.") And if I doubted it, I could go to Ikaros himself, where he had turned to stone as he fell into the sea. It sounded as though there were some fusion here of Minoan legend and some actual historical event—my wife and I thought at once of a daytime meteor—that had been woven into the story of Ikaros.

So we set out to see the stone Ikaros. The coast is rugged, grey granite going up abruptly. Ikaros himself stands there, like a cube poised on one corner, about a hundred yards offshore. He is distinctive enough, but is made of the same grey stone as the coastal rock. Onshore however, there is a hole in the rocks, and a quarter-mile stretch of the plain grey stone is burned black and charred. Under the impression that this might have been our meteor, which had exploded Ikaros in stone out into the sea, we came home with a sample packed in an empty cigarette box. But my knowledgeable colleagues discovered that what we had was not meteoric. Instead, it looked volcanic, possibly magnesium oxide, rather like industrial slag.

Now, Ikaros stands just outside the shaded oval on maps that mark the probable fall of volcanic debris from Thera. And when I asked about the date of Ikaros's fall, I was told that it was not too long after Minos had conquered Mykonos and Ikaria. So for admirers of the theory of Marinatos and Mavor that the Thera explosion was the actual catastrophe that inspired Plato's destruction of Atlantis, here is one possible added piece of evidence from the Aegean Sea. The reported date is about right and intersects the Minoan legends; the location is about right if the explosion was actually somewhat more violent than calculations suggest.

So, in spite of my confidence that I had discovered the fictitious character of most of Plato's account, I ended up wondering whether some of the other pieces in his collage were not as contemporary as I thought, but might instead be traced back to tidal waves, volcanoes, and vanished cities in the Aegean Sea. And while I am still sure that Plato's "Egyptian inscriptions" are as fake as the "Arabic manuscripts" from which Cervantes claimed he translated the tale of Don Quixote, I am still waiting with some of my undergraduate enthusiasm for new archaeological reports from Crete and Thera.

Reprinted with permission from the January 1970 issue of the *Yale Alumni Magazine;* copyright by Yale Alumni Publications, Inc.

Chapter 9

The Text and Intention of Plato's Parmenides

One set of my Platonic studies has been devoted to exploring the relation between the textual details and the philosophical interpretation of Plato's dialogue, the *Parmenides*. My own general interpretation of this is given above, in the discussion of drama and dramatic dates. But the awkward fact is that where my interpretation calls for careful logical and stylistic construction, the best texts published to date lapse, though infrequently, into deviations from consistent logical form, apparent absurdity, and careless inconsistency. This left me in the awkward position of thinking I knew what the argument should say, but confronting a record which did not always say it. I set out to see whether further study of the sources and transmission of the text would improve or deteriorate the match between my reconstructed argument and the historical record of what Plato actually wrote. The present chapter is an introduction to this rather specialized investigation. It is a fair sample of the sort of Platonic textual study that flourished in the nineteenth century, and that we still need to continue.

In the winter of 1956, while spending a week in bed with a cold, I received by post a set of photographs of the Parmenides ms. Modena Estensis W.9.11. I had seen this described in L. A. Post's "Checklist of Plato MSS"; I was curious about it both because no one seemed to have collated or classified it and because George Valla, a scholar with mathematical talent and excellent taste in manuscripts, had taken a hand in its copying.[1]

To my considerable surprise, the text differed frequently from Burnet's reported readings of B and T, and from Diès's reports of readings of W.[2] And a number of those differences, in cases where the structure of the argument offered a way to judge, seemed to be better than B, T, or W.[3] I became curious as to how this had come about.

Actually, I could hardly have started at a greater distance from the source of these variant readings than I did. Stallbaum reported enough variants from his Laurentian *alpha* (Plut. 80.7) to show that this was a cousin of my Estensis ms.[4] Both turned out to be copies of Milan Ambros. D 71 sup., Bekker's s.[5] *Alpha*, however, was extensively corrected. In turn, I confirmed the fact that s is a copy of Milan Ambros. D 56 sup., a fourteenth-century ms, Bekker's r. Not only were most of the novel readings of s also in r, but a gap in s exactly matches two pages of the text in r, turned together by mistake.[6] Although part of D 56 sup. is "a copy of Paris C," its contents fall into two distinct parts, and the first part, which includes the *Parmenides*, is basically a copy of cod. Vatican. gr. 1029, a fourteenth-century descendant of Vienna W.[7] Where r differs from the Vatican ms (hereafter V), comparison with Paris C may be the explanation; this remains to be determined.[8]

That was where my tracing ended in 1957. In my *Plato on the One* (New Haven, 1961), I included some notes on the most interesting material I had found.[9] I had planned, in 1957, since I was passing through Paris, to consult the photographs of Vienna W at the Association Guillaume Budé. But those photographs were in Egypt that spring, and it was not until 1976 that I saw Vienna W.

A comment on historical context is in order here. The ideas of the coherence of Plato's *Parmenides*, the reliability of transmission of Plato's text, of the usefulness of symbolic logic for checking dialectical argument, were all very different in 1957 from the generally accepted if not necessarily better notions that we hold today. Richard Robinson had just argued that the second part of the *Parmenides* was incoherent *by any standard*. I was scheduled to give a late winter lecture in London, to show that the hypotheses were almost perfectly coherent when formalized in Rudolph Carnap's symbolic logic. Such formalization was then, however, still a relatively new and somewhat suspect technique. Further, there were objections from British scholars other than Robinson who were convinced that the real issue here was metalinguistics, not metaphysics. An early winter in Cornwall proved still too short for preparing an invincible fifty-minute presentation to my contra-Robinson formalization.

But at this same time, Gunther Jachmann put forward radical new ideas that, if true, would have upset all of the standard assumptions about the history and reliability of our Platonic texts. Jachmann finally concluded that large-scale Byzantine expansion and interpolation along multiple independent lines could only be corrected by "divination." And we should take "a couple of dozen" manuscripts as equally authoritative.

Now Jachmann's iconoclastic notions about extensive restyling of Platonic text were exactly what I did not need in connection with my

defense of a precise and valid original argument. For it was unfortunately clear that if Byzantine Platonists had been tempted to improve
on *any* Platonic work, the *Parmenides* would have been their first target for the project. And the direction of improvement, inspired by the
transcendent Neo-Platonism of Proclus, would have been to rewrite the
argument to preserve its validity in a post-Euclidean deductive form.

Today neither Jachmann's view of the text nor Robinson's of the
dialogue's incoherence have supporters. This may not be clear gain.
Plato's *reductio* proof stays unappreciated: that understanding without
reason leads to the very incoherence Robinson recognized but took for
the final rather than the semifinal word. Interest in what Plato's text
said is minimal; we publish papers now on *what it might have meant;*
the exact phrasing is treated as not important. Thus divination displaced from textual history has reinstated itself as the dominant style of
Platonic textual explication.

In 1976, in a context of considerably changed scholarly styles and
convictions, I had a chance to continue my tracing of this Platonic text.
I had collated W for myself from our Yale Microfilm and found it to be
the source of some twenty-odd improvements on the BT text, some of
which I had first encountered and admired in the Estensis ms.[10] I was
able to check W itself; this is very important for accurate reporting,
since five different hands—working with different sources and degrees
of intelligence—had combined their work in the *Parmenides.* There
were a good many more differences between W and V than direct
copying would lead one to expect. It turned out that V is not a direct
copy of W, as I had thought in 1957, but rather a copy of the first two
hands of the Prague Plato ms, Radnice VI. F.a, fourteenth century
(hereafter Prague).[11] Some of the most interesting and important new
readings of V where it differs from W are copies of corrections made in
Prague in the first hand. This means that the story of the family of W is
still not at an end. For I still have not identified the source from which
the copyist of Prague took variants and corrections from time to time
and introduced them into his copy of the W text. (A check on differences between W and Prague suggests that this source may prove to
be either Paris E or F [B.N. MS grecs 1812] or the Escorial Plato. And
this may bear out the judgment of the Budé Editors, that a colla-
tion of Vienna Y, a descendant of Paris B via Escorial., was worth
undertaking).[12]

By this time, my tracing had given me a good pedigree and clear
title to a majority of the new readings in the Modena ms that seemed to
me originally to offer a somewhat preferable text. Below is the family
tree that I have established for the W subfamily.

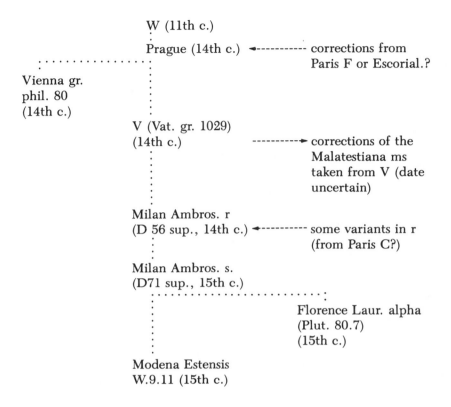

W (11th c.)

Prague (14th c.) ◄---------- corrections from
                             Paris F or Escorial.?

Vienna gr.
phil. 80
(14th c.)

V (Vat. gr. 1029)
(14th c.)   ----------► corrections of the
                                         Malatestiana ms
                                         taken from V (date
                                         uncertain)

Milan Ambros. r
(D 56 sup., 14th c.) ◄---------- some variants in r
                                 (from Paris C?)

Milan Ambros. s.
(D71 sup., 15th c.)

                             Florence Laur. alpha
                             (Plut. 80.7)
                             (15th c.)

Modena Estensis
W.9.11 (15th c.)

Having begun this account more or less *in medias res*, I must now go back for a moment to explain *why* I have had such a continuing, if sporadic, interest in the details of this text.

When, in 1956, I decided to formulate the argument of the *Parmenides* hypotheses in formal logic, I found that Plato had already almost done it for me. His argument was written out in a rigid deductive form. Each section opened with a "theorem statement," followed by a "disjunctive division into cases," a case-by-case consideration, and a final repetition of the original theorem.[13]

But somehow, for every general rule I thought I had found—whether for the choice of "if . . . then" conditional syntax, or for indications of topic change by special responses, down to the variant spellings of reflexive pronouns—there were some exceptions.[14]

But what was more puzzling, to me, than the exceptions were the regularities. There is an underlying repetitive, rigid argument structure. This is exactly what a later Neo-Platonist—Proclus particularly—would expect and admire.[15] And it is so different from any other extended passage in the *Dialogues* or the *Letters* that it needs exploration. There seemed to me three alternative explanations to consider. The first alternative was that this structure had been, at least to some extent, superimposed and stiffened by Neo-Platonic copyists. (In fact, it *might* even have been the result of some well-meant rewriting.) Since the texts of the mss B and T derive from a common archetype as late as the sixth century A.D., and W from the same archetype, though with extensive variants, such an "improvement" could go undetected.[16] I discovered, however, that by various operations of textual reconstruction we can show that the text already had this logical rigidity even before the advent of Neo-Platonism in the third century A.D.[17]

The logic looks like a parody.[18] A parody, however, may be relatively serious, or relatively lighthearted. If the point Plato wanted to make was a serious one, such as criticizing Eudoxus's metaphysical position, we would expect scrupulous and precise handling of its deductive logic. (An *invalid* deduction, as Richard Robinson pointed out effectively, has no relevance to either the thesis or the logic used in its construction.)[19] If the point were a less serious one—for example, to show the potential inconsistencies, including babbling, that followed from Megarian logic—we would expect a much more casual, even careless, construction.[20] In fact, if Plato were joking, we might expect some *deliberate* inconsistencies—omissions, misreasonings, other jolting lacunae in the Way of Truth—in the argument. How many such signs there should be is difficult to judge, since the project presupposes a very eccentric sense of humor.

From our best current texts, it is clear that this issue is not easy to decide. Some very able Plato scholars have regarded the hypotheses as a joke, while others respectfully treated them as a revelation.[21]

The sort of thing that makes a decision of serious or nonserious intention difficult is the following. In hypotheses 1 and 2, there are 16 "theorems." Fifteen open with a "theorem statement"; one does not. Of the fifteen opening theorem statements, fourteen are followed by a questioning, "theorem indicating" response; but one, the fifteenth, is greeted by something else, which completely violates the pattern. The "if . . . then" conditionals, by and large, are unexciting standard potential optatives. *But* some dozen times per hundred, they appear instead as "emotive future," where nothing in text or context warrants screams of anticipation. Because of a suggestion, in a paper of the 1950s, that the Plato mss preserve the author's original distinction between the two spellings, *syn-* and *xun-*, a look at the spellings of the reflexive pronouns seemed in order.[22] This is largely unsystematic and random. And in at least six places responses that should mark divisions in the steps of argument are lacking.[23]

Now I don't intend to argue that parodies of formal logic *can't* be funny—whether that judgment rests on contempt or reverence for formal logic.[24] But Plato's *Euthydemus* had exploited this potentiality already, a decade and more before the *Parmenides* was written.[25] Would any author have felt obliged to perpetuate this joke again, with an added wealth of circumstantial detail. I think not.

There did seem to me one test that might decide this question of the author's intention. If we are dealing with an original that was serious in intent and precise in execution, discrepancies between later manuscripts will be due to cumulative errors in copying. A remark of Paul Shorey's bears on this: "this text," he said, "is impossible to copy exactly."[26] A casual count in 1960 tallied over three thousand errors in thirty copyings of the text.[27] If both this thesis of original rigor and the fact of copying difficulty are the case, we should expect bits and pieces of the correct original text to be conserved uniquely—and haphazardly—in each independent line of descent. And we would also expect that, as we reconstructed progressively earlier versions of Plato's text, the precision and rigor would increase. On the other hand, given a carefee, absurd, initial version, we might well anticipate the *opposite* effect: that normalization and intruded solemn expectation would lead to an increase of order as copies became later. Or, at the very least, we would anticipate that any reconstructed earlier version would be just as haphazard as those that were later.

I decided to follow up this line of inquiry. For almost any other Platonic text, it seems likely that this technique would be indecisive. (For example, Prof. E. R. Dodds, in his edition of the *Gorgias*, reports himself as frequently undecided between the alternative styles of the Vienna F and the BTW version.)[28] But, as I have noted, in the present case the underlying proof pattern often makes it possible to specify what would be the "correct" text if we assume the author to be serious and not joking.

The results seem to me to bear out my expectation. As I expected a priori, bits and pieces are uniquely conserved in a number of partially independent sources.[29] The result is an improvement in the text. Though it is not a great improvement, this is a brilliant-cut gem of argument, which for all of the predictable underlying symmetry of its facets deserves any restoration we can make of its dazzling surface refractions.

Reprinted by permission from PHILOSOPHY RESEARCH ARCHIVES, vol. 8 (1982) (Chapter I of "The History and Interpretation of the Text of the *Parmenides*").

Part III

Platonic Thoughts about Aristotle

Chapter 10

If Aristotle Had Become Head of the Academy . . .

I

The thesis of this chapter is that Aristotle had in mind two systematic changes in Platonism which he thought would make it the completion of systematic speculative thought. Since the changes, though drastic, were systematic, most of the insights of the dialogues and Academy discussions would have remained intact when reinterpreted as coherent parts of an enlarged Aristotelian-Academic scheme.

The problem with Plato's view, as Aristotle saw it, was how to connect *logical* and *temporal* causality. Such Platonic analyses as that represented by the Divided Line in *Republic* VI, by the deductions of the *Parmenides*, or by the Myth of the True Earth in the *Phaedo*, ran at right angles to the temporal order. That is, they organized forms, structures, objects, and images on a vertical axis running from Being to Becoming. That axis, on its two higher levels, represented an *eternal present* with no provision for projection into or refraction through a past into a future.[1]

If this seemed a defect needing correction, two simple systematic changes could have done it. The most important change is represented by Aristotle's new theory of causality. Aristotle's four causes can be pictured geometrically with the use of coordinates. The *vertical* line is a Formal-Material causal axis, which corresponds to the Being-Becoming Platonic order. The *horizontal* line runs from efficient to final causes, thus representing a temporal sequence from past to future that intersects the logical order in a progressive present, a "now." Aristotle characterizes this causal line as change in a constant direction from "potentiality" to "actuality."[2] The axes and causes are:

FORMAL

EFFICIENT · FINAL

MATERIAL

The vertical axis, we have said, matches Plato's Divided Line.

BEING: THE GOOD
                FORMS (INCLUDING "SPECIES")
                STRUCTURES (DIANOIA)
BECOMING: NATURAL SUBSTANCES (WORLD SOUL; SOULS)
                ELEMENTS (QUANTITATIVE)
                APPEARANCES AND FANCIES

Using a kind of philosophical geometry, we can rotate the Divided Line ninety degrees to the right, so that the Form of the good lies as a future goal along the time axis.[3] The forms then become *ideals,* attractive goals given temporal relevance by the desire they create. That desire, in turn, is not an abstract limitation of pure form but the concrete attraction of a perfect Prime Mover.

A second change is to make Plato's system *specific.* Each kind of thing in Aristotle's scheme is attracted toward its own specific type of self-realization; species act as fully determinate goals, to be realized by each mature type specimen. Thus "all things desire God," while true, applies only to the most remote principle of final causality in the system. The male piglet does not have a natural drive toward becoming an Athenian statesman, much less a god, but toward becoming a boar. A determinateness of specific form is supposed to be necessary to exercise proper teleological attraction.[4]

The first systematic revision causes very little strain. Since it can be represented as a modification of the Platonic position as a whole, the sequence and interaction of parts will stay recognizably the same.

However, the second change is more complex. Aristotle's temporal causal axis is taken as introducing separateness of individuals, substances, societies, and kinds, where the atemporal Platonic scheme stressed continuity. (We will return later to a precise statement of the logical difference that separates Aristotelian from Platonic analysis of the genus-species relation.)[5] In later Western thought, Platonists will criticize Aristotelians for being unable to handle any "borderline case." (And not only Platonists: John Locke is eloquent on this point.) Neo-Platonism transfers some of this Aristotelian separative property to its logical space. (For my own purposes of diagramming main sequences of causally related types of entities, I have also introduced some Aristotelian crystallization and insulation into my "Platonism.")

The scholar who saw most clearly that Plato's doctrines for the most part anticipate Aristotle's modifications was, I think, A. E. Taylor.[6] In the latter part of his *Aristotle,* after a rather appreciative treatment of the *Organon,* Taylor has an inventory of the Platonic doctrines that he finds Aristotle claiming as his own invention. (And even in logic, the class relations basic to syllogism were already set out, Taylor thinks, in the *Phaedo.*) The ethics echoes the *Philebus* in its doctrine of the mean in relation to moral virtue and in its critique of hedonism. The role of the Prime Mover as object of desire is so close as to be a paraphrase of the treatment of Eros in Plato's *Symposium.* The astronomy is a less than scientifically literate reformulation of an elegant mathematical model into a tangled mess of physical spheres. The art of rhetoric, as Aristotle develops it, purports to correct Plato's *Gorgias,* and in fact does so, but with ideas adapted from Plato's *Phaedrus.* And the list can go on.

The point is, however, that in each case Aristotle introduces his own causal teleology, with the related method of organic analysis from functional wholes through proximate organic parts to *explain* these Platonic adaptations.[7]

What Aristotle needed to do, as he saw it, to complete his project of developing a final science of philosophy was to supply the teleological explanations that give concreteness to Platonism's logical hierarchies and give directed specificity to Platonism's general temporal processes. Aristotle found closure throughout the natural world: there are no borderline cases, there is no origin of species, the cosmos needs no divine cosmic adjustments, the parts of animals are without exception functional.[8] This fact of closure seemed to go beyond any explanation that the Academy had supplied.

Thus, if Aristotle had, in 347, become the Head of the Academy, in charge of its structure and policy, there probably would have been no obvious discontinuity in doctrine. The reason is that a project proposed as completing Plato's system could have added Aristotelian final causes to give sharper specification, while keeping intact (but now as peripheral), the logical metaphysics and mathematical physics of Platonism. The development, though, would certainly have been accompanied by an increasing departmentalization, as Aristotle's "analytic" method displaced "dialectic," and "mathematical structural analysis" ("God always geometrizes") was replaced by qualitative "functional organic" anatomies.[9] But I can see that Aristotle could claim that Plato had been right at every point, though Philosophy had since gone beyond him.

In line with this claim would have been the fact that Plato himself did not formulate his ideas with rigid consistency. Insights that seemed somewhat anomalous could often have provided openings for Aristotle to claim that his own work was developing such insights by Plato. An obvious example here is the tension between the apparent function of Platonic forms in the tranquil *Phaedo* and the demonic *Symposium*. (It would be helpful to understand how Aristotle saw this point if we had more fragments of *Aristotle's* versions of the *Phaedo* [his *Eudemus*] and the *Symposium* [his dialogue with that same title.])[10]

But Aristotle did not become The Head of the Academy. He went, instead, with his project of revision firmly in mind, to Assos. There, presumably, he wrote his critical essay *On the Ideas*. One can read the fragments we have of that—and I would so read them—as a statement that the problems posed in Plato's *Parmenides* were not resolved by the interpretations which had found favor in the Academy at this time.[11] This is a crucial first step in Aristotle's proposed revision. His own causal theory will, he thinks, explain why nature has *more* closure and order than process or procession (Speusippus and Xenocrates, respectively) could account for.[12]

Plato's forms, however, did not always fit into the logical space of the atemporal Being-Becoming scheme. Particularly in the *Symposium*, Plato shows them functioning as ideals rather than as types or kinds. (In the *Republic* this role of form as ideal is served by the model state constructed in the dialogue. Thus this demonstration of the right way to develop political science also postulates the form as ideal.)[13]

Suppose these suggestions are taken, as they were by A, as a key to the solution of the "participation" problem. Then the Forms must not simply be logical abstractions, but goals with attractive power, acting in time as future targets guiding present changes from potentiality to actuality. This sort of causal action must be somehow substantial, not merely logical nor purely formal.[14]

An Aristotelian will evidently think of completing the Platonic account by transferring the Form of the Good from a remote *formal* cause (where its status is like that of a logical *summum genus*) to a remote *final* cause (a temporally attractive *telos*, an ideal). By the simple metaphysical geometry already mentioned this can be represented as a ninety-degree rotation of the Divided Line to the right in Aristotle's causal coordinate system, thus transforming the Form of the Good into the (substantial) Prime Mover as unifying cosmic final cause.

THE GOOD
SPECIES
STRUCTURES
SUBSTANCES /STRUCTURES SPECIES THE PRIME MOVER
t–   to   t +

This transformation leaves the sequences and causal connections of Plato's logical scheme intact, while it gives his extralogical sporadic dynamical insights a new and important incorporation.

(Aristotle felt—correctly, perhaps—that there was a sort of external relation between the literary dynamics and the demonstrative demands of the Platonic dialogue. In fact, the two seemed to him to go in opposite directions: the driving force of the *drama* displays and depends on the forms as *ideals,* attractive powers; the *demonstrations* and *refutations* depend on the forms as systematically related *kinds* and *types.* Although it is the *Republic* that Aristotle specifically criticizes for this split (in *Politics* II), the place where it is most apparent is rather the *Phaedo.* Socrates' life has been devoted to the *pursuit* of forms, though his final conversation rather presents an *analysis* of them.)[15]

As I have noted, A. E. Taylor was particularly sensitive to Plato's anticipations of what have generally been put forward as original Aristotelian insights. Without as yet evaluating Taylor's negative appraisal of Aristotle's originality, we can recognize some justice in the underlying factual data on which it rests. Because of the similarity in sequence and connection of the Platonic *logical* order of things and Aristotle's reoriented *teleological* order, the Platonic *causal sequences* will remain intact, though the new notion of the *kind of causal efficacy* relating them gives the scheme a radically modified interpretation.

(We will see later that the same relation holds in the Academic accounts of cosmology where, as in the *Timaeus,* causal explanation is transformed into what an Aristotelian would call *efficient* rather than *formal* causality. The world order will still be the logical one, but the causal sequence will be seen as running causally from past to future, in the opposite direction from Aristotle's teleological order. Thus *creation* in the *Timaeus* frame of reference contrasts with *contemplation* in the Aristotelian.)[16]

Aristotle's methodical use of distinctions led naturally to a departmentalization of the Lyceum. Thus in Aristotle the relations of forms as Plato defined them could be selectively studied as the logical patterns asserting inclusion, exclusion, intersection and nonintersection. The result is the analysis of syllogism in the *Analytics;* this in contrast to Socrates' concern with the physical impossibility of an even triad or a cold fire,[17] in the *Phaedo.*

Three consequences follow from Aristotle's transformation, as I have reconstructed it. The first is a new retrospective whole-to-part method of analysis, appropriate to a world where species are fixed.[18] The Aristotelian Order of Nature, as I have noted, invites contemplation; it does not change, and its patterns—the species—bear no trace of a creation, whether by generation, making, or action. Since final causes are essentially complete (if they were not, they could not exercise the specific attraction that they do), they do represent selections among possible alternatives, but closed and actual units with functional perfection. This suggests that the proper analytic method will involve a constant assessment of *privation*. In zoology, for example, the young animal striving to grow is to be understood as a deprived adult. Its organs and actions are potentially, but deficiently, nature's aim.[19] (Necessarily and fatalistically, the study of old age and death must follow this same plan, as the individual carries beyond maturity, and begins to deviate more and more widely from ideal functioning. The high point of individual self-realization thus comes, for living things, at mid-career.)[20] In the case of human beings, maturity is complex and precarious, admitting a wide range of varied moral and intellectual development. But here, too, there is a single elite best ideal of human maturity. (Differences are then to be explained by different degrees, causes, directions of deviation. Slaves have no power of self-determination; children are so plastic that they as yet lack character; women are biologically incapable of full human maturity; workers lack the leisure essential to political and intellectual self-realization. Statesmen and politicians come out rather well, but it finally seems that only the contemplative philosopher is *fully* human. It is almost as though full happiness had only been attained by Aristotle himself at his maturity.)[21]

Since there is a conservation of order, analysis need not look for alternatives. Every part of an organic or quasi-organic whole is functional, hence the problem is not *whether* it has a function, but *what* the function is. (Though in the cases of society and works of fine art, the development of the full natural forms with functioning parts comes only after a history of experiment and discovery.)[22] There is an aesthetic economy in the completed form that ensures that each functional order has a maximum closure and functional value for its component parts. There would be no point, in this frame of reference, to raising such a question as whether there may be *no* teleological reason that explains *why* a flatworm has such large, crossed, eyes; or why the sessile mollusc called the pecten has any eyes at all.

With social organizations and works of fine art, the method will work as well, *provided* there can be an initial sorting-out of specimens that are in fact functionally organized from those that fail to be. In part, historical development helps with this selection, as tragedy, for example, develops toward its "more mature, natural" form. Or, again, a collection of constitutions may help discriminate stable from deviant forms of social organization.

The thing to be emphasized here is Aristotle's association of teleology and completed self-sufficiency. This is a *critic's* method, not an inventor's or creator's. It works excellently for the finished works in an art museum or a balanced social community; it does not do well in an art studio or a society caught in rapid evolutionary change.[23]

Somehow, the substantial attractive action of God and the specific forms depends on their determinateness, each with a kind of *autarchy*.[24] This quality is realized completely by the Prime Mover, and desired but only approximated by all the rest of nature. It is in this context that one can say "all things desire God." (The forty-seven or fifty-five subordinate movers, for example, while they enjoy their activity, still desire rest in a proper place. But since their bodies by nature have a circular motion, and there is no differentiation of terminal from nonterminal places in a circle, just as there is no differentiation of earlier and later in a cycle, their desire to be the Prime Mover will never be wholly satisfied. Yet they like zipping along.)

The difference between logical and teleological orientation gives rise to very different treatments of the realm of *structure*. Platonic forms, in the logical order, can characterize individuals only as they are schematized. A function, grasped by *noesis*, needs specification by *dianoia* before it can determine an instance. These specifications are not deviations, but added mediating determinations. For Aristotle, on the other hand, there is one ideal "normal" structure for each ideal specimen, and alternative quantitative realizations are relegated to the status of accidental deviations. Structures are a realm of quantitative abstraction, partially mind dependent, and—if Aristotle is right in his *Metaphysics* M and N—without any causal function.

I can see how one strand of Plato's own published thought might lead directly to the Aristotelian reinterpretation. In the *Statesman*, the Eleatic Stranger distinguishes two kinds of "measure." The first is measure of a descriptive sort, comparing greater and lesser—this is what the Pythagoreans study. The second, which is what is used in arts and crafts, is "normative" measure, which compares the right amount with excess and defect, "too much" and "too little." In this connection, Plato promises a future discussion of the theory of normative measure; but that discussion, *The Philosopher*, was never written.[25] What we have instead of such a general theory is Plato's demonstration, in the *Philebus*, that normative measure causes value in mixtures: an excursion in practical application rather than the promised general formulation.

Let the "right amounts" of normative measure be identified with Aristotle's "final causes" and it might seem that this could supply the theoretical framework which Aristotle thought Plato needed. The "measure" carries with it an *optimum* size, shape, and set of parts, rather than limiting a range of alternatives.

The role of the mean, the method of analysis as a study of deviation and privation, the relegation of mathematics to a sort of technological discipline, and the idea of an order of nature closed and suited for God's contemplation, all would follow out this extension of Academic thought. And it would exactly admit the interpretation that Taylor gave of Aristotle's relation to Plato: that in each case, he simplified and reorganized insights that Plato had already provided.

In this way, the history of the Academy would have been like that of the Lyceum. (Although I think that finally, in Rome, Neo-Platonism would have replaced the Aristotelian teleology with something like Plotinus's return to the logical-ontological order.)[26]

II

Meanwhile, in the Academy, Plato himself and his associates seem also to have felt the need for an account of the *temporal* causal efficacy of the logical formal system. The difficulty of using a purely *formal* scheme to account for participation and change is set out sharply in the odd-numbered hypotheses of the *Parmenides*. The sharp contrast of Being and Becoming, what always is and what is temporal, sets up contraries in the *Timaeus* in a way that demands mediation. (In this "Academic" group, I certainly would include Speusippus and Eudoxus; but I am *not* so sure about Xenokrates.)[27]

Now, just as a rotation of the Divided Line to the right through our systematic space will make the Form of the Good temporally relevant as an ideal—a "future" attractive power—so a rotation to the left will make it temporally relevant as a creative power, bringing the present into being from an evolving past. Instead of a Prime Mover, then, this transformation gives us a God who is a Demiurge, what Aristotle would count as an efficient, not a final, cause.

The *Timaeus* thus represents an alternative solution to the problem that concerned Aristotle.[28] And this alternative solution seems to anticipate many of the systematic features of twentieth-century "process philosophy." There are still conservation principles, but the creative flow of time also leaves room for novelty. Plato's God admires the aesthetic quality of the cosmos He has made, and from time to time steps in to adjust and repair it.

The two ways of relating what we may call the "main sequence of entities" are exactly opposed. Aristotle's order of nature is fixed and determinate. There is relatively little place for emergence of creativity—none, if we use a time scale adequate to the cyclic rise and fall of civilization, with the repeated discovery of arts and sciences. The *Timaeus*, on the other hand, leaves room for novelty within very general quantitative laws conserving symmetry and momentum. And Plato's other late works, the *Philebus*, *Laws* X, the Myth of Cosmic Reversal in the *Statesman*, and the baffling *Epinomis*, all move toward something like this ninety-degree left systematic transformation.

It appears that in the course of Academic discussions there was strong support for a systematic modification quite different from Aristotle's theory. An analogous discussion occurs in the thirteenth century in Paris between Augustinians and Aristotelians. The non-Aristotelian alternative sees the succession of entities as related by creation, rather than something more like contemplation. And such creation is marked at each point by selection among alternatives; and the alternatives, as I read Plato, include alternate structures that are equally functional and aesthetically satisfying. (So the best of all possible worlds would not, for Plato, be uniquely determined in detail.)

Aristotle's completion of Platonism leads to the view of the world as a perfect Museum with God as pure mind appreciating the type specimens and "critics' choice" art collection. Plato's *Timaeus* evokes a God much more at home in the workshops of ancient Athens that adjoined the Temple of Hephaistos at the northwest corner of the ancient Agora.[29] This God of the *Timaeus* admires the world in motion; realizes that its medium prevents its full perfection; and looks in surprised pleasure at its dynamic operation, as an *agalma*, a thing of beauty for the gods.

Aristotle's auxiliary deities are pure calculating machines, hard wired to their respective stars. Plato's are—apparently—creative forces, directing human destinies and deserving special worship. From the *Timaeus* through the *Epinomis* there is an increasing sense of the creative power of something divine in history. Any citizen of Plato's state in the *Laws* who advocated Aristotle's theology would have found himself in prison in a wild mountain tract.

Twentieth century process philosophy, which has reacted against the Neo-Platonic version of Platonism as a source of claustrophobia, finds more and more congenial anticipations of its view as it studies very late Platonic works. (Whitehead and A. E. Taylor are brilliant

examples. But they are far from alone; see, for example, Charles Bigger, *Participation* and Robert Neville, *The Cosmology of Freedom*.)[30]

III

A main difference in method between these two revisions is that
the *Timaeus* approach is synthetic ("constructive") and prospective, the
Aristotelian analytic ("anatomical") and retrospective. The causal approach of the *Timaeus* is concerned with success of full realization. In
an interesting detail, which Cornford tried to schematize—not altogether successfully—this difference appears in the logical analysis of
"family relations."[31] A logical family, *genos*, divides into smaller kinship
groups, *eide*. What is the relation of these? If one is thinking in terms
of a plan for successive steps of a construction, the *general* determination comes before and is explanatory of the later specification. Thus
Plato's God's decision to make the world One rather than Many, is an
explanatory condition prior to the later determinations of the kind of
oneness selected. On this view, the genus is a conjunction of the species,
which do not define it adequately taken separately. Thus for courage
(= G) we have that of a soldier (S1), of a child (S2), perhaps of an
animal (S3). And G = df S1.S2.S3. But if instead of construction the
logical model is analytic classification, it is the several species that define our world, and not the vaguer general compartments into which
we can sort them. Thus again for courage (= G), we have that of the
soldier (S1), the child (S2), perhaps the animal (S3). But this time,
G = slvvS2vvS3 (where 'vv' represents 'either or but not both'), as
though G is incomplete and less explanatory than the S-disjunction. If
we think of a dogfish as a selected type of aquatic animal to be created,
it is relevant to see it in relation to a catfish. But if aquatic animal is
only an abstract label for actual species, study of the catfish will add
nothing at all to the analysis of the type—specimen dogfish. In this
respect, Aristotle's logical method has a rule that goes in the opposite
direction from the synoptic dialectic of Platonism.

The record of the actual post-Platonic left-handed transformation
in the Academy is distorted and incomplete. This is due in large part to
the fact that its history was written by Aristotelians, and its primary
source materials not carefully preserved. (That it should be the Aristotelians who are intellectual historians of the Academy follows directly
from the role Aristotle gives to intellectual history, in contrast to an
Academy model of truth based on mathematics and astronomy). The
extant evidence does suggest, however, that Speusippus, in particular,

had developed the alternative to Aristotle's transformation in the Academy. For example, he is quoted as saying that the good comes last, if it is realized at all; for Aristotle, on the other hand, the good comes first: "actuality precedes potentiality alike in thought and fact." Speusippus thinks that "The One does not exist" (having in mind something like The One of the First Hypothesis of the Parmenides?); Aristotle's "one Ruler let there be" is his rejoinder. And, according to Aristotle, Speusippus somehow reconstituted the forms as "numbers." (What Aristotle means here may be explained in *Metaphysics* Iota, but if so I don't understand it.)

"The modern philosophers have made mathematics the whole of philosophy," Aristotle protests. But he is wrong; they had instead introduced a new, alternative philosophical solution to the problem Aristotle thought he had solved by recourse to teleology.

IV

The main problem Aristotle faced in the Lyceum can, I think, fairly be described as rhetorical. He was known as a former Platonist, and so could well be expected to offer a continuing development of Academic philosophy. But the Academy's interpretation of Platonism had, by the time he founded his own school, gone in what Aristotle considered just the wrong way. And yet there was an isomorphism of the Academy's and Aristotle's main sequences of kinds of entities and their causal order. A stress on similarities and analogies could challenge Aristotle's claims to new, critical, discrete moments of philosophic insight. What Aristotle had to do to establish his claim to originality was to emphasize the relative incompleteness of Plato's and the later Academy's position. As against Plato, this involved emphasis on two doctrines of the middle dialogues which Aristotle claimed he had revised. The first was the use of the *logical* dimension of the formalist system, rather than the teleological, as explanatory. Over and over again accusation, quotation, and paraphrase aim at establishing Plato's advocacy of a misguided *separation* of forms and instances. A "separation" in this sense exists whenever Plato asserts a logical, but does not explicitly supply a concrete causal, connection as explanatory. That causal connections may somehow be implicitly operating in Plato's scheme does not gain Aristotle's sympathy; he does not feel that Plato is entitled to such *implicit* causal relations until he explains both how they are possible and how that possibility is made actual. The result, however, often seems a most unfriendly reading, as Aristotle seems perversely to

deny to his teacher insights that are to be found in the dialogues—
and in some cases that are also to be found in Aristotle's work, claimed
as his own original contribution.

The annoying thing must have been that if *he* had inherited the
Academy, Aristotle could have presented his work as a development,
not a sharp break. This would have made possible a different, less
discontinuous, account of the historical progression of Greek philosophy from its original recognition of material causality with Thales to
its completion with the culminating appreciation of final causes by
Aristotle.

First printed in *Energeia: Études aristotelicienne offerte a Mgr. Antonio
Jannone*, Centre International d'Études Platonicienne et Aristotelicienne, Paris
1986, pp. 102–116. Reprinted by permission of the Centre.

Chapter 11

The Unity of Aristotle's Metaphysics

In the late thirteenth century, Giles of Rome wrote a treatise *On the Errors of Philosophers*. He wanted to counteract the influence of newly recovered Greek philosophy and newly available Arabic science on Christian thought. After stating his aim, he opens the book "And first comes Aristotle!" If we are to judge importance by who comes first, whether as hero or villain, Giles's ranking seems sound. Aristotle is given credit for forming our modern ordinary language and our common sense both by thinkers who see this as a virtue (for example, Henry Veatch), those who thought it a disaster (for example, A. N. Whitehead), and those who find it an interesting piece of erudition.

Aristotle's admirers, Alexandrian, Arabic, Scholastic, and contemporary, claim that he has a method and a world-view which avoid the opposed excesses of materialism and idealism, and which replace empty dialectic with sound empirical attention to a four-dimensional natural order. Some adventures of ideas at Chicago, Notre Dame, and Georgetown universities lend some support to the claim.

The key to Aristotle's achievement and its influence should lie in his science of metaphysics, which Aristotle himself called variously "first philosophy," "theology," and "wisdom." The purpose of that study was to explore common principles of being, logic, and thought, and to stabilize a method of causal explanation that would organize knowledge and reality.

We know, from various writings, that Aristotle thought of what we will call "metaphysics" as a science, which would study things that are wholly real yet unchangeable. We have a work, in fourteen books, called Aristotle's *Metaphysics*, a title given it because it was placed "after the *Physics*" in the standard Hellenistic arrangement of the works of Aristotle.[1] Clearly, if this is what its title claims it to be, it is one of the most important works in the history of philosophy. This judgment is reflected by the decision of the editors of Everyman's Library to offer a new translation as their one thousandth title.[2] Earlier, the judgment was backed up by the story that Eudemus thought "it was unfitting that so great a work should be published."[3] But is the title

141

right, or may we have here only a scrapbook of odd lecture notes and term papers?

The fourteen "books" clearly represent work written at various dates in Aristotle's career, and their organization is jagged, transitions and connections very often lacking. Another story about the book is told of Avicenna: he read the book thirty-two times without understanding; then he found a *Commentary* by Alfarabi, and with its aid understood on the thirty-third reading. My question in the present chapter could be restated as the question of whether Avicenna was right the thirty-third time or the first thirty-two. And this question is not simply rhetorical. The human mind has a great fondness for coherence, and tends to discover it even where there is very little objective assistance. A case in point occurred once in Australia, where some bored soldiers composed word-lists by opening a dictionary at random, then published the result as a book of poetry, with the title *Angry Penguins*. At least one critic gave it a good review. This is a reminder not to take claims about hidden order too seriously until the hidden harmony is made overt and explained to our satisfaction. And the baffling fact is, on naive confrontation, that the set of fourteen books of essays have more order than one would expect a Hellenistic librarian to be able to construct from miscellaneous left-over bits; but less order than one would expect from a master philosopher.[4]

One thing that makes this problem difficult is a disagreement as to what would constitute a satisfactory *solution*. For example, interpreters who assume that "metaphysics" must be *either* materialism or idealism, formalism or naturalism, will accept a claim of "unity" only when a work is shown to be consistently one or the other. Interpreters who think of unity in terms of a uniform style and single date of composition will demand kinds of tight transition and inner coherence that more tolerant stylistic critics would not insist on. Traditionally, "higher" critics, who find the work coherent when viewed from a great distance, substitute paraphrase for explanation as they approach finer detail, or compromise the distant vision of unity by admitting closer incoherence and rough finish. (Richard McKeon seems to be an example of the former, Sir W. D. Ross of the latter, type of explication.)[5]

In my present discussion, I intend to follow four lines of inquiry, corresponding to Aristotle's own four dimensions of "causality." The first line is strictly textual and philosophical: it rests on my discovery, in 1954, that definite stylistic devices mark off coordinate and subordinate problems in the lists of Books Beta and Kappa.[6] The second consideration is formal: a set of familiar Aristotelian distinctions exactly match the sequence of textual considerations, book by book. (These formal principles of sequence are first, the words-thoughts-things methodological triad explained by Richard McKeon, second a subordinate order in terms of the four causes, an order recognized in general by McKeon, and developed in more detail in a dissertation by Dr. Smigelskis at Yale.) My third set of considerations is rhetorical, having to do with the character of Aristotle as his efficient causal agency enters into the structure of the work. My thesis will be that the *method of composition* reflected here is one familiar enough to modern professors and lecturers, a thrifty reuse of older notes and "articles," which explains stylistic anomalies and poor transitions without casting doubt on the authorship or the author as overall organizer. (We probably all know colleagues or fellow students who never throw old term papers away. They are kept neatly filed, and when it is time to plan a new lecture or article, the first move is toward the file drawer, to see what can be incorporated. How much revision and polished transition is added depends on the use intended; for lecture notes, far less than for published articles, since the lecturer can ad lib—or thinks he can, though the thought is mistaken—anecdotes, transitions, updating corrections.) A second part of this rhetorical examination will be my claim that the "lecture course" as a literary form has certain potentialities, in Aristotle's hands, for climax, interrupted sequence, and surprise. Just as his shorter lecture units will sometimes pause, digress, then return to a new perspective that resolves a deadlock, the *Metaphysics* as a whole can be read as a development in which a pause for review sets the stage for a pyrotechnical completion of the course as it moves on towards its close.

Finally, in my pursuit of a causal analysis, I will ask what the final cause of the *Metaphysics* itself is. How does it relate to Aristotle's total philosophical projects, to his organization of the Lyceum, and so on. (My final conclusion, to anticipate, will be that there is considerably more unity in the work than Taylor, or Jaeger, or Randall, or even Ross, have found; but less than McKeon, or Aquinas, or Avicenna posited. Further, contra Zurcher and some of Jaeger's suggestions, I will argue that Aristotle himself was responsible for the overall selection and order of at least thirteen of the fourteen lectures making up the books of the *Metaphysics*.)

At the outset, as I said, it is clear that past interpretations have often rested on interpreters' presuppositions—philosophic, stylistic, or biographical. For the scholar who approaches this complex text with the idea firmly in mind that metaphysics admits of only two options, materialist and idealist, the work will be a disappointment. For, from either standpoint Aristotle seems to be inconsistent, either muddling what could have been a sound formalism by materialistic qualifications, or missing the chance to develop a coherent naturalism through a sentimental fondness for (adventitious) Platonic idealist motifs. A. E. Taylor reads the work in the former way, J. H. Randall in the latter.[7] A third interpreter who holds this two-option assumption, Josef Zurcher, argues that the amount of naturalism mixed into the *Metaphysics* simply proves that this is not the work of Aristotle himself, since antiquity knew *him* as a Platonist.[8]

Werner Jaeger seems to me to bring with him a biographical assumption, as well as the two-option view, using the former to resolve the problem raised by the latter.[9] His view is that as a young philosopher, Aristotle was a Platonist and an idealist, but as he grew older, he moved away from this towards a more empirical (and, in Jaeger's view, a "more mature") philosophical position. The puzzle we have been presenting arises from Aristotle or his editors having mixed together notes sections treating similar themes, but from opposed chronological stages in the development of Aristotle's thought, in the extended lecture. For example, at one time he has just one moving intelligence, but later he changes the number to either fifty-five or forty-seven. Now, I am sure no one will dispute Jaeger's perceptive observations on the differences in style, major and minor, that mark various sections of the *Metaphysics*. Nor is his notion of some sort of cut-and-paste piecing together of topical materials likely to be wrong. But the notion that naturalism is more mature than idealism is an externally imposed one. It could be argued that one of Aristotle's strongest attacks on Platonic idealism was his earliest, the *Peri Ideōn*, of ca. 345.[10] And there may be reasons for preferring the notion that, throughout his career, Aristotle tended to oppose, then balance, what he saw as two extreme positions. This dialectical technique would give the same effect of alternating standpoint, but without the biographical and chronological significance Jaeger attaches to the phenomenon.

Having established the divergence of past opinion, I would like to return to the problem itself, setting it out in more detail by briefly recapitulating the contents, in order, of the fourteen books themselves. I will try to make this description as like a catalogue of plumbing supplies as I can, without prejudging any unity that may underlie the ensemble.

Metaphysics Alpha writes a history of philosophy, organized as a progressive discovery of Aristotle's own "four causes." The causes, in his sense of "cause," are the formal cause of a thing—its shape or type; the material cause—its stuff or substratum; the efficient cause—the source of change which brought form and matter together; and the final cause—an end or goal toward which organisms develop, or a purpose artifacts serve. *Alpha* is a typical Aristotelian introduction to a topic via dialectically ordered history. But it is worth noting that already here, where the authorship is clearly Aristotle's own, the chapters representing individual lectures are put together in spots with thrifty use of earlier historical and critical essays.[11] The next book, *Alpha Minor,* or as a modern editor would number it, IA, is a short note on method, which adds something to the argument but may indeed be a later addition; this one I will not worry too much about. The third book, *Beta,* is one I do worry about. It introduces itself as a study of the problems of philosophy, first stated in general outline, then given more detailed formulation. If what we have in our total work is a coherent lecture course, then clearly *Beta* would be the key to its organization. But past interpreters have for the most part not found a coherent detailed outline here, nor one that matches the content of the subsequent lectures.[12] Books *Gamma* and *Delta* deal with logic and language. *Gamma* treats the principles of demonstration. *Delta,* treating various meanings of key terms, may be the "philosophical dictionary," which was one of Aristotle's early works, perhaps simply inserted here arbitrarily. Book *Epsilon* treats kinds of knowing, and locates metaphysics in the wider frame of sorts of knowledge. It suggested, to many later readers, that metaphysics should treat *only* those entities which are fully real but wholly unchanging, in which case it actually goes counter to the contents of the books that follow.[13] A trio of books, *Zeta, Eta,* and *Theta,* deal with "substances," things that are a combination of form and matter. These are part of a single theme, and are treated as the "backbone" of the *Metaphysics* by Jaeger and Ross. Book *Iota,* on unity, is treated as authentic, but misplaced. The whole search for explanations is a quest for a kind of unity; and this should be the final topic of a metaphysics course. Book *Kappa,* which now follows, is in three parts: it recapitulates the "problems" list of *Beta;* summarizes the solutions to two sets of problems, solutions given in books *Gamma* through *Epsilon;* and concludes by defining a set of terms from physics. The two problem lists are almost the same, and this forces us to suspend judgment among three possibilities.[14] We might delete *Kappa,* as a duplicate problems lecture that was put here by mistake; we might think of *Kappa* as the same lecture as *Beta,* but given at this point rather than at the beginning in an alternative version of the lecture course; or we might think of *Kappa* as a rather hasty and redundant set of notes for a review of the key problems, a review intended to come here and to refer back to, not displace, *Beta. Lambda,* the next book, treats the Prime Mover, reminding the reader that one of Aristotle's names for his first philosophy was "theology." But, just when we expect "metaphysics" proper to carry out the promised ontological analysis of substances that are "immovable and separable," *Lambda* deals with nature, change, and cosmology. This has led scholars to view it as a separate, complete treatise, rather forcibly inserted here. Books *Mu* and *Nu*, the final books, offer a sort of appendix on forms and numbers, showing that neither Pythagorean numbers nor Platonic forms are metaphysically functional. These (Books *M* and *N*, not forms and numbers) are kept by editors of the text. But they are certainly patchy; part of *M* is a repetition, almost verbatim, of part of the critique of Plato in Book *Alpha*; joining is worse than usual; the contents are not neatly sorted out as the outline suggests they could have been as between various versions—all untenable—of substantial or causal numbers or forms.[15]

One suggestion—and a rather conservative one—is that we keep *Alpha-Beta-Gamma-Epsilon-Zeta-Eta-Theta-Mu* and *Nu*, delete *Alpha minor, Delta, Kappa, Lambda*, and relocate *Iota* at the end. This is rather drastic editorial intervention, but after it is done, it still seems (see Ross's *Commentary*) that less than half of the major problems raised in *Beta* are treated in the subsequent text, and then not quite in order. It should be clearer now than it was before we did this detailed inventory of content that the case for the unity of our inherited collection fourteen treatises and the science Aristotle projected as "first philosophy" is a problematic one.

Somehow, *Beta* should hold the key. In the twentieth century, no readers have had the temerity to defend Wilamowitz's suggestion that *Beta* is a work in a lost literary form, the "School-Logos." The point of this form was to be a sort of challenge to the student, an essay or lecture in which the expert set forth as many problems as he could devise, *in a deliberately scrambled order*. The idea was to challenge and interest the student; and there was no implicit contract, as Wilamowitz saw it, to answer later, or even to treat later, all of the problems making up the pyrotechnical display. But from the comments of modern readers of *Beta*, even the sympathetic ones, one wonders whether the School Logos view would not be the best explanation of the findings of the incoherent maze that seems not to match any standard philosophic order, and that poses fifteen problems of which only half-dozen are ever solved or heard of again? (Wilamowitz also believed that *Beta* was only one of three extant specimens of his lost form, the other two being Plato's *Euthydemus* and *Parmenides*. Since neither of the latter qualify on closer examination, this weakens his case.)

My work with the *Beta* problem lists has persuaded me that there are certain problems singled out stylistically as major and coordinate. Does the outline thus singled out confirm, refute, or leave open the question of deliberate disorder?

Seven of the many problems thrown together in the first chapter of *Beta* are singled out by a *men . . . de* coordinating construction, while an eighth introduced by *te* and with a verbal in *-teos* also seems meant to be coordinate. These begin with the question of whether the study of being and the investigation of causes is the province of a single science or of more than one? (This is followed by two subordinate problems relating to the scope of such a science.) This first problem, at 995b. 4–13, thus includes Ross's problems (hereafter numbered R) R1–R3. A second problem, at 995b.13–18, is "and we must also say, whether there are only sensibles, or other substances besides these." This, using the *de* and *-teos* to indicate coordination (*kai touto de . . . phateon . . .*) is Ross's problem R-5. I will count 995b.18–25 as a third coordinate problem, assuming a lost or intended but omitted *de.* The phrasing is very like that of my second problem: (*peri te touton . . . episkepteon . . .*). This problem is "whether only substances or also their essential attributes are to be treated"; Ross's problem R4. At 995b.25–31, the phrase *pros de toutois* singles out as a fourth problem "what scientist treats same, other, . . . and the concepts of dialectical inquiry?" Ross does not number this question as one of his coordinate problems. The next stylistic indication of coordination comes at 995b.31–996a4, my fifth problem, introduced by *eti de toutois:* "what is each essential attribute, and has it one contrary?" This is broken into subordinate questions about principles: are they elements or rather genera, etc.? Ross numbers these specified cases as problems R6 and R7, and does not treat my fifth problem as coordinate. A sixth problem is stated at 995.b.31 (*malista de zeteteon . . .*), a problem in two main parts: (1) whether there are causes other than material causes? and (2) whether there is something apart from composite entities? Ross numbers this eight at the first question (marked by the *de*) but discusses it as though the second, introduced in the text by the more frequent *poteron . . .* , were the main point.

Comparison with the list in *Kappa*, and the very similar phrasing in which the sixth and seventh problems are posed, leads me to count the problem between them, a sort of 6a, as coordinate, too. This is the question "whether the principles are determinate in number or kind," Ross's R9 and R10. (The fifth problem is introduced *eti de toutois*, the seventh by *eti de aporian*, and the use of *eti* to introduce my '6a' between them suggests a lost *de.*) Now the list moves on, with my seventh problem at 996a.4–12, introduced by *eti de . . . aporian echon*, to ask "whether unity and being are themselves the substance of things?" This with two subordinate questions equals Ross's R11–R13. Finally, at 996a.12–15, comes my eighth problem, introduced by *pros de toutois . . . poteron*. This is the question, "are number, measure, and shape substance?" This equals Ross's R14 and R14a or R15.

This scrutiny of stylistic clues thus leads to a set of coordinate problems, which is in fact a philosophically coherent one. A first problem asks about the logic and language proper to metaphysics; a second group inquires into the kind of knowledge it will represent; a third set asks about its subject-matter proper, with one question each about its *principles, causes,* and *subject-matter;* while a final query challenges a set of "hyperbolic entities," postulated causes or substances that are not real or functional.

Two things in particular confirm me in my notion that this list is right. The first is that where Ross's listing suggests that the extant text carries out only two-fifths of the program announced in *Beta*, my list of eight finds every one of its problems resolved in later discussions, in the *Beta* order of treatment; and five of these eight resolutions include explicit cross-references back to the "problems" lecture.[16] The second thing that is good about my list is that the organization of problems into the three groups of questions about words, thoughts, and things, exactly matches Richard McKeon's notion that this is a standard Aristotelian organizing triad. In his account of the argument of *Metaphysics*, McKeon uses this principle of order but without relating it to the philological patterns of *men* and *de*.[17]

These same eight problems, substantially, make up the set given detailed discussion in the balance of *Beta* (which is not surprising), and also in Book *Kappa* (which suggests a carefully thought out list, repeated in a separate problems lecture). My conclusion on this point is, therefore, that the entire lecture series, from *Beta* forward, is introduced by a careful course outline, and sticks to it systematically. This match of problem and resolution seems to me far beyond the competence of a supposed Hellenistic editor, even supposing the infinitely improbably fact that he had exactly the set of notes and essays needed to fill out the program.

This brings me to my next line of inquiry. Are some of the features that have led to questioning the systematic unity of the *Metaphysics* capable of being answered when we consider the Aristotelian lecture as a literary form, and explore the method of its composition? (What makes this line of inquiry hard and risky is that we are not allowed to assert things about the form or the author which we cannot document *in the text itself.* That caution from New Criticism is a needed safe-guard against free association.)

The argument of the lecture series at large is that there must be a role in reality for forms and species; if there were not, science would be impossible, and there would be no stable order of nature. But if these formal entities are made so separate that they are 'out of touch with' their instances, we face the Platonic Problem of 'separation,' the impossible job of putting them together again.

The *Metaphysics* as we have it uses two successive types of order to develop this theme. First, it locates metaphysics in respect to the words-thoughts-things triad. Then within the things moment, the four causes are used successively to organize the discussion. Thus *Gamma* takes up the proper logic, *Delta* sorts out the proper language, *Epsilon* locates first philosophy among kinds of human knowledge and action. Here the second principle of order takes over. *Zeta* gives a highly technical account of formal causes, distinguishing Aristotle's own "species" from "Platonic forms" or Aristotelian "universals" or "genera." *Eta* returns to the material cause with its reminder that formal and material causes are correlative, so that one implies the other. *Theta* now takes up the role of efficient causes, the *power* that brings form and matter together. (This introduces a dynamic factor, where the analysis of *Zeta* and *Eta* tended to be static, using a bronze sphere as an example of form-matter rather than, say, an individual person or animal.)[18]

From the preview of the history of philosophy in *Alpha*, we ourselves, and most of Aristotle's audience, anticipate that Aristotle will somehow resolve all the remaining deadlocks by the introduction of his own philosophic discovery, the final cause. In fact, he seems to be aiming toward the ambitious thesis that "the causes of all things are the same analogically," a thesis that would establish the role of metaphysics very nicely.[19]

But most of us underrate Aristotle's rhetoric as a lecturer. With all the parts *but one* in place, he seems to pause to recapitulate the complex intersection of the three causes he has just analyzed, then in a flashback digression to remind us that while we *have* solved the problems of metaphysical discourse and knowledge, key questions of its subject-matter still remain. Returning, the introduction of remote (and proximate) final causes in *Lambda* will complete the analysis. Its crucial role is to point out the way in which species and forms function as causes for sensibles, namely, as final causes, in the sense of object of desire.

This means that one dimension of unity is still not adequately handled in *Iota*, and that this lack is meant to be emphasized by the repetition of the list of unsolved problems in *Kappa*. *Lambda* closes the gap, and *Mu* and *Nu* mop up leftover formal entities no longer needed as causes or principles.

This account of an architectonically brilliant but hasty slapdash construction of notes for a lecture series simply reveals on a larger scale what we already find with Aristotle's individual lectures taken as lesser literary units. For example, in a tightly set up Book such as *Metaphysics* A or *Physics* B, there is an opening with a clear outline. Then, taking *Metaphysics* A as one specific example, Aristotle goes back to his files of earlier talks and treatises, and pulls out bunches of notes that can be fitted into the series. (For example, in 345 he had given a critical lecture "On the Forms" to a group in Asia Minor. This reappears as a large part of *Alpha* chapter 9. He had written four or five sets of notes on Pythagoras and the Pythagoreans, and these are drawn on for paragraphs of chapter 6. And so on.) He then hastily blocks out the rest; he is, paradoxically perhaps, too impatient to polish the style, but too meticulous to want any minor objections or counterexample to escape him. Thus, there is typically a maze of parenthetical digression, quite out of scale in the total outline, as he clears up some annoying detail that has struck him. (Perhaps as good a case as any occurs in the *Physics* B lectures on causality: there, having remarked that only intelligent agents are called "lucky," he then digresses to explain the special case in which a horse might be called lucky, then digresses further to explain why Protarchus once called an altar stone a "lucky stone.")[20] He rewrites the old material somewhat and sometimes, so that it fits in "all right." (And he assumes he can improve the fit when he actually uses the notes for a lecture.)[21]

In my own way, like Jaeger, I suppose I have had a story in mind, with Aristotle as the hero; a story which explains the chaotic mix of chance and order in the *Metaphysics* and, less spectacularly, in his whole lecture style. I see him as inspired, at a fairly early age, by the insight that "the causes of all things are the same analogically." If *that* can be shown to be true, Aristotle will emerge as the conqueror of the whole domain of knowledge and of fact. But the proof requires nothing less than creating causal analyses of *every kind* of being and of knowing on the cosmographic map. Aristotle, setting out on this quest, had no time nor patience to retrace and polish; to invent diverting anecdotes; life was short for the project. And by his death at age sixty-five, it is amazing how close Aristotle had come to the complete proof he was after. The comparison of Aristotle and his sometime student Alexander is often seen as a contrast between a conservative pedant and a romantic conquerer.[22] But the fact seems to be that, of the two, Aristotle was the more ambitious, in his design of conquering all knowledge and reality; and more nearly successful in his ambition.

So I conclude, bringing together these various lines of inquiry, that the *Metaphysics* as we have it owes its organization to Aristotle himself. It is hasty pulling together, with jumps and gaps. Nevertheless, in the detailed style where it counts most—for example, in the lists of problems—there is a tight organization. In the at first unexpected placement of books *Iota* and *Kappa* there is a piece of understandable showmanship by a professional lecturer preparing for the greatest climax of his lecturing career. In the impatience that shows through, there is a sign of Aristotle's race against the pressure of time; of an obligation he feels to complete the search for causes that had guided the course of pre-Aristotelian Greek philosophy.

To make this claim more than a myth, one must be able to provide a coherent account of the four causes of the treatise called Aristotle's *Metaphysics*, which explains the unpolished matter that stands against the brilliant architectonic form. I have been summing up work, in the present paper, which seems to converge at just such an explanation. The result is one which should surprise both materialists and idealists: Aristotle is neither of these, but claims to offer a third, and a better, mediating position. His treatises that we own state that position clearly, if not in lapidary style.

Reprinted by permission from the *Midwestern Journal of Philosophy* (spring 1978): 1–13.

Chapter 12

Aristotle as a Mathematician

Studies clarifying Aristotle's knowledge and use of mathematics also make it clear that an appraisal and transposition into modern terms of the nature and value of Aristotle's work in this area is a complex problem.[1] In basic features, the problem is typical of those that Aristotle poses to twentieth-century philosophers and scientists.

This chapter is an application of a more general formula of transformation which seems to sharpen the issues and explain the opposed reactions involved in treating Aristotle as a contemporary philosopher. In my discussion, I intend to show that Aristotle can be read as a Pythagorean scientist if we concentrate on his applications of mathematics; that he must be read as an anti-Platonic intuitionist if we concentrate on his account of the nature and foundations of mathematics; that the way in which he conceives his theory and practice to be related exactly reverses our contemporary idea of what constitutes *explanation* and what constitutes pre-demonstrative *inquiry*.

Although it has never been hard to find a Platonic element in the other dimensions of Aristotle's philosophy, my first point represents a sharp break with past consensus where mathematics is concerned. Again, while the stress on construction in Aristotle's view of mathematics has been repeatedly noted, this has not been properly connected with his restrictions on the law of excluded middle. Finally, though contemporary reaction illustrates three very different appraisals of Aristotle—that he is wrong at almost every point, that he has brilliant insights but develops them to anticlimaxes, and that he is using an idiom that is wholly unfamiliar—I do not know of any general theory of the interaction of systems which shows how a single system can produce all three of these reactions.

These three points I take to be related in such a way that the first does not presuppose the second, nor the first and second the third. The reader is therefore asked to judge the case for the interpretation of Aristotelian mathematics in its own terms, apart from his reaction to the concluding suggestions about Aristotle and metaphysics in general.

I

Aristotle is so outspoken in his criticisms of the use of mathematics by Pythagoreans and Platonists that it seems pointless to read him as a later Pythagorean.[2] Despite his strictures in theory, however, he seems in his practice to be carrying on the techniques of the *Timaeus* throughout his whole system.[3]

The most striking Pythagorean feature of Plato's *Timaeus* is its assumption that certain basic mathematical formulae will provide the key to all kinds of phenomena. For example, any problems of structure or interaction should be analyzable into three parts, with the quantitative relation $a:b::b:c$, where a and c are extremes, "harmonized" by the mean. Or, again, the analogy of periodic cycles is carried into cosmology in the same way, even down to the motions within the individual animal brain imitating those of the cosmos.[4] These basic patterns provide a guide to inquiry: we are to look in any range of subject-matter, for the linking mean term and the proper cyclic periodicity. This seems to be the kind of inquiry that Aristotle rejects as a mere "collection of analogies" in *Metaphysics* N.

However, if we assemble Aristotle's own uses of the "mean" as a key concept, the result is surprising.[5] In the logic, it is the "middle term" which connects the extremes in an inference.[6] In the *De Partibus Animalium*, the several organs which are each more near an extreme than the animal as a whole, are harmonized and the mean between them is the functioning of an organism.[7] In the *Physics*, we find Aristotle insisting that physics requires three principles, because pairs of opposites cannot interact except through some third mean.[8] The outermost heaven, which by its motion keeps the processes of nature in regular continuation, as described in *Physics* VIII is a mean between the eternal impassivity of the unmoved mover and the diverse processes of generation within the heavens; one of the arguments for its eternity is that it has this mediating place, and a mean must have some factor in common with each extreme.[9] Plato's "measure" from the *Philebus* reappears in an Aristotelian counterpart in the mean position of moral virtue in *Ethics* II, and in *Ethics* V "justice" is defined by analogies to kinds of ratio. (Plato used a somewhat similar device in *Republic* X to schematize the structure of "cosmic justice," though Aristotle goes back closer to the Pythagorean aphorism that justice is a square number.)[10] In *De Generatione et Corruptione*, the presence or absence of a mean accounts for different velocities of the six basic chemical reactions.[11] In the *Meteorologica* (in the final book which is sometimes thought not genuine), and also in *De Gen. et Corr.*, compounds are the mean which is the resultant of opposing vectors of natural motion, and this gives them their stability. (The echo of Plato's image of God using violence to join the components of matter, because they were fissionable, is faintly audible in this idea.)[12] It is recognition of the appropriate similarity as a mean which makes us understand metaphor in poetry, since this is a transference of names on the basis of some common similarity.[13] Psychologically, genius in poetry is sensitivity to such means, just as in science it is the ability to see middle terms of demonstration.[14] The phenomena of the psycho-physical level of a life cycle, in the *Parva Naturalia*, are analyzed in a way which will justify the usual Aristotelian location of closest approach to a final cause at the mean point of the cycle, not at either end.[15] And so on.

Among other cases of the omnipresent "mean" covered by my "and so on" is that of motion in a trajectory, which is a mean between and resultant of circular and linear motion. This leads to Aristotle's use of the mathematical notion of proportionately related cycles as the a priori form in which to treat periodicity within cosmology, if one is to follow the Pythagorean treatment. As a matter of fact, both the analysis of efficient causality and the account of induction in Aristotle displays this schematism of cycles. Circularity appears in the rotation of the outer heavens and this, with variations in solar energy that accompany it, is the source of seasonal cycles, and the basic cycle of transmutation of elements.[16] The subcycles of reciprocal change of place among bodies with rectilinear motion, and the lives of individual organisms, are connected by links of efficient causality to these other cosmic processes. Life cycles, for example, occur because in our part of the world coming-to-be never ceases to be, yet the organs of an animal are made of compounds not in their proper relative places, and they deteriorate with time. If the *De Motu Animalium* is Aristotelian, the stimulus-organic response mechanism it describes is basically cyclical; if it is not, its doctrine seems needed to complete the physiology.[17] In science, since a consequent can never be inferred with certainty from its antecedent, dependable induction is limited to those cases of cyclic change in which the same term becomes consequent and antecedent in turn: the inference of antecedent from consequent does provide certainty.[18]

A reader of the *Timaeus* can hardly fail to be struck by the apparently Platonic frame of mind these repeated metaphors show, when they are assembled from Aristotle's various writings. As a third case in point, Aristotle cites a Pythagorean "Table of Opposites" in *Metaphysics* A.[19] This table seems a device for contextual definition of key terms: by arranging a set of terms in two columns, their spatial relations are made analogous to their similarity or opposition in meaning. Such a "verbal matrix" was presumably an extension of similar diagrams used in computation, study of proportions, or genetic theory where combinations were listed.[20] In any case, the "semantic field" of meaning it seems to imply is very Pythagorean, and reminds us of Aristotle's deprecation of their "collections of analogies."[21] Yet Aristotle makes five subsequent references in the *Metaphysics* to a *systoichia*, clearly a verbal matrix, and uses this diagram as the starting-point of inferences, especially in M and N.[22] Whether the intended diagram is Aristotle's own, or is, as some scholars have thought, the Pythagorean table itself, does not change the point at issue.[23]

It might be urged, however, that Aristotle's "mean," "cycle," and so on, are not meant as *quantitative* properties, so that their transgeneric application is not a *mathematical* analogy.[24] Since, however, in the syllogism it is *extension* of terms in question (originally with diagrams where segments represented relative breadth of extension); in the physiology, measurable qualitative intensity; in the chemistry, reaction time; in the treatment of compounds, proportion of components; throughout the references to cycle, measurable temporal periodicity, etc., this attempted interpretation cannot be convincing.[25]

However, if we extend the concept analogically, the Prime Mover, the twofold potentiality and causal nature of art and science, and the active mind give us the two extremes and the mean most basic in Aristotle's ontology.

I submit, that if we had only these doctrines preserved as the teaching of Aristotle, we would not hesitate to identify him, along with Speusippus, as a thinker typical of the Pythagorean phase of the Academy.

This catalogue of items is meant only to point out that Aristotle does use applied mathematics in the whole range of his inquiries, so that his practice seems at odds with his theoretical position. What it does not show, but what seems to be true, is that Aristotle uses the method well. (D'Arcy W. Thompson regarded his extraordinarily Platonic chapter on "Transformation" in *On Growth and Form* as a development of an insight in the *Historia Animalium*.) This squares very well with the evidence that Aristotle was wholly competent in pure mathematics and interested in the Academy's newer theories of astronomy.[26] As will be suggested below, Aristotle's mathematical talent was considerable; when we have a history of set theory in the Greek period, this will become clearer.[27]

Consequently, if Aristotle rejects a "mathematical" approach to science, we cannot explain this by assuming him ignorant of what he was rejecting. Either the rejection constitutes an unconscious inconsistency between his theory and practice or it represents a judgment based on extensive firsthand experience in this type of thinking.

II

Though Aristotle's practice coincides with that of the Platonic tradition, he builds mathematics on different foundations, and he rejects the Platonic theory as to the nature of mathematics and the conception of mathematical entities.[28] His criticism is very hard to understand unless one recognizes two things about mathematics: First, that alternative accounts of its foundations are possible; second, that one of these is the "intuitionist" view of mathematical thinking as construction.[29] Since pure mathematics itself has been dominated by the Platonic tradition ever since Euclid, the periodic suggestions that it is not really concerned with discovering properties of entities, as the Platonists say, have made little impression within the field proper.[30] This tends to create the presumption, unless one is aware of the philosophically possible alternatives, that a discussion is either Platonic and right, or is not mathematics or wrong. That a constructional interpretation could be consistently maintained was defended theoretically by Kant but seems not to have made much impression on historians of philosophy and mathematics until the present century.

If we now study Aristotle with contemporary discussion in mind, many of the problems that seemed most hard to nineteenth-century philologists are clarified and can be resolved in the light of recent speculation.

The passages on mathematics in which its constructional character is most clear are (1) those dealing with the infinite and infinitesimal in the works on nature, and (2) those identifying the causes of mathematics in the *Metaphysics*. The former set of passages argues against attributing actual existence to entities which cannot be actually exhibited or constructed.[31] The latter set includes an identification of the efficient cause of mathematical knowledge as the idea of a constructible diagram in the mind of the mathematician, and of its formal cause with the quantitative properties of actual substances (properties treated as separate by the mathematician, though in fact they are posterior to substances which underlie them).[32] The axioms and postulates of a mathematical system are not formal but material causes, and result in actual mathematical knowledge only through specific construction. Existence assertions in the postulates are justified insofar as it is intuitively evident that the defined entities have existence as attributes of real substances, but in the absence of this intuitive certainty, we would not have a demonstrative science.[33]

This all sounds very like contemporary "intuitionist" discussion, and the criticisms of Plato come close to duplicating current criticism by intuitionists of formalists, at least where infinities are concerned. But this attempt to identify Aristotle with Kant and Brouwer probably will not convince the reader who remembers that Aristotle makes the law of excluded middle a metaphysical principle and a logical one, while the "intuitionists" of the present day deny it.[34]

It is therefore worth noting that Aristotle also denies this law when we are reasoning about possibilities. If "All P is possibly Q" be true, then "All P is possibly non-Q" follows by immediate inference in Aristotle's logic.[35] Future situations, such as the outcome of a construction not yet made actual, are assimilated to this rule in the following way: a disjunction, p or ~ p, is *as a whole* true of a future event; but *at present*, neither p nor ~ p is as yet true of it.[36] This offends the sensibilities of formal logicians, and yet it is a necessary formal device in any logic which can treat contingency: certainly, it will either rain or not rain tomorrow, yet at the present time the state of tomorrow's weather may be indeterminate. The question of whether contingent situations exist is metaphysical, not logical; but Aristotle's assertion that they do exist requires the present restriction in his logic.

In addition to the rules of modality cited, the distinction of immediate inference between contradictories and contraries restricts the possibility of "existence proof" in Aristotelian logic. While "Socrates is either well or non-well" is true, and while "every man who is not well is ill" is also true, the inference from "Socrates is not well" to "Socrates is ill" is invalid if Socrates does not exist.[37] Consequently, an argument that "every number is either odd or even" and "the number equal to the square root of zero is not odd, hence this number is even" is *invalid* without the added proof that "there exists a number equal to the square root of zero." (Since "number" is abstracted from sets of substances, and arithmetic deals with constructions, with the "units" that result from this abstraction, this "number" does not exist; but the critical point is the inconclusiveness of "proofs" of the type cited.)

This set of methodological restrictions entails a non-Platonic conception of the foundations of mathematics, and a consequent change in the meaning of "existence" or of an "existential operator" in mathematical science.[38] It explains the repeated stress on the nonconstructibility of the "inaddible numbers" and "number-forms" of Platonic ontology, since it restricts Aristotle's own presentation of arithmetic to set-theory, without transfinite sets.[39]

This transmutation also provides the clue to the otherwise unintelligible assertion of Aristotle that for Plato "the forms are numbers."[40] What Plato actually says, in the later dialogues, is that in practice the presence and construction of forms is a question of "measure."[41] What Aristotle is arguing, in the context of the *Metaphysics* as a whole, is that the Pythagorean-Platonic position is right in one sense, but is not an adequate anticipation of Aristotle's own concept of formal causality.[42] An Aristotelian "formal cause" becomes actual only when it appears in the space-time realm of efficient and final causality.[43] Consequently, it is the Platonic forms at their point of fusion with concrete process which will be closest to "forms" in Aristotle's sense, and at this point of fusion, Platonists identify the operative form with "measure."[44] If, as their uses of mathematical techniques suggest, they mean "measure" in a quantitative sense, then, since for Aristotle the measure of something is a set of homogeneous units, which are counted and represented by a number, this is equivalent to identification of "numbers" and ingressive forms.[45] Therefore, Aristotle seems to be substituting for the Platonic doctrine a statement equivalent to it in Aristotelian terms. The point of this substitution is to see whether Aristotle himself must concede the existence of forms or numbers as separate substances and causes within the framework of his own analysis of substance and causality.[46] Naturally enough, therefore, he translates the position into a paraphrase embodying some of the equivalences and distinctions of his own system. If science is a search for causes, if formal causes are actual only when concrete, if measures are sets of homogeneous units, if Platonic forms when they approach concrete realization are transmuted to measures, Aristotle's paraphrase follows. The subsequent criticism centering on the "units" of these sets shows the impossibility of an Aristotelian acceptance of this doctrine. It is beside the point to show that this is not what Platonic mathematicians meant, and that the objections are therefore irrelevant: for Aristotle has already indicated that they run into difficulties if they mean something else by "forms," "measures," or "causes," and the adequacy of this refutation must be measured by noticing the prior elimination of alternatives throughout the *Metaphysics*.[47]

More generally, Aristotle's position seems to lead to the rejection of passage from values as one approaches a limit to values at the limit if the approach can never be completed.[48] Presumably, this would rule out Pythagorean "points," Platonic "minimal planes of contact," Anaxagorean infinitesimals, Leibnizian monads, and Whiteheadian minimal slices of space at a moment (with which he replaces Leibniz's interpretation of *delta x*).[49] His reasoning on this point is most clearly shown in his rejection of Plato's *Timaeus* as physical science. Plato, in analyzing the world into minimal triangles, then describing it by integrations of these, has committed a typical mathematician's fallacy: not noticing that the existence of these minima is dependent on and posterior to the existence of actual substances in which they are present. Plato's initial act of abstraction has left out something crucial which can never be restored by multiplying mere mathematical triangles.[50] In a similar way, causality in nature is effective between substances, and to ascribe causal efficacy to quantities is to accept an erroneous ontology.[51]

The purpose of these comments is to indicate that Aristotle's mathematics proper reflects a non-Platonic concept of the nature and foundation of mathematical science, not mere ignorance or misunderstanding nor lack of any appreciation for the work of the Academy.[52] The position Aristotle takes is a very interesting one, in that he seems to be deliberately avoiding the paradoxes that beset Platonic formal logic and semi-Platonic set-theory. Ultimately, he restricts ontology by limiting postulates which assert existence to abstractions from actuality; this provides intuitive clarity and guarantees consistency and interpretability. But that guarantee will not extend to abstractions from possibility.

III

The combination of the first two points of the present discussion is an apparent antinomy. If the account of the nature of mathematics is right, numbers are neither substances nor causes, and applied mathematics seems irrelevant to scientific demonstration in physics, ethics, or any other science except the limited category of composite mathematical studies, such as optics, harmonics, and the theory of the rainbow. An Aristotelian scientist might well refer to the *De Anima* and explain this fact by showing that the natures of things are recognized by *intuition*, a faculty which presupposes the *abstraction* of mathematical thinking, but supersedes or supplements it.[53] Whitehead has pointed out that stress on classification, not on measure, characterized science in the Aristotelian tradition; of course, this is not literally true, but it does underscore a lesser emphasis on mathematics than the Platonic-Augustinian tradition showed. Yet Aristotle uses mathematics in every aspect of his philosophic work; mathematical formulae and analogies appear to be expected a priori by him, and looked for, in everything from physiology to formal logic and ethics.

The resolution of this apparent break between theory and practice is given by Aristotle in the final chapters of the *Metaphysics*. The Pythagoreans, like his other predecessors, were too wise to be wrong altogether, and, while the shift in his conception of the foundations of mathematics leads Aristotle to an extensive criticism, he ends, as is his habit, in accepting part of the position as a valid contribution to his own philosophy.[54]

In solving his final problem, of the status of numbers as causes, Aristotle follows his usual balanced approach. It has *seemed* to many of his readers, particularly those with strong Platonic sympathies, that his books M and N do involve a wholesale rejection of the causal efficacy of number. But, without the key to Aristotle's paraphrase given by recognizing his shift in the concept of foundations of mathematics, the Platonic reader tends to want a sharp logical opposition between this criticism and the original, so that he can reject Aristotle.

It is true, Aristotle concludes, that the cross-generic analogies of mathematics show something.[55] What they show is, as we can gather from the diagram (this is the *systoichia* referred to above), that there is a natural appropriateness or likeness between things that are in different genera, insofar as beauty and existence are tightly related.[56] In a universe where final causality is constitutive of every substance (though not analogically) certain mathematical properties which are the constituents of beauty will accompany operative causality.[57]

Consequently, there is not a total irrelevance between the fanciful Pythagorean collection of aesthetic similarities and the truths of scientific demonstration. On the contrary, in trying to identify the causes in a given subject-matter, looking for mathematical regularity—for symmetry, order, and measure—is a very scientific preliminary stage of inquiry; for these properties will indicate that a final cause is present, and where it is to be sought. But, for Aristotle, this is not yet an explanation until the indication revealed by mathematical properties is followed and clarified, so that we discover what a substance is by the further intellectual operation of rational insight into its purposive structure, which enables us to recognize its proper causes.[58] It is these causes which are responsible for the quantitative characteristics, not vice versa, so that, with some special exceptions (such as optics) mathematical terms can never serve as middles in precise scientific demonstration.[59]

In this way, Aristotle can justify his practice as an appropriate use of mathematics as a technique of inquiry, yet reject the position that it provides explanations of causes suitable for scientific demonstration.

This relation of inquiry to proof seems to the modern reader to be exactly the reverse of our own convictions: Aristotelian classification is for us often a useful preliminary technique of inquiry, when we are deciding what to measure, but we use mathematics for our final demonstration. I propose to suggest some of the consequences of this reversal at some later time.

Reprinted with permission from the *Review of Metaphysics* (1954): 511–521.

Part IV

Ideal Form In a World of Gadgets

Chapter 13

The World of the Greek Philosophers
and the Sense of Form

In this account of an encounter with the surviving traces of the world
of the Greek philosophers, and my own discovery of their relevance to
the ideas that originated and were tested there, I have three purposes in
mind. The first is to start a discussion of ancient thought in its context;
such topics as "the world" are somewhat out of style, and yet our more
specialized studies presuppose such a world and can go wrong if the
general presuppositions are mistaken. My second purpose is to persuade
us that it is necessary for us to keep track of collateral information in
other fields of research tangent to our own; my selection and classification of archeological items serves here as case study. The effect of increased specialization and precision has led to a decrease in the size of
individual "items" considered important enough to publish separately;
and this in turn has lead to an exponential increase in the amount of
information one must somehow scan and appraise in order to keep
track of material in other fields that is also relevant for us. The problem
of storage of information, and access to it, is not limited to the natural
sciences, where current attempts to use computers for this work are
going on; the humanities, too, are giving serious consideration to the
technological devices we can use, before the rising tide of information
flow inundates us all. My third purpose is to report on my own experience during a year in Greece which began with the assurance that I
knew about Greek philosophy and that archaeology was irrelevant to
it, and ended in a discovery that, on both these counts, I had been
wrong. In the course of finding that there are at least four types of
relevance between idea and artifact, I also found myself with an uneasy feeling that the sum of my information was not adding up to an
ancient world that matched any standard image of it—neither
nineteenth-century austerity nor twentieth-century flamboyance.

    Let me say at once that I am not setting myself up here as a
specialist in archaeology; my ideas and examples are taken from a year
in which I combined writing about philosophy with being a tourist in

the tradition that runs from Pausanias through Mark Twain. The items I have selected, in spite of my rather formal classification into graded types, are not the result of any systematic or exhaustive search, but a sample selected more by luck, footwork, and general curiosity.

There is one undeniable sort of relevance that archaeology has for any student of Greek philosophy: it offers a vivid conviction that ancient Greece was real, and its philosophers were really there. Hume was right in his contrast between the force and vivacity of a firsthand impression as opposed to an idea; and the different feeling for the historical reality of the ancient world that results from being there and seeing actual sites and traces is, of itself, a justification for a visit to Greece by a philosopher, however convinced he is that environment and thought are independent of each other. For the philosopher on tour, some statues, inscriptions, and artifacts have special "human interest" because they are connected with earlier Greek philosophers; these are indexes fixing an exact place and time for the men whose thought we admire. But these items of atomic indication have only extrinsic and accidental relevance to philosophy itself; to keep track of a scheme of graded relevance I will call them items with relevance of *grade one*.

Even on this flat, precise level, we need to keep up with changing findings, which may result in new discoveries, and in new judgments as to what the precise facts are. John Burnet, for example, cited a fragment of a statue of Anaximander found at Miletus as an index locating this philosopher in history; and also as indicating that the story of his political activity had some confirmation here by fact.[1] But new examination by an art historian has shown that the statue is that of a woman, and hence not of Anaximander after all.[2] There is a loss to us here, but it is rather slight. Correspondingly, there is some gain in noting the unchallenged fact that Gorgias was commemorated by at least two statues at Olympia. The base of the later one survives, with a dedicatory inscription, and also a defense of Gorgias for having, earlier, set up his own statue to himself.[3] Well, this does clinch the fact that Gorgias was real. It may even be tangible confirmation of the public impact, wealth, and influence of the Sophists of the older generation. What importance we are to attach to the fact that Gorgias was criticized by someone for his undue sense of his own importance is not immediately evident; perhaps this depends on how closely we agree with his own appraisal.

Another example of a fact with this sort of human interest, and relevance of grade one, was found in the Athenian Agora. One of the stories told about Socrates was that he spent much time in the Agora in the shop of a cobbler named Simon.[4] The American School archaeologists found, in the remains of a cobbler shop of the fifth century, the base of a cup, inscribed "Property of Simon," and on this basis it is believed that this was the shop of the friend of Socrates.[5] This gives a vivid human touch, as we visit the spot and picture Socrates just here talking with his friend. It also suggests that we might look again at the titles of the "Socratic speeches" Simon is supposed to have written down; also, that all of Socrates' "talk of cobblers" likely rested on firsthand observation; and the find certainly tells against the flashy but unlikely thesis that Socrates was a social climber and a snob, who only favored influential people with his company.[6]

The intrinsic relevance of a fact is, unfortunately, no index of its importance. If there were greater certainty in attributing the design of Italian coinage to Pythagoras, these coins would be important, though not highly relevant to the history of ideas.[7]

Items of this kind convinced me that even such items of "slight" intrinsic relevance might be important enough to notice; and I soon found that I had to recognize a higher degree of relevance from some archaeological items. I was very pleased, as a tourist, by the Agora Museum, with its tools, plates, cups and coins; I was particularly happy to recognize some items that philosophers had referred to as illustrations of their concepts. I had already been surprised to find, when I was trying to understand Plato's reference to physical objects as "minted space," what a different connotation "physical object" took on when I compared it to coinage of the Athenian rather than the modern American mint.[8] And the odd but functional shape of the classical pruning hook is an eye-catching illustration of function dictating form.[9] In such cases as these, actual items give us a way of attaching concrete referents to terms, and of verifying our own notions of intended meaning and reference; and I will assign them a graded relevance of type two. A volume treating Greek philosophers—particularly Plato— among the arts and crafts could be of some, if peripheral, importance for giving a more precise grasp of the meanings of some terms, concepts, and similes in their philosophies.[10]

Without itemizing examples here which could range from eel traps to astronomical apparatus, I will note one puzzling point that surprised me about this class of facts as a whole: the workmanship of useful objects was often wretched. The striking of coins, where some slave of the mint slammed his die onto the silver anyhow—and sometimes nearly missed with it altogether—was not atypical. At least as surprising was the fact that dice were not even close to being cubes, in Athens or in Corinth. They had tapers and anomalies that no American game player would trust for a single throw! This contrast of workmanship between the meticulous coin die and the casual coin, the precise applied geometry of the Partheonon and the unlikely failures of dice makers, was unexpected, and I noted it as a puzzle for future cogitation.

But it was not only possible to fix meanings of terms better where archaeology supplied intended referents; in addition, sets of items sometimes had very suggestive relations to general propositions, both of and about Greek philosophers, particularly where they seemed likely to have been in the background as illustrating or confirming new—or old—hypotheses and assertions. This is a closer, but more problematic, grade of relevance than the two discussed already; if its existence is established, it should be called relevance of *grade three*.

The most striking example of the way in which large sets of small items can reverse interpretation of, or belief in, a philosophical generalization is the new appraisal of Aristotle's "we Greeks are men of moderation" in the twentieth century. The nineteenth century took the statement at its face value; it fit well with the austere, symmetrical structural remains that their archaeologists were studying and restoring. But new combinations of fact, from law cases to ostracism sherds, have convinced our century that either "moderation" means what we would rather call "excess," or the statement is a lie.

There are some less spectacular questions that I have in mind which show this third grade of relevance between idea and archaeology. I will cite three, which have a peculiar interest. In general, it is interesting to notice that suggestions and hypotheses which seem at first incorrigibly vague, almost meaningless, turn out to be capable of sharpening and testing against definite evidence; in particular, the three cases I have in mind result in the surprising finding that life in ancient Athens was much more like our own than one would expect.

In Greece as opposed to ancient India, the atomic theory was a popular and technical success. Why? One thing that has always struck me about this theory is that a practical world full of gadgetry gives it much more intuitive plausibility than it could have in an environment devoid of ingenious mechanism altogether. Could it be that there was more ready-to-hand confirmation of this sort in the West than in ancient India, and that this contributed to the different receptions of the suggestion that all nature is a congeries of complex mechanisms? We still don't know about ancient India; but until fifty years ago, the part of this thesis that concerns the West would have been rejected as absurd. Who ever heard of gadgetry in the leisure-class, aristocratic ancient Athenian atmosphere? But here a set of facts confirms the generalization that gadgets were a recognized and well-established fact in Athenian life, and disproves the myth—which begins in the classical philosophers themselves—that there was no place in their society for ingenious machinery.

Perhaps here a definition of gadget is in order: I mean by this a small mechanical device that, with a surprising ingenuity of mechanism, performs some action it surprises us to find capable of being mechanically performed. (A Florentine toy gold bird that flaps his wings and whistles is a good example; toys and gadgets are overlapping categories.)[11] And from Minoan to modern times, the archaeology of Greece offers a collection of gadgets thus defined—culinary, theological, political—which someday deserves its own history.

My set of artifacts begins with a strange sixth-century jar found in the Athenian Agora. The outside has openings for hollow tubes that coil through the interior, like the water-heating coils of coal furnaces in my younger days. The purpose of these was, however, cooling rather than heating; immersed in cold water, this would flow through the coils and cool, without diluting, a jar full of wine.[12] Over the next century and a half, we find (though two of these finds are not from the Agora itself) ceramic water-clocks set for three minutes and for six; the setting and accounts, if not yet the pieces of a wonderful oil lamp needing only one annual filling; molds for mass producing small clay figurines; the base of a public sundial with a new design; ingenious juror's ballots, pairs of wheels with a shaft, one shaft hollow, the other solid; a child's small potty-chair; a new design of sausage grill, where lugs prevent the skewered meat from rolling off or turning; one item I have not seen, but know from firsthand report, a bowl with an Amazon on the rim designed to spout wine or water from her single breast when the bowl was filled (this is an adaptation of a design frequent in Minoan pitchers); the relics of a lottery machine (the slotted backboard, metal tickets with name, a brass ball).[13] With this evidence, we can now combine references in literature that are relevant. We already find Plato repeating a story about a crackpot inventor; Aristotle, in the *Constitution of Athens* meticulously itemizing the apparatus used for a day in court. (The latter equipment included hundreds of lettered acorns, twenty lottery-machines, name tickets, colored staves, a model of the chambers where cases were tried, the wheel-shaped ballots already mentioned, and a ballot box I will return to later.)[14] Perhaps we need more evidence for a conclusive demonstration that a feedback between atomism and Agora actually took place; but the impact of this set of small-scale devices certainly confirms the notion that such a feedback was possible. My colleague, Mr. Arthur Falk, suggested that the case would be stronger if the pore-and-effluence model of atomism found any counterpart in machine design; in the devices I happen to know of, there is only one relevant item. That is the ballot box described by Aristotle; this was fitted with a lid that had a shaped slot exactly right to allow one, and only one, juror's ballot to fall into the box at a time.

But my confirmation of the proposition that there were Greek gadgets is particularly interesting because the facts go counter both to the standard nineteenth-century image of the Greek world (in this view, the Greeks are too serious and aloof to have any time for such novelties) and to the twentieth-century image (which finds the Greeks at once too dominated by a leisure-class mentality and too flamboyantly engaged in using their leisure time for politics to divert their energy to such minor technological matters.)

A second, overlapping, set of items in the Agora Museum also has the sort of relevance I have called *grade three* to the Sophists and their conventionalism. Throughout the *nomos-physis* controversy, there was always immediate evidence in the Agora itself to illustrate and support the claim that society's standards of value, and even its public world, rest on arbitrary enactment and convention. There have been found sets of standard weights and measures, marked "Official"; seals of inspectors; the headquarters of the Market Police who did all they could to give the operation of enacted customs the inexorability of laws of nature.[15] Currency (represented by some tools and bars from the ancient mint), metric standards, justice in jury trials (the elaborate artifices to secure honesty in court), all represented a multiplicity of arbitrary definition and regulation.[16] Indeed, the Agora enclosure itself had been marked off arbitrarily by planting inscribed boundary stones, one of which still stands, reading

HOROSEIMI

TESAGORAS

rather like our own

PLAN AH

EAD

signs.[17] There appears no doubt that there was a whole structure of commonly recognized facts that the Sophists could presuppose, facts that would make their dictum intelligible and plausible to the ordinary Athenian, however contrary to his prejudices this new exaltation of "convention" might be. I had held quite a different notion of the balance between free enterprise and public regulation; Plato's comment that landlords should be supervised to cut down on the holding for ransom of travellers came closer to my original idea. And philosophically, it is not irrelevant to find that the new conventionalism did not have to rely on extrapolation from travellers' accounts about odd actions of remote barbarians, but had an immediate local plausibility. The role of metric standards in creating "agreement" about a "public world" appears as a familiar fact in the *Euthyphro* of Plato.[18]

I was surprised to find these groups of items pointing toward a much greater likeness between Athens and modern New Haven than I had expected. But I could not, somehow, fit this fact together with the other things I had seen as a tourist: Delphi, the Athenian Acropolis, Olympia, Epidaurus—where sculpture, architecture, choice of site showed exactly the "classical" sensitivity to form, precision of technique, and absolute sense of right size scale, that the nineteenth century had tried to generalize into the determining qualities of the culture as a whole.

Perhaps, I thought, my trouble in seeing how these sides of life had fitted together came from thinking about ancient life with a modern sense of time. There has been a good deal written about the arbitrary tyranny of mechanical time, as it displaces the "life time" or "work time" of an earlier way of life; it might well be, I thought, that a society without many mechanical clocks could be much more loosely articulated, somehow, in the way its component classes and parts interacted and held together. For life on some Greek islands, at present as well as in the past, I am sure this difference in time-sense holds, and that it does really involve a different feeling from my own about causality, sequence, and the degree of regularity one can expect in society or nature. The Postmaster of the one island I knew well, for example, had a budget of hypotheses to explain why a message phoned from his office to Athens radio had not reached the S. S. United States at sea. The ship could well have changed course to pick up last-minute cargo; might, naturally, have decided not to sail at all; or might have shut down its radio for the voyage because the operator was drinking. I don't feel qualified to decide which world is *better*, the one where boats have personality and creativity, or the one where they have exact, efficient schedules. But I can say that the former worlds simply cannot have the kind of precise prediction, advance planning, or tight synchronization by watch and calendar that we expect in our own.

This island example is not irrelevant to my main theme, since it confirms my generalization that difference in time-sense does give rise to differences in articulation and interaction. But I am pretty sure that the time sense of an ancient Athenian was already sensitized to mechanical time and not drastically different from my own. In cities and palaces, there is already an ancestor of the mechanical clock in the Minoan libation jars, many of which were found at Knossos. These are jars which pour a constant fine stream of oil or wine, and empty and have to be refilled with exact mechanical regularity; their considerable number already must have put clock-time into operation for the religious officials attending them.[19] By the first century A.D., the Tower of the Winds made its appearance as an important feature of the Roman addition to the Athenian Agora. This handsome octagonal tower was a display piece, combining eight external sundials, an inner weather vane, and an elaborate water-drive clock—which could be consulted by the public at any hour of the night or day.[20] That mechanical clock, setting the pace of the city with its arbitrary, analytical divisions of each day, was not just a sudden innovation. In 433 B.C. the astronomer Meton had put up a new public sundial where the Assembly met on the Pnyx.[21] By about 350, a very impressive large-scale water-operated clock was in operation near a northern entrance of the Agora.[22] The small, six-minute water clock found near the old courtroom by the American School is of about the same date.[23] Putting these items together with literary references, indicating that courtroom speeches and cases, theatrical competitions, assembly meeting times all were regulated by sundial and klepsydra, it appeared that the fourth century in Athens was already running on modern time. The harassed lawyer of Plato's *Theaetetus*, running to keep up with the clock as his time "ran out," has much the look of a modern American.[24] And the fact that "fractions of a day" were defined by a "standard day" meant that mechanical timekeepers were displacing the more natural, but more variable, risings and settings of the sun.[25] This set of items, given more impact as my guide book recorded mechanical clocks of this period elsewhere in Greece, completely contradicted my hypothesis of a different sense of time.[26]

If archaeological facts can be relevant to the study of philosophy as indices fixing exact persons and events, as artifacts helping to make terms and concepts clear by providing concrete referents, as sets of items capable of verifying or discrediting propositions about and in Greek philosophy, there may be still another order of relevance. Where the archaeologist has been able to completely recreate an ancient site, in its detail, this may give us a way of understanding and confirming philosophic *systems* which purport to explain and reflect the whole world. Such concrete reconstructions of whole segments can be said to have a relevance of *grade four*. Notice that, as items become more relevant, they form larger and more complex sets; their importance for us is greater, but their use is much harder, and they tend to invite vagueness and subjective free association. I think I can summarize the conclusions I have drawn so far with some precision. That indexes and referents of illustrations may be important, and are in any case interesting, for the student of Greek philosophy is neither vague nor surprising. That there existed, in ancient Athens, enough familiar mechanical devices to give the atomic theory immediate intelligibility, is surprising; but until one tries to pinpoint the exact extent of interaction, not vague. The same is true of the finding that artificial convention permeated the whole legal and economic structure to a degree that must have given the Sophistic stress on custom immediate comprehensibility and a claim to be taken seriously. Even that evanescent thing, "a sense of time," proves to be capable of confrontation with sets of facts which indicate that it was already beginning to be very like our own.

My final excursion is more tentative, more important, and less clear. In looking at the models reconstructing Olympia and the Acropolis, and spending some time identifying details at Delphi, I had an uneasy feeling that the sense of order here was not my own, that the relation of surface and substance was much more external than I had expected. This would mean, if it proved true, that the crucial ordering relations in ancient philosophy were presupposing, as the definition and illustration of their systematic theses, a considerably different world from the one I had assumed.

I am sure that ancient Olympia would have seemed to us a shattering center of disorder. A beautiful setting had been cluttered up with miscellaneous items and trophies of every description, from a stone inscribed "BYLLUS LIFTED ME OVER HIS HEAD WITH ONE HAND," to the statues of Zeus, (the Zans), payments of fines for cheating in the Games. With its ubiquitous busts of foreign potentates, of heralds, of politicians, of Gorgias, it must have been unpredictable and confusing.[27] (What would Hegel have done with this information? Would he have had to give up his contrast between the "scientific" Western and the "dream-like" Oriental mind?) Apart from two main avenues, I had the impression that any path anyone followed would pass around, by, and through a succession of things forming no coherent order or sequence: a tourist hotel with bath, a rotunda in honor of

Phillip of Macedon, an athletic commissioner in effigy, perhaps a small likeness of the noisiest herald of, say, 360 B.C. There was a planning commission, and perhaps they had some radial plan; but lines of sight and travel are straight, not circular, and it should have been easy to tell that their approved plan would produce vistas of incongruities. Nor is Olympia alone in this effect. At Delphi, to take another example, a pilgrim climbing the Sacred Way and pausing in the shadow of the Temple of Apollo must have found himself in a veritable warehouse of second-hand armaments and miscellaneous stauary.[28] Matching ancient accounts against the square cuttings still visible in the stone floor, I got a picture of benches piled high with dented helmets, boat oars, old shields; repeating in artifacts the collected jumble of trivial decrees immortalized in four hundred odd inscriptions on the wall lower down the Way. And this is not an idiosyncracy of sites where many city-states were each determined and entitled to get their own buildings and heroes into the act. For the detailed reconstructions of the Athenian Acropolis, identifying the tablet, statue, or bench once mounted in each of the cuttings that occur every few feet in the rock, show the same baffling lack of order.[29] But there were officers in charge of building and decoration, and they were satisfied.

Just here may be the point: our notion that a beautiful natural scene, an elegant frieze, or a graceful temple *logically requires* a compatible, not a distracting, foreground was apparently not ancient Greek at all. Our mint would never tolerate Jefferson nickels with only a quarter of the portrait stamped on; our dice players would throw, as far away as they could, the pairs of classical noncubic dice which upset our assumed equivalence of a priori probability and relative frequency. Our admirers of modern furniture cheer the passing of *de luxe* overstuffed, with its lions' feet and extraneous golden tassels. But I suspect that an ancient Athenian would not react in these ways at all. The purity of marble that we admire in the Elgin Marbles is pock-marked with drill-holes for the attachment of bronze fittings: chains fastened to the nose-rings of cattle, harness and reins of chariots, anatomical details of satyrs. Traces of pigment on other friezes remind us that the Greeks added bright stones, paint, and gilding to their finest statuary, friezes, and column capitals. The foreground of their most important shrines, symbols of eternity, were filled with chauvinistic epigrams and tasteless heaps of trophies.

We should not dismiss this as some sort of unexpended barbaric energy. There is nothing barbaric about the sites and temples, statues and reliefs, to which this color and clutter was juxtaposed. Somehow a different sense of metaphysical distance from our own is at work here.

There is a "distance" between surface and substance so great that the two are almost externally related to each other. And other feelings for distance than our own seem to be reflected in the closer sense of relevance of the ideal to the actual, the greater tolerance for poor approximation. The Athenian coin, with the elegant goddess lacking her nose, provoked no recorded execution of employees or overseers at the mint. Why should it? Everyone saw what the design ideally would be, and accepted the fact that the artist's die was an ideal very remote from the concrete silver surface of a coin. Apparently the thickets of small statuary did not interfere with a comprehension of the Parthenon, nor the brass fittings seem out of place flashing against the clear lines of its frieze.

This final observation of mine is in need of a good deal of checking. Perhaps it is idiosyncratic; perhaps it will fade when there are more concrete sites or when the present ones are confronted longer, in more detail. But if it is right, let me indicate what bearing I think it has on Greek philosophy. The fact may be that Plato and Aristotle in handing over the order and direction of the world to forms or final causes are paying these entities less of a metaphysical compliment than we assume they are. Is the form really omnipotent in relation to the natural world to which it gives direction and value? Does it set a target that pinpoints aim, with no tolerance for deviation? This notion would go counter to all of the examples we have seen of the variability in approximation of instance to form, the indifference of symmetrical structure to what passes before its facade, or glistens on its surface. We would do better to envisage the role of forms or final causes on the model of ancient Athens, not a modern assembly line. And in ancient Athens, the Acropolis, which gave the city its unity and rose above it as center of identity and ideal, did hold together Theater, Academy, Agora, Assembly. But it did not cast a shadow of eternity over the city that unified it, as the nineteenth-century scholars suggest. When we recapture the concrete texture that related the parts of ancient Athens to the shared ideal, without taking away from each its autonomy and color, we may be in a better position to appreciate the exact meaning of the role of form in classical philosophy.

And so I come, by what Mark Twain would call a natural and easy transition, to three conclusions. The first is that we would lose something if we were to stop talking about such broad, nonspecialized notions as "the world"; we need these broad-spectrum ideas to reinfuse romance, color, and wider relevance into specialized analyses of high precision. The second conclusion is that there are at least four grades of relevance that hold between the findings of classical archaeology and the study of classical philosophy. The same thing applies, I am sure, to what is being discovered, discussed, and decided in other fields tangent to our own. This being so, it will be necessary for us to keep track of what these other specialists are up to. My third conclusion is that we can use information about the Greek world to pinpoint events, fix meanings of terms and similes, test general hypotheses and see how their setting did or did not give them intuitive plausibility, and even, perhaps, be able to supply the models of reality that classical philosophic systems presupposed. Both confrontation and gradual approach have made me feel that those models were a world with different distances and textures from our own. I wonder, for example, whether the systematic relation of reality sending directives to appearance might not have evoked the same interpretation of reason and necessity in an ancient Athenian that my Postmaster in modern Greece supplied for his abstract idea of Athens radioing messages to the S. S. United States at sea?

Chapter 14

Classical Gadgets, the Hardware of Early Western Science

My own interest in the history of science, as distinct from the history of ideas in general, dates to an interaction of heredity and environment in Athens in 1962. The heredity component is a congenital fondness for gadgets which I seem to have inherited from my great-grandfather Buck, a nineteenth-century inventor. The environmental component was the many ancient gadgets tucked away without comment in the showcases of the archaeological museums I visited that year.

I had been brought up in a tradition that believed the ancient Greeks to be pure theoreticians, contemptuous of arts and crafts, devoid of mechanisms or mechanical inventiveness, austere characters in bedsheets working in philosophy. (How much of this attitude traces back to my elementary school days, in the University of Chicago laboratory school curriculum originally designed by John Dewey, I can't say.)

But the gadgets were there; in profusion, with splendid ingenuity and inventiveness, a whole dimension of classical culture not only unrecognized but inconsistent with most standard histories. There was a sixth-century wine-cooling jar—*psykter* with inner coils to cool the wine without diluting it: this model is still offered for sale by Hammacher Schlemmer. There was the special sausage grill, ancestor of our modern barbecue gear. There were lottery machines, fragments of self-moving puppets, souvenir toy animals, ivory tickets to the theater.

One odd thing about this material was that it did not function as a modern observer would expect it to. The inventors and mechanics whose work this was had an aesthetic rather than a pragmatic interest in slot machines, gears, steam power, and the like. Further, until the first-century A.D., no one *wrote* about this gadgetry. (One student in Aristotle's school did write a short essay on direct drive and mechanical advantage, in the third century, but that seems all.) It was apparently a convention of the time that this was not material to write about. Luckily, in the first century A.D., Heron of Alexandria put together a great anthology of inventions drawing on five hundred years of crafts tradition; copies of this, with schematic diagrams and allegorical Renaissance ornamentations, are in print today.

My specific theme is the previously unnoticed or underrated interaction of technological inventions and abstract ideas in four strands of ancient Greek intellectual history. The strands represent them in psychology, cosmology and timekeeping, machinery for political purposes, and nonanimate sources of power.

More important than this very specific interaction, however, is the implication of this tradition of minor technology for our appraisal of the history of science in general in this early stage. Following up my archaeological notes with rereading of classical literature has made me reconsider several of the commonplaces that historians of science, from Plutarch to Sarton, repeat uncritically. (1) For example, I don't think there ever was a period when Greek science was "pure" speculation with no hardware. It follows that the possibility of science without observation and apparatus cannot be established simply by appealing to incorrect, revisionist, Neo-Platonic claims that ancient Greek science was of this character. (2) I do not find a leisure-class disinterest in arts and crafts in the writings of the Greek philosophers. On the contrary, an index of Plato's references shows both interest and competence to a surprising degree. A hostility, sometimes overstated, to a proposed substitution of arts and crafts for liberal education does occur, but this was itself a "leisure class" proposal, and criticism of it cannot be used to interpret classical thought as rationalization of undesirable social attitudes and structure. (3) The thesis that a society with slave labor will not have mechanical inventiveness can hardly be defended in the face of the classical inventions of geared analogue computers, power gearing, the steam engine, and the coin operated slot machine, all of which we find in the ancient world. But for the present, I want to develop the more specific historical theme of idea-invention interaction in ancient Athens and Alexandria from the fifth century B.C. to the third century A.D.

Work by Derek Price on the "antikythera machine" makes the reconstruction of this analogue computer detailed and solid. I have run across sources bearing on the history of automata—an item that may be science fiction attributing the invention of a full-size horseless chariot to a Syracusan dictator in about 360 B.C., and an account of a parading mechanical snail that actually slid into Athens in about 309. References in later medical works to the use of a screw in surgical equipment have made me change my mind as to whether the toy chariot designed to turn at a right angle would actually work. I now think it probably would.

Professor Derek Price has suggested that there is some innate human urge to simulate living creatures mechanically. Through a long tradition ranging from magic to mechanism, there certainly is such a drive in the West. Originally, small painted or moulded figures were designed to come to life magically, accompanying the Egyptian king, for example, in his journey to the west. Perhaps the works of the legendary Daedalus mark a new intersection of mechanics and simulation. For his statues were self-moving, and had to be tied up or they would run away. Later tradition claimed that their motions were controlled by quicksilver, but nothing definite is known about them, except for the impression they made. But a tradition of mechanical simulation flourished in ancient Greece. Its achievements in designing automata—self-moving puppets—led to the name "amazing things" for these creations, and had, I suspect, an important role in the development of Western psychology.

It will be important to remember that a "soul" (*psyche*) was supposed to be responsible for two things: motion and sensation. Thus Thales could say that "a magnet has a *psyche*, because it moves iron." But does it follow that a windup toy has been given a soul by its designer? Well, it does follow if anything self-moving is also "alive"; or if there is no "vital principle" involved, but every *psyche* is a mechanism, so that there is no difference in kind between a person and a windup toy.

The whole project of simulation was finally recorded in the treatises on automata of Heron of Alexandria, in the first century A.D. Working backward from this final anthology, we find two themes carefully traced that particularly intrigued professional mechanics, self-moving chariots and automatic theaters. The puppets that are listed as "wonderful" by Aristotle, and that figure so prominently in Plato's Myth of the Cave, can to some extent be reconstructed from Heron's inventory of devices of the chariot designer and the theater builder.

Heron's first section deals with schematic plans to make a small chariot propel itself in all of the patterns that a real one might trace. A gravity-drive motor, consisting of a falling weight tightening a string wrapped around the axle, is the motive power. To slow its fall, the weight rests in a box of sand with a small outlet, very like an hourglass. Simple patterns of winding give straight ahead linear motion. Reversing the winding will program the chariot to stop, then run back. A redesign of the wheels can set up a chariot that runs in a large or small circle. But the most sensational effect, effected by an extra pair of wheels that are lowered and jack up the whole machine, is a motion *at a right angle*. (The same device was patented in 1965 by a Detroit truck manufacturer.)

The same falling-weight power provided the motive force for the ambitious design of an automatic theater. This project of simulation, in which a five-act play was performed automatically by wooden actors, is as ambitious a project of duplicating art mechanically as one can imagine. By Heron's time, a scenario—the Nauplius—with spectacular effects had been chosen as the standard display piece. The neatest principle at work here will be recognized by anyone who ever had a push-toy with three legs painted on the wheels. (This three-leg-and-pivot pattern, the *triskelos*, occurs as ornament on silver coins of Sicily and Asia Minor from the fourth century B.C. on.) In this way, three dolphins attached to a wheel, spun as it travels across backstage, will jump; three-armed nymphs with hammers will nail Odyssesus's ship together upstage center; a swimming Ajax with three arms will move ahead until a lightning-bolt from above the stage flashes down, and he disappears.

This challenge piece of simulation gives us a number of clues to the self-moving automata that fascinated Aristotle and Plato. Apparently there were dolls with jointed arms, legs, and mouths controlled by strings; there was some windup device, probably a twisted leather thong; and as this unwound, a peg striking the "nerves" (*neura*, nerves or bowstrings) made the puppet wave, jump, and grimace. There are extant shells of dolls of this type, but none with the "works" intact, and it is not clear from the enclosing bodies just how the inner "selves" worked. What is clear, however, is the tremendous impression these creatures made on Greek psychology. Aristotle, in particular, trying to explicate a theory treating the soul as mechanism, refers to them. In explaining that philosophy begins in wonder, Aristotle has examples of three kinds of things that are wonderful: the changing length of day (a natural phenomenon), the incommensurability of the side and diagonal of a unit square (a mathematical relation), and self-moving marionettes (an artificial invention). In the *De Motu*, Aristotle himself or a student in his school analyzes animal behavior by a stimulus-response arc concept, which he argues for on the analogy of the bowstring nerves of puppets. In the *De Anima*, Aristotle brings in the statues of Daedalus to illustrate one earlier psychological theory.

In a culture that had no windup toys, mechanical theaters, or marionettes, it seems quite clear to me that a mechanistic analysis such as the one that follows from the atomic theory would not be very plausible. I wonder whether this may account for the failure of atomism in early India to gain any adherents: it was a theory, but it was without disciples and was not a school. In any case, the interaction of ideas and artifacts is clear enough in this dimension of gadgetry to entitle our automata to a chapter in the history of science in the West.

It is interesting that our own century has not gone in for automatic theaters, nor for mechanical persons that look alive and engage in general conversation. There may be something we are afraid of in over-realistic simulation.

Modern enthusiasts for social engineering, an art intended to take advantage of our new computer technology, will be interested to learn that some of their classical forbears had much the same ambition, though with more elementary implementation.

The Greek Sophists appear in the fifth century, urbane travelling educators, arguing that human values do not rest on some innate "human nature," but rather that they are the product of legislation and social convention. Although it is often said that new anthropological information about exotic cultures was responsible for this glorification of convention, it seems at least equally likely that experiments aimed at "automating honesty" inspired the thesis that value creation is by social control.

At some point in the fifth century, there was a sudden enthusiasm for "socially useful invention." By the end of the fourth century, relative disenchantment had set in. But in between lay an enthusiastic attempt to control political, legal, and business functions by inventions that would make dishonesty impossible. Perhaps in the background, the introduction into Greece of coinage of guaranteed standard quality and weight in the late seventh century was an inspiration. The Athenian Agora was filled with regulative devices and regulatory personnel. The seller and buyer worked with standard weights, duly inspected by the Market Wardens and certified as official. There were standard measures, likewise officially established and required, for wine, for nuts, for olives, and so on. Clearly the notion was that official standards could outlaw petty dishonesty in business. The extent of this regulatory urge was not fully appreciated, however, until the modern excavations of the Athenian Agora. Case after case of standard weights (some ornamented with likenesses of Hermes, patron of thieves) of official nut measures, of wine buckets of standard size, now grace the Agora Museum, giving vivid proof of an unexpected density.

If hardware could be harnessed to ensure fair trade, could mechanical ingenuity also work out socially useful inventions for selection of public officials, or for jury selection? Again, there was a vigorous interaction of idea and invention along these lines. The actual history involved needs some background for its appreciation by a modern audience, however. The apparatus was intended to implement two operational definitions, of "democracy" and of "impartiality," which were neanderthal-like notions very different from our own. The Athenians believed that democracy involved equal opportunity for every citizen to compete for public office, a sound idea, but went on to identify equal opportunity to run for an office with equal probability of being selected for it. They believed that in trials by jury, it was important to ensure the jury's impartiality, again a sound notion, but they went on to equate impartiality with immensity, because of some misguided opinion that a jury too large to be bribed would therefore be fair. The concomitant hardware had its specifications written into the section on jury selection of the Athenian constitution, and the section on selection of officials. The central device was the *kleroterion*—a lottery machine. For jury selection, the members of the eligible jury panel presented metal tickets; these were inserted in rows in a slotted rectangular backboard; a ball was drawn from a hopper in which there was a mix of black balls and white; and the draw determined selection or exclusion of ticket owners, column by column. In this way, juries of 201, 501, 1001, could be impanelled. Other finds from the courts show continuing pursuit of the automation of honesty theme. My own favorite among them is the special ballot used by jurors. Apparently, secrecy of one's vote was very desirable. As a result, identical wheel-shaped devices were used, one with a hollow, one with a solid shaft. A juror held his pair, one in each hand, with the shafts concealed, and cast his vote into a box with a wheel-shaped slot in the top that would admit only a single ballot at a time. A maze of model courtrooms, colored staffs, tokens for pay entitlement, official clocks, and six-colored dice contributed to the randomizing objectivity of the procedure.

For election to political office, again the name tickets and lottery machine were the chosen instruments. For each office, a name ticket was chosen at random from the pile of name tickets of all eligible citizens, and a black or white ball was drawn to confirm or reject the appointment. In this mad way, almost every office was filled: water commissioners, prison wardens, supervisors of flute girls, members of the legislative assembly. It is perhaps not surprising that Socrates and his philosophic successors, looking at "democracy" in this mechanized version, thought that there ought to be a better way! But in the absence of archaeological and literary information which has been coming to light, it was often assumed that the "democracy" criticized by Plato and Aristotle was our own modern model—with our voting machines displacing the older *kleroteria*—and some very uncomplimentary things have been said about these philosophers for their criticisms of political equality.

The honesty by invention movement began about the time that Hippodamas, town planner and utopian, proposed prizes for useful political inventions in his model constitution. It had peaked and faded by the time that Aristotle wrote his *Politics*, in which he rejected Hippodamas's idea as "merely encouraging meddling" and not likely to succeed. Faded, but not gone; for one of the more touching finds in the Athenian Agora dates from the first century B.C.: a mounted standard roof tile to protect the customer from a possible shoddy contractor!

Hippodamas would have admired, and Aristotle disregarded, our modern bank vaults, voting machines, counterfeit-proof money printing plates, automatic toll gates, and many similar things.

There is something about seeing the universe from a special superhuman standpoint that has a strong appeal for the theologian, the natural scientist, and the inventive gadgeteer. In ancient Egypt, one expression of this impulse took the form of board games set up as cosmic road maps, seen from some transterrestrial point of view. In ancient Greece, models to scale imitated celestial motions.

The idea that the motions of the stars and planets could be duplicated by a model, and the further notion that such a duplication would have explanatory as well as predictive value, seems first to have occurred to Anaximander, a Milesian engineer, in the sixth century B.C. Trying to explain the relation of planetary movements to the day-and-night cycle, Anaximander devised what has been called a "stovepipe" model. Suppose our earth is a disk at the center of the heavens, and that around it there are circles of hollow stovepipe (Anaximander compared them to hollow spokes of a chariot wheel), made of some opaque material. These circles of pipe are at different distances and move (in the opposite direction from the daily motion of the outermost heaven) at different rates. The pipes are filled with fire; but because they are opaque, we see this only where it shows through "breathing holes" in the moving circles. Proper adjustment of this device can make the model simulate and predict the motions of planets, the sun, the moon, and the constellations.

Anaximander's cosmological model was only one of his inventions of scientific instruments. He also made what was perhaps the first map of the earth, some sort of star map, and he designed a new type of sundial for marking seasons. Apparently, it didn't occur to him that his astronomical model could be self-moving; that idea came almost a century later, bringing with it the advent of mechanical clock time.

The later attempts at building self-moving universes to scale depended on an earlier Minoan invention. By and large, the Sea-Kingdom of Crete was *not* mechanical—elegant, civilized, unscientific, somewhat barbaric. But its Palaces had many sacred altars, where gods were to be pleased by constant libations, in fine flowing streams, of oil, or honey, or wine. The offerings, to be acceptable, had to be made by priests, and while this protected their professional monopoly, it also took up considerable time. Presumably in response to this challenge, a new invention appeared: the *rhyton*, an automatic libation jar. A small hole in the point of a hollow drinking horn, set in a frame above the altar, took care of ritual libations while the priests were free to watch the bullfights in the Palace courts.

In the *rhyton*, the sinking level of wine or oil, as it flowed out, was a primitive measure of time. Modified in various ways, the *klepsydra*, a water clock, evolved from this ancestral *rhyton*. (By about 585 B.C., *klepsydra* technology had evolved so far that it was used in an experiment to measure the diameter of the sun compared to that of the arc of the heavens from dawn to midday.) This water-clock technology, in turn, suggested a way of giving motion to a celestrial globe, descendant of Anaximander's cosmic models. If a cable attached to a sinking float was wound around the shaft of a rotating globe, as water flowed out of its container and the float sank, the globe would turn at a rate that could be adjusted to match the daily rotation of the skies. The idea seems at first to have been thought of only as a display piece (Derek Price's work on the history of the clock bears this out), and it may have been as such a display that by 361 B.C. a grand float-and-globe "clock" was built in the Athenian Agora. From this date on, the even flow of water and the resulting even turn of the artificial universe put the West on mechanical clock time. Somewhat later, this triumph of mechanical "equable flow" over the more eccentric periods of days, nights, and seasons was written into the Athenian Constitution, where (if a textual guess of mine is correct) an official ("legal") day was defined as the equivalent of a modern six hundred minutes of *klepsydra* time. Plato, in his *Theaetetus* (written shortly after 369 B.C.) already records the clock-watching neuroses of the lawyers in court, and contrasts this to the "freedom" of the philosopher.

Some historians, Trevor Roper most notable among them, hold that accidental causes play the most important roles in human history. (Aristotle said almost the same thing somewhat earlier, when he wrote in his *Politics* that "the proximate efficient causes of revolutions are trivial.") Surely the adventitious sequence of interactions by which ancient Athens found itself running on mechanical clock time is a confirmation of this theory. Beginning, as we have seen, with ingenious and lazy Minoan priests, running through Milesian engineers building worlds of stovepipe and fire, advancing to the aesthetic display of water-driven globes, time itself descended from theological to cosmological, on to political and commercial, as proto-clocks evolved and travelled from Knossos to Miletus to the Athenian Agora. The sundial, with its potential unequal measurements of fractions of daylight and night, was still a competitor in 433 B.C., when a new one was installed in Athens by the astronomer Meton. (Aristophanes commemorated that by portraying Meton onstage as a crackpot inventor.) But it was a set of other persons, in a different line of descent of the scrap iron and hollow pipe cosmology, who via applied gadgetry gave us a regular clock time that left the seasons behind it but synchronized well with the stars.

What strikes the modern reader of Heron's anthology forcibly is that the potential for modern industrialization was already present in this ancient time. Given the social regulation of the water-clock, the functional ingenuity of the coin-operated slot machine, and the application of steam-power to a small revolving mechanism, we are practically in the nineteenth century. (The resemblance is heightened by the small scale model "automobiles," accompanied by fictitious accounts of self-propelled full-size horseless chariots.)

Why the development stopped where it did for over a millennium is a fascinating question for the historian, whatever special field is in the foreground of his history.

The usual explanation is that in a society based on slave labor, labor-saving machinery would not be recognized as "useful"—apart from some applications of mechanical advantage to architecture. My own notion in 1966 was a rather different one. Slaves were so inexpensive to purchase and maintain that their displacement by machinery was not economically attractive, as I figured it. And the *idea* of mechanics and science applied to supplying inanimate power sources was still nebulous, and did not include the notion of applications that would be "useful" as distinct from "interesting."

The archetypal case in point is the *aeolipile*, a model steam engine with jets and a central bronze ball, designed to puff and spin in the center of a banquet table. The idea that a change of scale and some use of pulleys could harness this power to the sort of job a slave turning a spit was doing did not occur to anyone. The owner had, of course, a much less vivid and personal interest in labor-saving than the slave in question. And some vestige of vitalism, identifying power with living things, must also have inhibited the imagination of the mechanics who failed to apply their new designs.

A clear picture of what an Alexandrian "engineer" did consider useful, a picture primarily interesting for what it fails to include, is Heron's article on the uses of steam power. Having designed a boiler, it is handy for heating water; it can direct a blast of hot air into a fire; it can sound a trumpet; and it can make a mechanical bird sing! This exactly matches my thesis that the mind set of the classical mechanic was aesthetic rather than utilitarian.

On the other hand, a review of the evidence has made me reconsider my thesis that it was *only* the lack of an idea that delayed the industrial revolution. For there was one situation in which an upperclass classical citizen did have a firsthand obligation to perform work; and in that situation, labor-saving applications of every kind seem to have been forthcoming. It was the priests whose office required such varied duties as continual pouring of libations, or sale of water to worshippers in the temples, or sprinkling of purifying water, whose function apparently could not be delegated. And it was exactly this class that showed an atypical genius for inventing machines that saved labor.

For example, the *rhyton* has already been mentioned as an ancestor of the water-clock. An easy harnessing of gravity to constant libation-pouring protected the priestly monopoly on access to the gods, without much intrusion on leisure. Along the same line, the Egyptian priests were supposed to perform a purification by ritual sprinkling of water on worshippers. But a storage tank with a pipe and perforated wheel very like a shower head that sprinkled water when the wheel was spun made it possible for the worshipper to perform this for himself. In the Greek temples, a ritual washing before sacrifice was part of the ceremony—with the priest collecting his fee, one supposes, as he dispensed the water. By Heron's time, however, both the ablution and the collection are taken care of by a coin-operated slot machine. The coin, a silver stater, falls through a slot onto a plate; the plate is pivoted; it opens a valve, releasing water into a basin; the coin slides off and the valve closes.

Part of this priestly ingenuity traces back through a tradition of magic and miracle abetted by mechanism. (For example, a magical Egyptian statue would at one time designate which son of a deceased Pharaoh would succeed him by lifting its arm and tapping the successor on the shoulder as he walked past. And a Greek adaptation of right-angled gearing seems to have controlled the positive or negative response to requests for a miraculous "divine sign" in the form of a revolving bird).

But, if the priests so unerringly hit upon applications of every sort of power and advantage to labor-saving when it was their labor being saved, I think we must admit that the use of slave labor was in fact an important inhibiting factor in the development of classical mechanics and technology. In spite of a possible long-range saving in expense, there would not be the immediate incentive for the slave owner to try to adapt such a notion as that of a fire-powered metal tractor (which occurs in the Jason legend) to an actual device that would make life easier for his enslaved gardener.

So, finally, it seems that in the past, the assumption that mechanical advance and ingenuity will always be linked to inanimate power sources, and labor-saving machinery, has operated to distort the actual history of both mechanics and science in ancient Greece and Alexandria. Instead, the fact is, that there was a great deal of ingenuity and inventiveness; but it was not directed to those enterprises that we think of today as worthwhile. It was not even directed to enterprises that were "useful," but rather to projects that were "amazing" and "amusing."

Chapter 15

Scientific Apparatus Onstage in 423 B.C.

This chapter offers supporting evidence for the true but unstylish thesis that Western science entered Athens in the mid-fifth century B.C. like a tinker's cart, hung about with jangling and gleaming hardware. That thesis, in turn, is a vital link in an inductive proof that Western science has never actually developed apart from close interaction with measures, models, and machines.

The traditional view, common to histories of science and philosophy and to more general interpretations of classical culture, made the use of models, observation, and apparatus the crucial difference between 'science' in its classical and in its modern form.[1] This did not quite match the actual documents and achievements of classical work from Archimedes through Ptolemy, and more detailed study led to a new and different consensus.[2] Since 1952, the empirical character of post-Aristotelian science has been recognized, and it has been explained as the result of a confluence of Near Eastern computational, observational technique and a more austere classical qualitative, speculative fondness for theory construction. The date of fusion is put at about 323 B.C., the death of Alexander the Great.[3] On this recent view, apart from an incidental early coincidence, science in Greece before 323 would still have been the austere, antiempirical enterprise which earlier historians thought typical of classical science in general.

Neat as this scheme is, both historically and philosophically, further investigations now lead me to doubt its accuracy for the fourth century, as evidence shows that science in this period was already interacting with models and mechanisms, in a way that compromises its postulated rationalistic "purity." If the dialectical pattern of Hellenic pure rationalism—Near Eastern pure empiricism—Hellenistic empirical science holds historically, the rationalistic, antiempirical phase must be limited to about a century, from the arrival of Anaxagoras in Athens (ca. 467) to the compilation of Plato's *Timaeus* (ca. 367, surely begun earlier).[4] That lends a new, unappreciated magnitude to the role

in Western intellectual history of such thinkers as Anaxagoras, Arche-
laus, Socrates, and Plato in his younger days; for it would be just here
that the essential Hellenic component of the later synthesis appeared,
to be gradually weakened in the mid-fourth century, and synthesized
after 323.

But was there such a selective transplantation, separating "science" in Athens from the empirical strand of the Milesian tradition,
and giving it another direction?[5] Was a partial compromise being made
in the fourth century, as the "purity" of this scientific thought was
modified by importations of equipment from Italy and Asia Minor?
Interesting as this would be—and, in a way, plausible—it seems to me
it did not happen.

The evidence here presented for my view is primarily the role
played by "stagey" scientific properties and mechanisms in Aristophanes' Clouds. There is throughout the play an intrinsic association of
"new learning," atheism, and mechanical apparatus; and an audience
is presupposed already familiar enough with that association to appreciate the grotesque properties hung about in the Phrontisterion, and
the way Strepsiades misinterprets them.

Since my focus of attention here is the fifth century, I will relegate
to a note my reasons for insisting on the "impure," "mechanized" character of "science" in the latter three-quarters of the fourth century, and
center on Aristophanes' evidence that the same idea—apparatus interaction held in 423 B.C.[6]

There are four points about the Clouds that I think brief citation
can establish clearly. First, that the connection of science and hardware
is pervasive in the imagery and plot of the play itself, not merely the
subject of a few contrived jokes. Second, that the unscrupulous
intellectual—typified by Socrates—uses this equipment to intimidate
and dazzle the uninitiate. Third, that Aristophanes rejects all such appeals to models as a non sequitur; he finds them no more plausible
evidence for giving up traditional belief than the pots of a kitchen
posing as celestial hemispheres would be. Fourth, that Aristophanes
recognized that the appeal of "gadgetry" was dangerous. Part of the
education he undertakes that does rub off on Strepsiades is the notion
of using gadgetry as an "art of mischief," to further injustice. Thus the
destruction of the Phrontisterion by fire includes, implicitly, the notion
of its equipment melting as part of the happy ending.

(To anticipate the objection that this dependence on models may
have been only an idiosyncrasy of Socrates, not an attribute of the new
system of ideas he represents, we can look at another of Aristophanes'
plays. The walk-on bit played by Meton as "mad scientist" in the Birds,

with his equipment for staking out lots in upper air, has this same strong thematic association of typical new intellectual and cumbersome new mechanical gear. This combination is therefore proper to the type specimen Meton and Socrates resemble, not just an eccentricity of the latter.)

The whole tone is set at the outset of the Thought-Shop scene by Socrates in his elevated basket. More usually, it would be a god who rode aloft on the theatre's machine, and Aristophanes does not let the audience miss the connection of "higher-thought" mechanism and Socratic *hybris*. "Why dost thou call me, O Mortal?" asks Socrates in l. 2231. Strepsiades shortly comments, "Then it is from the basket that you show contempt for the gods" (l. 2261). We were already partially prepared for this by Strepsiades' hearsay account of the wise men in the school, who say that "we are coals beneath the cooking-bell of heaven" (ll. 97–7). This homely hearsay paraphrase introduces the two notions that the new Shop has some sort of cosmological model, and that it is really trivial.[7]

The suspended basket at l. 218 is the climax of the initial tour in which the Disciple recounts the ingenuity of his Master, and points out the "cult objects" that characterize the new sciences. One of Socrates' subtle masterpieces is recounted that sets up the initial association of apparatus and injustice, at l. 179. To get food, Socrates bends a skewer into a compass, pretends to be studying geometry, and hooks his neighbor's sacrificial meat from the altar with it.[8]

The gaudy map of l. 206 anticipates the more sinister model of l.380. Merry is surely right in envisaging the stage set: "placed about the School are sundry philosophical instruments, such as some sort of celestial globe to designate *Astronomy*, an abacus to represent *Geometry*."[9]

At l. 380 "The Vortex" appears; he rules instead of Zeus. (Cf. ll. 828, 1471.) Impiety on the part of Socrates, imbecility on that of Strepsiades, and topical commentary by Aristophanes all intersect in this stage property. A clay jar symbolizing physical process is the patron deity whose statue stands here in the school. The scale and function of this model are established by its balanced contrast with the statue of Hermes, to which Strepsiades turns for counsel near the end of the play.[10] The "thing here of clay" has misled him; he mistook it for a god (ll. 143–741). Strepsiades, who is stupid and a nonscientist, sees before him only a gigantic tapered goblet or jar when Socrates points out the cosmic model; but his ambition and gullibility lead him to take *that* as the shape of the new father of gods. Aristophanes invited his audience to share his notions that cosmic models are ridiculous but intimidating to the uninitiate, and that they have an evil power in the hands of the new thinkers of the day. (His property man, if he provided a black or red tapered jar on the same scale as the statue of Hermes, would have given visual emphasis to the point.) A consideration of what must be presupposed about an audience able to appreciate Socrates' addiction to his model, Strepsiades' enthusiastic misunderstanding of it, and Aristophanes' sardonic personification of this odd artefact, underscores my central thesis.

But it requires nothing so grandiose as cosmic models to make mischief; even relatively "neutral" tools turn to evildoing devices in the play. We have already heard of Socrates' ingenious transformation of compass to skewer, and his theft from the nearby altar, under cover of pretending to study geometry. Strepsiades, trying at Socrates' urging to think in the new way, finds a similar solution to the problem of evading his debts. His first impulse (749f.) is to "hire a witch," who will steal the moon from the sky, and so by magic postpone indefinitely the date the interest is due. But then, to escape a lawsuit, he hits upon the notion of taking a "burning-glass" and using it to melt the wax from the legal tablets. He is inept; the gadgetry is far-fetched, unlike Socrates' geometrical compass, and the intended result involves simple injustice without impiety. But the contagious character of the scientific association of ideas and new tools is well brought out in the "burning-glass" theme.

Strepsiades' final rejection of the new higher learning, at line 1472 (after his son has just repeated that "the Vortex reigns instead of Zeus," l. 1471 repeating l. 828), again has the model Vortex as its focus. Repenting his folly in mistaking this thing of clay for an immortal god, he turns to Hermes for advice. (The literal identification of god and goblet was of course Strepsiades' own; for Socrates, it is clearly a *model* of a new atheistic cosmic power; but Aristophanes keeps insinuating that its credibility as a model is no greater than its credibility as a literal sacred object to be worshipped.)

Another association of ideas is the equation of the apparatus with the cult objects of the Mysteries. "These must be held as Mysteries," says the Disciple who opens the *Phrontisterion* door (l. 143). The air of the Disciple, as he points out "that is astronomy . . . this is geometry," is that of the hierophant explaining a tableau. The resemblance is emphasized by beginning with the students as a group prying into "things under the earth," and ending with Socrates riding the god-machine.

These are some of the passages that one can cite to show that the association between science and its trappings is treated as intrinsic in the play, presupposing an audience for whom that association is already familiar. And I am sure that anyone charged with designing sets and properties for a production of the *Clouds* would find himself quickly convinced of the crucial part played by the scientific gear in the spectacle.

This is not the only evidence, of course, for the contention that there was no discontinuity in the history of science between phases that depend heavily on concrete models and tools (the sixth century, the period after 323, and I think the scientific work from about 387 to 323), and a fifth-century phase in which science disregarded them; but it does offer one footnote to support the thesis that the partnership of new ideas and new apparatus was in effect and generally recognized in 423.

The further implications of this for studies of the history and nature of Western science are highly complex problems of interpretation; but we must begin by having our facts correct, if we are to understand them.

First published in YALE CLASSICAL STUDIES, vol. 22: *Studies in Fifth-Century Thought and Literature* (1972), ed. by Adam Parry, copyright by Cambridge University Press, with the permission of Cambridge University Press.

Chapter 16

Plato's Relation to the Arts and Crafts

In our last conversation, Professor Miller and I talked about the importance of travel in Greece and of a knowledge of its historical context for the student of Greek philosophy. We both agreed that we two, at least, were wandering scholars, who learned from travel and adventure as well as from silence and analytic thought.[1]

Just offhand, as examples of classical ideas that look one way in the abstract and another in their original setting, we cited four. When we read about classical canons of beauty—restraint, balance, symmetry, purity—we do not think of the garish gold and vermillion ornamentation, the adjacent dense clutter of trivial *stelae*, that went along with the austere Attic architecture as part and parcel of the real classical instantiation of "the beautiful." Our standard myth of classical lack of mechanical genius and distaste for gadgetry is contradicted from the first display case to the last in, say, the Ancient Agora Museum of the American School. Our vision of "democracy" suffers a rude shock from confrontation with political hardware of that ancient phase. And Aristotle's smug "we Greeks are men of moderation" must mean by "moderation" an energy and engagement that we would more likely describe today as "mania."[2]

One tension between modern reconstruction and historical original lies in our accounts of Plato's (and Aristotle's) attitude toward arts and crafts and their practitioners. Where the sedentary expositor has ordinarily remained content with an anthology of aspersions, the wandering scholar is brought up short by the frequency with which artifacts—whether those of fine or useful "art"—remind him of references in Plato. Buying a fifteen-cent "pruning knife," still handmade in its classical design, along the Street of Hephaistos in modern Athens, one thinks at once of the reference to the *drepanon* in *Republic* I as a clinching example of the way "form follows function."[3] The small money-changing tables, minor league competitors lined up outside the National Bank in modern Athens, take us back to the detail in Plato's *Euthyphro*, where the pious priest can follow the mathematics of patterns only on a counting table.[4]

195

The result of this vivid feedback is to make one wonder just how alien Plato was from the arts and crafts, and whether a second look is in order in the light of his evident interest and his range of references that include practically *every* technical field of the time.[5]

That second look is particularly important because critics—Marxist, pragmatist, anti-elitist—have developed all sorts of baroque hypotheses about the connection between a Veblenesque contempt for honest work on Plato's part and his formalist metaphysics and aristocratic political theory; and between that same leisure-class mentality and Aristotle's Prime Mover.[6]

There is indeed some striking textual support for this attribution. It is all the more striking because its snobbery and irascibility often seem a quite gratuitous going out of the way to put down honest workmen. Aristotle proposes to take their voting franchise away from "mechanics"; Plato finds all arts and crafts "servile" and "unscientific," even detrimental to full mental or physical development.[7]

I would almost have to concede the case without reexamination if it were true that later Platonists, from Plutarch through Proclus, had correctly understood Plato and Aristotle on this point. For example, Plutarch makes his Archimedes a Platonic sage, and attributes to him a disinterest in the material world and its mechanics that would make even a Zen Buddhist stare.[8] But something odd seems to have happened between the original doctrines and these later explications. For example, I have just been looking at a Plato scholion, probably originated by some scholar of the third or fourth century A.D., which offers as "Platonic" a classification of all exercise as "necessary evil." That weird scholion alone would make me distrust Hellenistic explications.[9]

The key to the case is suggested, I think, by the fact I noted before, that there seems something *gratuitously* hostile and polemical in the deprecations of craft and art. The reason is that in Plato and Aristotle we are hearing only one side of a heated conversation. There were professional educators who proposed to *substitute* useful crafts for the "impractical" liberal arts in the curriculum. And it is in response to *them*, not in moments of passing general ill-will, that we find angry, acid reactions to the proposal. In other words, the negative comments are not intended to deny that arts and crafts have utility, interest, some cognitive value, and so on, but they are intended to deny that *only* arts and crafts—as opposed to mathematics, astronomy, dialectic, or political theory—have utility, or value, or even interest. And any positive moment is likely to appear only in *implicit* references and evidences of skill on the part of Plato and Aristotle, rather than in any general explicit concession or expressed admiration that might seem a capitulation to their opposition.[10]

We have just enough of a record of the other side of the polemical debate to reconstruct an outline of what this opposition was. For advocacy of the practical arts as something worth knowing, we can cite the portraits of Hippias. He shows up at the Olympic games with a robe, shoes, staff, a ring, and a display oration all of his own construction.[11] Or we can look at the references to a now lost set of pamphlets by Protagoras, who had written them on every craft from cooking to wrestling.[12] In one sardonic contrast between the Sophist and the Philosopher, Plato dismisses as irrelevant the fact that the latter is not very clever at flavoring a sauce; a totally stupid remark, unless some audience might have thought either that sauces and sciences *were* mutually relevant or that attention to sauce was wiser than attention to "philosophy."[13]

Some other data show how strongly the negative side of this proposal to make education "useful" was presented. This negative case is the thesis that "liberal arts" are empty and educationally irrelevant. There is Gorgias's display speech "On Nature" claiming to show the uncertainty and instability of metaphysics, or science, or cosmology.[14] By juxtaposing selected doctrines from past experts, Gorgias claims to show that nothing exists, that if it did, we could not know it, and even if we knew it, we could not communicate our knowledge. Protagoras thought it a total waste of time to inflict the study of mathematics—as opposed to rhetoric, poetry, and law—on future democratic leaders.[15] He even wrote a pamphlet on this subject (in addition to his short essays on crafts), pointing out, apparently, that pure mathematics exists only in a world of fantasy. His title "On the Contact Between a Hoop and a Beam" makes fun of the geometer's fiction that a straight line tangent to a circle touches it at only one indivisible geometric point.[16] If pure geometry is that far off target when we try applying it to as similar a "real" situation as a two-by-four beam resting on a copper barrel hoop, it is hard to see where there is any place for it in practical political or legal theory. Indeed, the Pythagoreans who tried to reduce things to numbers must have been mad, on this Protagorean view. Isocrates, a later and more disciplined educator, still thinks the study of political *theory* irrelevant to political *practice,* and accuses Plato's Academy of a great deal of "idle chattering" (which, says Plato, is what "the many" call dialectic).[17] A practical man, committed to political power contests but still speaking for the Sophists, Callicles explains in one of Plato's dialogues that "a little Philosophy is a good study for young men; but too much unfits them for public life."[18]

In these demolition jobs, we hear the main guns of a new idea of education that ran exactly counter to, and attacked, the "liberal education" approach of the Academy. And we must remember that this new idea was backed by men who were, at that time, recognized intellectuals with considerable authority. It is no wonder that the counterattacks we also hear are sometimes as much of an overkill and satire as, say, Gorgias's parody of philosophy or Isocrates' condescension to political theory. In fact, very similar exchanges between somewhat similar positions have taken place in educational philosophy in our own century. The debate between Dewey's pragmatism and Hutchins's liberal arts humanism was very like a resurrection of the earlier Athenian controversy. Perhaps even more like it, however, would be a debate as to whether we should replace liberal arts education in our secondary schools by vocational training, giving up abstract theory and instead teaching skills in more immediate social demand.

Given this history, we can see why it is difficult to disengage Plato's acquaintance with, appreciation of, and attitude toward the arts and crafts from this contextual polemic, and why *implicit* evidence *might* show a far more friendly attitude than he felt free to avow explicitly. But the question remains of *what we find in fact* when we neutralize the polemics and look at the textual and contextual evidence that remains.

The first piece of evidence is simply a tabulation of the frequency of reference to arts, crafts, and artifacts, in the dialogues. The mere quantitative result is amazing: Plato was, apparently, one of the most enthusiastic of the sidewalk supervisors in the Agora of ancient Athens. Taking a casual and partial sample of references to crafts, the following items appear: Bath attending; Blacksmithing; Building (with masonry); Carpentry; Butchering; Carving; Cabinetmaking; Clothesmaking; Cobbling; the art of Commerce; Cooking; Barbering; Coppersmithing; Dyeing; Embroidery; Flutemaking; Thread spinning; Gold refining; Statue carving; Minting of coinage; Navigation. . . . And this does not yet mention the more frequently cited arts: the General's (art of Warfare); Hunting; Medicine; Lawgiving; Measuring; or even Weaving.[19] This is an odd fact if indeed Plato means his dismissal of all arts and crafts as "vulgar and irrelevant" seriously. A more complete and finer-textured index of references only makes the oddity more striking.

One might at first think that this facile use of references to *technai* was a trait of only one stage in Plato's thought. Perhaps in his earlier period, when he was echoing the historical Socrates more closely, the arts played a major role, but then moved out of the spotlight. The idea is interesting, but finds itself refuted by the existence—by very rough count—of two hundred and six references to arts and crafts in the *Republic*. Well, remembering Winspear and Silverberg's interpretation of

Socrates as would-be capitalist betraying his class of origin, we might suppose that this frequent Platonic citation occurs only in the middle dialogues, as an advance beyond the historical Socrates.[20] But that will not work either; for the brief *Laches* has twenty-one references to the arts, the briefer *Ion* ten, the transitional *Euthydemus* twenty-four, and the *Charmides* a surprising thirty-four references. Nor can we say that Plato's "analytical" later dialogues show him to have outgrown his earlier habits of analogies and references to crafts and arts. The *Timaeus* has thirty-five, which, considering its subject-matter is not surprising, indeed a bit unexpectedly low; the *Statesman*, however, comes up with twenty-six, and the notorious *Sophist* scores sixty-two! One moral of this emerges clearly enough; Plato found the arts and crafts useful for some purposes of philosophic explanation, and that usefulness did not appear or disappear as his method and style shifted from the *Charmides* through the *Republic* to the *Sophist*. While he clearly did not think the arts and crafts identical with either science or philosophy (though some of his characters do from time to time—Erxyimachus, in the *Symposium*, for example, repeatedly calls "science" what is only "art"),[21] he did not think, either, of doing philosophy without them.[22]

How deep this interest goes is another matter. It is one thing to refer, *in passing*, to technology—today, for example, we are always doing this when we say that something is being done "by computer." But it is a different thing to understand an art from the inside, as a craftsman would. (Rather than saying the job was done "by computer," the technician would say "on an IBM 3004.") Where we have enough text and context to judge, Plato frequently shows an insight that seems to go beyond that of the mere observer, to a level of close observation, and probably firsthand execution. It is no surprise that we can document this firsthand awareness for the gentleman's arts of hunting and of war; and perhaps one would expect anyone with philosophic curiosity in Plato's circle to also have considerable familiarity with medicine.[23] But this control of fine detail also appears for carpentry, and even more for spinning and weaving.[24] In fact, Plato preserves details, in his account of the weaving art, that we find in no other ancient literary source, and that make perfect sense to a modern expert in home weaving.[25] I am sure that, after Hippias's boasting about *his* weaving skill, Plato would have allowed himself to be boiled in olive oil before admitting that he had ever tried his hand as a weaver! But, if arts and crafts were for a time—as the Hippias and Protagoras doxographies attest—a faddish thing for an Athenian elite, there is no adequate reason to disbelieve the textual evidence that Plato knew as many technical details as Hippias could have about this art. Today, of course, it is

carpentry rather than weaving that is the "in" thing for our intelligent-
sia. Some reasons for this cultural difference might be plainer if we
knew more about ancient Greek carpentry.[26]

Two points have now been established concerning Plato's relation
to contemporary arts and crafts. The first is that references to them are
always present; the second is that those references have, on occasion, an
air of firsthand technical knowledge which is hard to set aside. This
brings us to a third, and final, question. What is the philosophic function of this set of references to the crafts? Or, if there is not just one
function, what are the several functions?

The character of the references themselves suggests that there are,
indeed, several different functions, which vary between early, middle,
and late dialogues. In the earliest dialogues, the citations occur in contexts where the problem emerging is to refute Sophistic and popular
notions identifying *virtue* (or *knowledge*) with *technical skill.* The
clash is certainly sharp in the *Charmides,* where Critias equates temperance with knowledge which is ethically neutral. It is more like a
pitched battle than a clash in the *Euthydemus,* where verbal technique
is applauded, by the audience, as the ultimate in philosophic excellence. It is stated in a particularly clear form in the *Hippias Minor,*
where if we accept Hippias's notion that "better" means "more technically adroit," the man who lies on purpose, with sound technique,
would come out "better" than someone who told falsehoods uninten-
tionally. In these earlier dialogues, while references to skills are used
sometimes to contrast the expert and the non-expert, they also contrast
skill with true wisdom or virtue; the references are brief, wide-ranging,
with a whole world full of examples of "arts" which are indeed kinds of
"knowledge" but none of which can be "virtue" in Socrates' sense.

In the *Republic,* Plato's Divided Line expresses a new, more precise classification of levels and stages of cognition. One way of reading
that line is as a series of stages in education and concept formation,
from a mythical private world of fantasy, to an objective vision of the
good. But to "understand" or "explain" the relation of time and eternity, the cave and the sun, it seems that all four of the levels of the line
must be represented. Thus, the good appears directly, on its own top
level, in the dazzling simile of the sun; it is located on a timeless,
abstract *dianoetic* map by the Divided Line; it appears at the end of a
long corridor of dark ascent in the Myth of the Cave; and it is linked to
the public world of space and time by a road of technology in *Republic*
VII, the "Way with tokens" of an ideal curriculum.[27] Yet throughout
the *Republic,* this moment of reference to crafts, essential for dialectical completeness, still takes the form which it had in the early dia-

logues of citing many arts—whichever one comes to mind first when an example of *techne* is needed—with very brief expansion of the citation. For every problem, institution, or idea Plato finds a connection with common funded human experience in some almost passing analogy to a useful or fine art.

In the later dialogues, the arts play a different part in the argument, and receive a different treatment in the literary structure. In most cases, they are now contrasted not so much with *knowledge* as with *semblance;* the problem is not so much the dogmatism of the craftsman who, because he knows something, fancies himself wise in everything, as it is the contrast with the professional skeptic whose contention is that no one is "wiser" than anyone else in any way.[28] Now, the existence of expertise in the arts (testable by their relative accuracy of production and prediction, for example) refutes any relativistic reduction of all knowledge to perception or to conjecture.[29] Further, the existence of successful arts is the basis, in the *Statesman,* for a transcendental proof of the existence of objective normative measure.[30] The arts, without changing their status as specialized technological skill, thus tend to reverse their roles in the argument: they become an onstage testimony for the possibility of some "knowing" which is not purely subjective and relative, and of some "evaluative measure" which is objective as well.

At the same time, a 3 × 5 card index of references to arts and crafts becomes misleading for these later dialogues. The density per page (whatever page we use—Stephanus, conjectured Thrasyllus, Burnet) becomes low because Plato hits on the device of using arts and crafts as either *framework* or *extended running simile;* once this is established, spot references become less necessary. For example, throughout the *Timaeus,* the god who makes the cosmos is a demiourgos—metallurgist, smith, potter, sketcher. His tools and media are changed from time to time, but the framework simile, once introduced, makes repeated item-by-item allusions to "craft" unnecessary. In a similar way—though this has been less appreciated—the *Sophist* is framed and enlivened by the running imagery of a great hunt. In fact, the Stranger from Elea who is brought in to "track the wily creature down" reminds me of the team of bounty hunters hired, in another time and context, to gun down Butch Cassidy and the Sundance Kid.[31] In the *Statesman,* a summary takes the form of the extended comparison of statesmanship to the weaving of a fabric, carried to the unusual technical detail already mentioned.

However we explain this literary development, the explanation involves a new recognition on Plato's part of the importance of operational definition. A democratic ideal of "equal participation in making policy" can be a "good" idea, and yet be implemented—as the Athenians did in fact implement it—in a way sure to result in incompetence, and chaos, and corruption. A metaphysical notion that the laws of nature ought to have formal simplicity, which first appears in the *Phaedo*, is finally operationally tested by quantifying these laws in the *Timaeus*.

Yet, particularly interesting to the modern reader in his prescience, these later dialogues recognize a negative potential in rampant technology. The *Critias* projects the result of technical skill left unrestrained and run wild, dominating nature, embarking on global conquest, inducing chronic intemperance and bad taste. While Atlantis had *techne* to a degree that "seemed more than human," it lacked philosophy; and eventually, through the operation of divine justice, it was sunk beneath the sea.[32]

So far I have simply assimilated the "fine Arts" to the other arts and crafts in this overview. Plato, however, recognized their distinction. On the negative side, he went to some length—for example, in the *Ion*—to reject the still current notion that Homer and other poets should be thought of as encyclopedias of information and technology.[33] While in one sense their sensitivity to the beautiful rather than to the accurate or the useful gave them a higher calling than they were commonly accorded, in another sense their imaginative indifference to cold restraints of fact made them producers of mere semblance. "Poems should seem, not be," is a sentiment Plato would certainly have supported; what he would have thought it meant, as opposed to the notion of a twentieth century fellow supporter, might be quite another matter.[34]

But in addition to *this* contrast between genuine productive crafts and entertaining fine arts, we are aware that certain very disquieting things happen if we measure the exact details of fine art as closely as Greek craftsmen had done, or even as closely as Plato had analyzed the art of weaving. That elegant simplicity of the Parthenon, where columns appear absolutely equally spaced, cylindrical, and vertical, the floors seem level, and so on, rests on multiple complex deviations from "exact" rectangular or linear measure.[35] (The Atlantean temple, with exact dimensions of 2:1, had, said Plato, "something barbaric in its appearance."[36] A traditional Greek temple plan would be 1 to the square root of five.) Greek music, too, beginning with the transparency of its framework of "concords," plunged into a mathematical complexity of ratios of prime thousandths to one another when it expanded to include the variable complete modal scales in the integral ratios of mathematical theory.[37]

In his last dialogue, the *Laws*, Plato combines an aesthetic sense with a new notion of a maximum potential for social technique. Since the useful arts rest on measure, and on ratio, the ideal population for a model city may be some number—in this case, 5,040—which is capable of maximum technical flexibility.[38] Whatever social divisions and measures—of soldiers on frontier patrol, of gardeners in the country parks, of producers of papyrus for the paper plant—we may need, can be built neatly and integrally out of this selected numerical substructure. This is a technical implementation of the thesis argued in *Republic* VII that all arts and crafts presuppose counting and measure.[39] In the design of life for the colonial town of the *Laws*, the legislators finally bring fine art, useful art, and human life together. They indicate this in their farewell to the visiting tragic poets who are not allowed to perform. "Best of men," they say to them, "we ourselves are also tragic poets, creating in our state a drama of human life. Do not suppose, therefore, that we will welcome your interference as our competitors. . . ."[40]

This final word, in which technology and beauty come to terms, may do less explicit metaphysical justice to the arts and crafts than the *Republic* had. For in the figure of the Divided Line, it was clear that the kind of "knowing" represented by common sense and *techne* was not only a useful stage in learning and designing a society that could combine efficiency with nobility, but that it was necessary.[41] Without the arts projecting forms and paradigms into space and time, neither nobility nor philosophy would be humanly attaina'le. Technology without theory, art without philosophy, may dominate the realm of what is spatio-temporally actual—may, indeed even destroy it—but by itself, it cannot envision the ideal.[42] Philosophy without technology can contemplate eternal verities and values, but it cannot design their actual human, spatio-temporal realization.[43]

Thus, in a visit to modern Greece, the true Platonist will not disdain to study either the Classical artifacts which are survivals of ancient technology, or those modern crafts which are the ancient arts barely changed. We can admire it all: from the elegance of the Parthenon, through the homely but ingenious wine coolers and sausage grills found in the ancient Agora, to the modern hand production of pruning hooks on Hephaistos Street by classical technique with blades in the classical *drepanon* design.[44] Plutarch, reading Plato in another, more pessimistic, setting and a more joyless day, found in him a counsel of enervated, snobbish catatonia and escape. But Plato in his own time, as his invention of the Academy proves well, was the West's greatest and most engaged educational *technician*. From his writings we can see that he noticed and enjoyed the authenticity and action of the world of fine and useful arts through which he passed each time he crossed the Agora, en route from his Academy to the Acropolis—or to the Theater.[45]

Reprinted from W. Werkmeister, ed., *Facets of Plato's Philosophy*, (*Phronesis* supplementary vol. II), copyright Van Gorcum, Assen, 1976, by permission of the publisher. These papers were presented at a Memorial Symposium for Robert D. Miller, Tallahasee, Fla., May 1973.

Part V

The Feminine, Genres, and Once Again the Hemlock

Introduction to Part V

This section fills in Plato's thoughts by supplying more context of antecedents and contrasts. The topic of women, which was treated in earlier discussion of the *Republic*, is used as the focus for contrasting Plato's philosophic formalism to the three main alternative contemporary metaphysical systems. The topic of style tries to show how philosophic motives shape the choice of literary form, and how Plato and Aristotle represent paradigmatic examples of what have been the two main Western traditions ever since. Finally, an account of the trial of Socrates takes us back to the crucial event that led Plato to devote himself to the writing of philosophy, from the early dialogues of inquiry to the magnificent system of the *Republic*, and beyond. This final section, therefore, leads back naturally to Part I.

Chapter 17

Four Definitions of Women in Classical Philosophy

The origin of this chapter was the claim, made in Stallknecht and Brumbaugh, *The Compass of Philosophy*, 1952, that what seem questions of fact are often, instead, functions of alternative, and systematic, philosophic definition. The relevance of this theme to women in antiquity struck me particularly vividly in 1983, when I was simultaneously preparing a lecture on Plato's *Republic* and captions for an exhibit of ancient coins showing four conceptions of women. The deduction is particularly interesting in comparison with Sarah Pomeroy's study *Goddesses, Whores, Wives, and Slaves*, and with the N.E.H. curricular material her group assembled, *Women in Classical Antiquity: Four Modules*. My work is completely independent, a philosophical deduction from a study of the classical systems outlined below in my Epilogue. I must admit that I am surprised both by the approximate match of my results and Prof. Pomeroy's, and by the consistent—but, so far as I can tell, metaphysically gratuitous—negative attitude toward women of philosophers of my "atomic" systems. I am grateful to the N.E.H. for support in planning a course exploring "Classical Definitions of Women in Philosophy and Literature."

I

One thing that complicates any discussion of women is that there can be a difference in the presupposed notion of what we are discussing, that is, in notions of what women really are. The result of a difference as basic as that, when it goes unrecognized, is an annoying failure to agree even about the most evident matters of fact, beauty, justice, or budget.

This effect of crossed latent definitions can also be described as the collision of alternative paradigms. A "paradigm" in this sense is a single model or example that is taken to be typical of a whole class of theories or subjects—for example, of the class of women as a whole. In classical philosophy, such effects are very clear when different thinkers bring with them different notions of what counts as a definition or typical case of "reality." I hope to show that the same effects are there when, instead of talking about what reality is, the different notions have to do with a special part of it, that is, women and what they *really are*.

The study of paradigms has recently concentrated on cases from natural science. In this domain, paradigms seem to dominate one at a time. For a while, some single favored model and theory is generally accepted; but then there is a change, and it is displaced by another single alternative. However, in philosophy and the humanities, and probably in the social sciences, the situation is more complex. Here, alternative theories and paradigms seem to operate at the same time in a given culture. This explains, in part, why questions in these areas are so controversial. (I will suggest later, though, that within this plurality, there may be one paradigm most widely accepted, and then rejected in favor of any plausible proposed alternative.)

II

Four classical coins can serve as illustrations of the four principal paradigms I find in Greek and Roman philosophy and drama; each illustrates an attitude toward women based on an implicit general definition.

The first coin is an Athenian tetradrachma, with the head of the goddess in profile. The portrait itself is an idealization, a type and an austere one. The implication clearly is that a female deity can regulate society, deserve worship, and preserve authority in just the same way that a male god can.

The second coin has a "woman as beauty queen" motif. It is a Syracusan tetradrachma. Here in three-quarter face there is the portrait of a very human nymph, Arethusa. Nymphs, one recalls, were much more affectionate, more capricious, and less important than Olympian goddesses. (The human aspect is underscored by the report that a particularly attractive princess served as the engraver's model for his nymph on the coin.) The suggestion is that women deserve *affection*, where the Athenian paradigm rather brings with it the suggestion that they deserve our *respect*.

My third coin design, a Gorgon, from Neapolis, pictures an alien being, a female monster. This comes from a background of legend and belief that sees women's nature as different in some deep way from men's; and as frightening in this deviant nature. (I am sure Gorgo, properly placated, seemed a protectress of her native town. But I doubt if she inspired either much affection or reverence from it.) Oddly enough, in the great Greek Age of Reason of the fifth and fourth centuries, this notion seems to be avoided by the philosophers at just the time when it comes onstage in tragedy.

I had some difficulty choosing a fourth coin type to illustrate the idea that women are objects (sex objects), property, and often a social and legal liability. My colleague, John Burnham, came up with a two-coin solution. The first is a Roman denarius, portraying a troop of Roman soldiers carrying off Sabine women. The Romans trudge along, each with a plump Sabine slung over his shoulder—like a hunting party coming home with game. The second coin is a Greek drachma from Thasos—in legend a pretty wild island—on which an erotic satyr represents the "sex object" standpoint. (Women as liability seem not to be portrayed in the coinage record. I would have liked a classical Xanthippe.)

III

The first of these designs goes well with the definition of women which we find in Plato's *Republic*. There, in Book V, he argues that women share a common ideal human nature with men, and, therefore, must have the same rights and responsibilities. The idea is, he admits, unfamiliar; and he expects that it will seem ridiculous to many of his audience. However, it follows solidly from Platonic metaphysics, and the Academy admitted two women. (In other contexts, from time to time, Plato forgets this, and does make chauvinistic remarks about women.)

In his late *Seventh Letter*, Plato says that to understand something, three things are necessary: a name, an abstract definition, and at least one concrete example; and thus philosophy gives us definitions, while we find examples in art and drama. To match Plato and Athena in literature I think Sophocles' Antigone as tragic heroine is appropriate. In particular, her *courage* is as heroic as that of any earlier masculine epic hero. (Courage, as the name *andreia* suggests, was popularly regarded as a distinctive and almost exclusive male virtue. We will presently find Aristotle citing evidence to show that this is the case even among cuttle-fish.)

The second notion of women, pictured in the nymph and beauty queen coins, is developed in Aristotle's natural and moral philosophy.

They are of the same biological species as man, but remain immature (Aristotle's favorite example of causation is "man is the father of man"), hence lacking the capacity for full human excellence. On the other hand, they are affectionate and attractive, though capable of mischief. The social implications of this biological view are spelled out clearly, if briefly, in Aristotle's *Ethics* and *Politics*. (Richard McKeon's suggestion, in 1976, that the discussion of women's "nature" in Aristotle's "practical sciences" introduces a different sense of *physis* are not convincing, particularly in the light of the *Historia Animalium* passage which McKeon included in his *Basic Works* selections.) There are additional examples of this viewpoint in the medical tradition and in some other works from Aristotle's school, the Lyceum.

On stage, this view is perfectly illustrated by the women in Aristophanes' comedies, "Cute little critters." The example fits particularly well in present context, because in one play, "The Women in Congress," Aristophanes' women discuss some of the same themes that later figure in Book V of Plato's *Republic*. The comedy was earlier than the dialogue, and Plato seems to think that many of the ideas in the play, intended to be comical, in fact make good political sense; but no one is likely to confuse Aristophanes' heroine, Praxagora, with Sophocles' Antigone.

Women as dark and alien in nature occupy a dominating role in Greek folklore and religion, and a dualism of Male and Female principles is important in early Greek philosophy and cosmology. But for some reason, the philosophers of the fifth and fourth centuries seem to avoid, almost to reject, this definition with its associated paradigms. (Empedocles, haunted by the Orphic mysteries, tries to compromise with the female nature when, in discussing reincarnation, he claims "I remember I was once a girl. . . ." He would have been more consistent if he had recognized a cosmic polarity of male and female comparable to his basic cosmic opposites of Love and Hate.) Perhaps this is because, particularly after the Sophists and Socrates, these philosophers are *rationalists*, and inclined to ignore rather than accept the challenge that would be offered by women as irrational, nonhuman, supernatural. On the other hand, the recognition of this theme is central to some of the most powerful characters in Greek tragedy. There is Medea, who kills her children for revenge on their father. There is Agave, who in a frenzy ends the *Bacchae* carrying her son's head on a pike staff. There is Hecuba, maddened by her misfortune, transformed into a dying dog with yellow eyes. And there are more. Aristotle calls Euripides the "most tragic" of the poets. O'Neill notes that while we have no other record of Socrates' attendance at the theater, he seems to have gone to every new production of a Euripides play—though at least once he walked out on one. But neither Aristotle nor Socrates presents a world-view that could include the women of Euripides.

Women as property and liability figure in classic law and custom. The idea that there is no such thing as "human nature," but that all values are conventional creations of society, was a central philosophic theme of the Greek Sophists. Given their view, it followed that what women are is defined by what law and customs say they are. And law and custom pretty much said that they were possessions and subordinates, best kept confined to the house. (The most remarkable feature of an adultery case, as we know from a speech written by Lysias, was how on earth the Athenian wife ever managed to get acquainted with another man in the first place!) They were not allowed to dispose of property on their own, though in some cases of divorce, male relatives could recover a dowry. Family policy was made by the husband, and was final. (This law was changed by the Greek Parliament in 1983). Notice that this paradigm is different from the Aristotelian view, which holds that there is a shared human nature, but women realize it less completely. There is no appeal to "nature" recognized by Sophistic cultural relativism. (Twentieth-century descriptive social science would, *if it were consistent*, adopt this same point of view. But feminism, even in social science, tends to go beyond simple description of the current status of women to introduce prescriptions for improving it!) Women, certainly as wives—and also, attested by Roman comedy, as non-wives—as a hindrance to happiness is a theme foreshadowed in the ethics of Democritus; immortalized in the stories of Xanthippe and Socrates; and brought, by Epicurus, to explicit philosophic formulation. (In fact, the Epicurean philosophy is a long way from its popular representation as "wine, women, and song." Quotations from Epicurus make this abundantly clear.) An extensive gallery of women who are sex objects and property for sale is offered us by Greek Middle Comedy and Roman comedy. A plot pattern set by Menander in the Hellenistic period was taken over as the standard comedy plot in Rome; and we have a collection of extant examples by Plautus and Terence. Specializing in kidnapped and enslaved young women and enamored young men who can't afford to buy them, this set of plays gives kaleidoscopic, if somewhat monotonous, illustration of this fourth theme. (Graphic art offers even clearer sets of illustrations. A Pompeiian brothel had wall paintings illustrating the wares it offered; remarkably explicit, though opinions differ on how erotic. See M. Grant, and A. Mulas, *Eros in Pompeii: The Secret Rooms of the National Museum in Naples*, Bonanza Books.)

There is a play by Aristophanes that is a dramatic case study of what I have called "paradigms in collision." This is the "Women's Club Meeting," a meeting called to plan vengeance on Euripides for the jaundiced portrayal of women in his tragedies. The upshot is that the Aristophanic-Aristotelian model prevails.

IV

While I was organizing this material, a further notion about paradigms occurred to me, which I mentioned briefly earlier. I noted that the philosophers of the Age of Reason in Greece seemed willing to defend and debate three of the four definitions I had distinguished, but *not the fourth*. Powerfully expressed in tragedy, inherited in legend, celebrated in religion, the notion of women as ecstatic non-natural beings simply was not explored. And in fact one reason that led to the accepting of the other definitions was that they all disagreed—though in different ways—with this traditional but philosophically unpopular fourth.

Now, in twentieth-century philosophical discussion there seems a similar avoidance of the Aristotle-Aristophanes implicit definition. This is particularly striking since exactly that paradigm is "paradigmatic" for contemporary popular art—comedy, soap opera on television, comic strips, popular paperback romances—and for contemporary life, as seen, at least, in advertising. Also innumerable movies fall in this category. But women as pets and cute dependents are firmly excluded from our philosophic speculation. Perhaps here we see the rejection, certainly in the interest of needed change, of a paradigm that had become too nearly dominant. Certainly the contemporary work in women's studies which I have read includes recognition of each of the other three paradigms as worth serious study, but not this fourth.

Chapter 18

Philosophy and Literary Style: Two Paradigms of Classical Examples

The general consensus of philosophers today, with some existentialist dissent, is that literary criticism and the appraisal of argument are distinct enterprises, and that they should be kept so. Even studies of Plato (Murphy's interpretation of the *Republic*, Robinson's of the *Parmenides*, Crombie's of all doctrines) separate "literary devices" from "philosophic argument," assuming that it is easy to separate the form of an argument from dramatic development. A more liberal group of philosophers may, if pressed, admit that in some special cases philosophy has overlapped the category of poetry; but they would regard this as accidental and atypical.

My intention here is to show, to the contrary, that the student of philosophy must either be, or consult, the literary critic if he is to understand any piece of philosophical literature. The differences remain crucial, but the relevance of critical considerations—of form, character, unity of plot—cannot be ignored if we want to understand philosophy.

All philosophic writing is literature, and as such it can be looked at through the lenses Aristotle used in viewing "productive science": the author has ideas which he must communicate through the medium of language and overall ordering form. Aristotle himself, of course, would dissent. He thought he could draw a line halfway, between philosophy that can also be analyzed as poetry (notably the Socratic dialogue, which he admired) and philosophy incurably unaesthetic (notably the verses of Empedocles, which he detested). But this sharp-line project cannot be consistently carried out; it turns out, for example, as W. E. Leonard showed, that Empedocles' verses rank very high as cosmological epic poetry. And in the very nature of the case, it is clear that every author is also a speaker, every argument a development of an "action" in some probable or necessary sequence, every stylistic device appropriate or inappropriate to the overall "object of imitation."

As critics adapting tools used for poetry to analysis of philosophic literature, there are certain differences that we must take into account. In works of philosophy, thought is the unifying part of the development rather than overt action and change of fortune. The critic is dealing here with literature more like novels of discovery than of adventure. The thought, furthermore, must meet the extraliterary demand that it remains valid outside of the story itself. (In this peculiarity, philosophic literature is like science fiction and the detective story.) This imposes a need for kinds of order and sequence that we might roughly call logical, in addition to sequences that are valid aesthetically. Further, the central character, unless he gives clear warning to the contrary, will be supposed to be the real-life philosopher; we expect a kind of sincerity here that could be quite irrelevant in poetry.

But given these adjustments, the methods of the literary critic apply to philosophic literature, and apply in places that are as unexpected as they are philosophically important. For example, I will show that the perplexing question of the unity of Aristotle's *Metaphysics* cannot be treated properly without establishing the character of the speaker and the specific canons of form of the Aristotelian lecture.

The history of philosophic writing can be written as Aristotle wrote his history of the drama. It opens with a search for forms to fit insights, a period of experiment. We find a range of forms from almanac with Thales to epic with Parmenides, from oracular epigram with Heraclitus to geometrical symbolism with Pythagoras. The search for proper form seems to stabilize in two generic types in the fourth century B.C. On the one hand, philosophers who see philosophy as shared inquiry, a continuing search, follow Plato's example and use dialogue form. On the other hand, philosophers who see their writing as instruction, as an explanation of the *results* of investigation, use various species of the long or short treatise and the Aristotelian lecture. Within each genus, there are species that differ. The dialogue as it is written by Cicero and Hume is a different style from its Platonic original. The autobiography counts as an offshoot of this dialogue tradition, setting up a more direct interpersonal conversation between author and reader, as in St. Augustine's *Confessions* and the *Meditations* of Descartes. There are a few ventures that fall outside of these two main traditions: the epigram returns in Nietzsche's *Zarathustra*, the epic in Camus's *The Stranger*. But on the whole, dialogue and didactic treatise seem to have become stabilized as the best vehicles for the writing of philosophy.

The first tradition, that of dialogue, is clearly attractive to the admirer of literature. It is equally attractive, but sometimes baffling, to the philosopher who wants to extract a body of doctrines and solutions detached from the dramatic dimension. Aristotle's several expressed frustrations with the *Republic* in his *Politics* are a classic example. The reason for this difficulty is that the form and doctrine are not simply separable. The dialogue, well-used, has a kind of self-instantiation and counterpoint: thought motivates characters, and their actions instantiate and reflect on the validity of the thought. In dealing with the tradition of dialogue, I think my main problem is to convince the advocate of philosophy in the didactic mode that the so-called "literary devices" are relevant to the logic of the so called "philosophic argument." The literary critic is predisposed to accept this; indeed, to him it seems almost self-evident. (The reverse will be true when we turn to philosophy presented in the finished lecture or critique; the philosopher will see coherent aesthetic form in it, but the literary critic will try to deny that he has any business with, let alone any obligation to read through, this kind of writing at all.)

As samples of criticism applied to the dialogue form, let me show briefly the interaction of drama and argument, and the device of self-instantiation, at work in two of Plato's dialogues, the *Meno* and the *Hippias Minor*.

The *Meno* continues to receive attention today. The dialogue bears directly on our own contemporary question "Can values be taught?" It offers a first step toward an answer by suggesting that they cannot; but it does this without doing what the later Platonic dialogues do as they force us into sweeping metaphysical commitments or dissents.

The logical structure of the *Meno* is that of a destructive dilemma. If virtue can be taught, Meno assumes (and Socrates accepts the assumption) that the method of such teaching must either be by precept or by example. Meno has been trained by the master of teaching by precept, Gorgias. By nature and family he was a well-endowed student. We would expect, therefore, if the precept method works, that Meno would know what virtue is; or, at the least, that his excellent education would have made him virtuous, a fact that would count as evidence in the discussion. (Note how argument and drama interpenetrate at this point: Meno's "character" will or will not constitute an implicit existentially quantified proposition that nowhere figures abstractly and explicitly in the "philosophic argument.") But Meno can neither define virtue, nor is he a virtuous person; in fact, Plato presumably chose him as respondent because historically he was so unvirtuous. At the outset of his conversation, he displays ignorance, impatience, unfairness, and petulance.

Well, what about teaching by example; by daily contact with public life, and by taking great men of the past as exemplary? Anytus, willing to defend this method even to Socrates' death, is brought onstage as its spokesman. He, too, fails to embody the ideals he admires; and is forced to admit, angrily, that history does not confirm his passionate belief in the efficacy of example.

Socrates, in summing up, suggests that they test the hypothesis that virtue is knowledge. If it is, then it can be taught; and any possessor of such knowledge, being made virtuous through having it, would want to teach it. Yet in the two test cases presented in the dialogue, Meno and Anytus, the teaching has failed to operate; and Meno has to admit that he cannot find a single instance of a teacher of virtue. On the other hand, in the course of discussion, Socrates' experiment with the Slave Boy has shown that Meno's assumption that "teaching" must be didactic transfer of information is false, by actually teaching some elementary geometry by another method. And it becomes pertinent to ask whether the *Meno*, taken as a whole, does not contradict the abstract thesis that concludes its argument. For, if Meno himself improves in virtue through the shared inquiry with Socrates, though the improvement is short-lived, there does exist at least one teacher of virtue, and it is false to say that virtue cannot be taught. It will remain true, though, that the "teaching" was not done either by precept or example, but by "Socratic method."

Now, I hold that in this very dialogue Meno is shown to improve in virtue; and that various literary devices are used to direct our attention to this improvement. He improves because he shares in the discussion; his improvement is an extremely relevant item in relation to the problem being discussed; and I see no way of separating the "dramatic" from the "philosophic" dimension of this imagined encounter.

This device of self-illustration typifies the dialogue form, whether the dialogue is constructive as with Plato or sceptical as it becomes in the works of Hume and Cicero. The wonderfully sardonic opening of the *Lesser Hippias*, when we return to it after surviving the argument's logical involutions, shows the interaction of idea and action in a two-sentence vignette that one can hardly set aside as inadvertent or irrelevant. Hippias's prestige as an intellectual must have annoyed the Academy. The dialogue, aimed at showing Socrates to be a better man than the information-stuffed Hippias, centers at first on a literary question. The question is, which character in fiction is better, Homer's Achilles or his Odysseus? Hippias dislikes Odysseus, because "Odysseus lies deliberately." Socrates now asserts the thesis—which is a deliberate lie on his part—that the voluntary liar must be wiser and better than the involuntary one. The upshot is that, in this case, Socrates' lie seems to be true—at any rate, he comes out ahead of Hippias. The point and standpoint are set up in the very beginning, when Socrates says that

Hippias is wise, and Hippias accepts the compliment. For one of them has told a voluntary, the other an involuntary, lie.

Clearly, Plato's dramas are the right form to embody his conviction that you cannot teach answers without engaging the student in the questions they answer; that philosophy can't be transmuted into an objective spectator sport to the degree that mathematics or astronomy can. On the other hand, Platonic dialogue has a clear notion of the direction in which answers do lie, and perhaps an even clearer notion of where they do not. They lie in the direction of the theory of forms, forms which are the goals of inquiry. As an objective logical problem, the relevance of these forms to persons and things is probably insoluble. But in the dialogue form, we have it set before us as a fact, as argument shapes action and the ideal attracts the actual.

The second traditional genus of philosophic literature, the didactic form, has been repeatedly commented on and analyzed as though the form contained no varied species, and as though the character speaking could be only an impersonal, didactic voice of thought. But the identification of the specific form, the discovery of its unifying principles, and the motives for its choice suddenly become baffling just where we most want to follow what is going on: and the way in which criticism helps in these extreme cases brings out its general relevance to philosophic literature in the didactic form.

A problem of honorable antiquity is the question of the unity, or lack of it, in Aristotle's *Metaphysics*. Although we are not too eager to tell this to our undergraduates, there is good external reason for an initial doubt as to whether the text we have and the content of the projected science that Aristotle called "first philosophy" are the same. The title is a later editor's label for the treatises that "come after the *Physics*"; the contents show stylistic evidence of very diverse dates of writing; and Book Beta, which should be the key to the work since it announces itself as a treatment of the problems of first philosophy, is a maze of questions which do not find subsequent answers. (Ross finds, for Beta, that only five out of twelve of the problems as he enumerates them are answered in the subsequent text.) Something must be wrong here, either with the text as a whole, or with our expectations concerning Beta. But on the other hand, the fact that five of Ross's list of problems *are* explicitly solved and are referred back to in later books indicates that there must be *some* relevance between the program and its execution.

Wilamowitz first proposed the thesis that the puzzle results from our loss of a classical literary form, the "School Logos." The purpose of these *logoi* he postulated as an initial pyrotechnical challenge to the student, exhibiting the range and number of problems he must face, and exhibiting them in deliberately disordered patterns. Its literary artistry should then consist in the range of questions posed and in their presentation in a contrived random order. Are there any other instances of works in this unrecognized lost literary form? Yes, Wilamowitz thought, the second part of Plato's *Parmenides* presents itself as a clear case; and the Platonic *Euthydemus* is another example.

I must say that, on its intrinsic merits, the "unrecognized school-logos" hypothesis is very strong. It has not been judged on its merits, because philosophers have hoped for so much more from our *Metaphysics* text that they did not want to believe it, but I think we must either find a better alternative to this thesis or accept it. What would constitute a better alternative? Either external evidence that whatever form the original version had has been shattered in transmission, or internal evidence that we can find coherence within a perfectly recognizable species of the general didactic form. I will argue for the latter; I believe that there are formal properties specific to Aristotle's lectures, not typical of all species of the lecture form, and that any error we may have made in analysis has only been to place the material in the wrong species within the right genus, not to mislocate it generically.

My first step toward refuting the "School Logos" thesis is an indirect one. In a study of 1961, I proved that while the *Parmenides* hypotheses are in an unfamiliar form, right enough, it is a form of axiomatic-deductive demonstration, not aporematic disorder. The sequence that gives order to this thought progression can in fact be displayed as formally valid by using the rather noncommital "material implication" connective, borrowed from modern logic. (This takes only a sentence to state, but actually took me about six years to establish.) *Why* Plato chose this form here is a different question; *that* he chose it, however, can be so clearly shown that we lose one supposed example of the School Logos. And fairly simple literary analysis also shows that the *Euthydemus* exactly fits standard dialogue form. Thus *Metaphysics* Beta is left as the sole surviving specimen of the postulated lost literary genus.

I would like now to return to this question by way of another book, *Physics* II, which Aristotle evidently was pleased with since he cross refers to it in other works as his definitive treatment of causality. A simple experiment will convince any reader that there is something structurally eccentric about this prize lecture. The experiment is this: to read it once quickly, making an outline of the main topics; then to read it again, line by line, writing down an outline to a proper order of subordination. The first reading is easy, the outline seems clear; but the second time around, the outlining is frustrating. Half a day may still find the deliberate note taker still undecided about where to put into his outline the stone called "lucky" because it was used for an altar. These results reflect two marked traits of the author's character, both of which show in the form. First, he can block out large-scale organizations of material clearly. Second, he will not take the time to polish up his notes either by indicating that certain sections can be quickly read because they are subordinate, or by treating such subordinate points in articulated detail. A combination of an ambition to achieve total overall order, an impatience with polished style, and a reluctance to overlook any minute counterinstances, is projected here. Thus, the detail results from a desire to take account of all the data—whether ordinary language, opinions of experts, or seeming factual anomalies—that might count against the main point. Only, as these considerations become more subordinate, their treatment is more cryptic, until what could be a treatise on geometry compresses to a parenthetical enthymeme. And this is done without stylistic guideposts for the hearer or reader. The overall form is suited to a great project, the details of which may represent loose ends, mentioned in passing, to be tied up later.

In passing, we should note that the text we have is the transcription of what were oral lectures; and the manner of delivery can offer means of indicating outline and emphasis that escape the written record. The most important of such devices include: (1) special diagrams to be shown and pointed to—we find these presupposed particularly in the Ethics lectures; (2) gesture; (3) timing—pauses before returning to a major theme, for example; and (4) emphasis and voice volume. In connection with timing, I have just realized in writing this that I myself always tend to go too fast, and slow myself down by puffing a cigarette—quickly at mere sentence ends, slowly and perhaps twice for ends of paragraphs (This was true up to 1980). I could develop this theme of unrecorded elements of lecture style at greater length if it were helpful for the solution of the present problem. But I'm afraid it is not. For when I tried the idea that oral presentation, with emphasis and gesture, could have made the written text of the third problem in the detailed Beta list lively and clear, the result was an hour of anguished boredom for my captive Aristotle seminar.

This brings us back to *Metaphysics* Beta. I suggested that the formal structure of *Physics* II might also apply here, and that since the lack of polished indications of coordination in the former was a result of impatience rather than a deliberate deception, the same explanation might hold for Beta. The lack of clarity in many passages results from the fact that Aristotle's Greek offers him far fewer distinct ways of indicating subordination than his topic outlines require. It is not that he fails to indicate the balancing of his major coordinate topics, with a *men-de* or equivalent construction, but that he must repeat the same device to articulate other balanced sections that are subordinate in the total outline. I would describe the result as a style which has weak or partial indications of organizations.

Working from this basis, I find that stylistic indications single out an eight problem main outline in Beta. These problems come in three groups: the first treats metaphysics as discursive, the second treats the kind of knowing it involves, the third treats its subject-matter. This exactly matches the scheme that Prof. Richard McKeon proposed as that of the *Metaphysics* as a whole. My list, further, is a set of problems all of which are successively resolved, in order, in the subsequent books of our *Metaphysics* text. This is a much higher level of coherence than Ross's organization, which gives something like five out of twelve as the number of key problems actually treated; in fact, my eight out of eight is just what we would expect if Aristotle himself, and not some Roman editor, had organized selected essays to follow out this initial outline.[1]

But what about the unresolved subordinate problems? They vanish without resolution or further mention when the assumptions that generate them are shown to be false. For example, the second problem of Beta, whether there are any substances apart from sensibles, includes some eleven questions one must ask if the objects of mathematics form a group of genuine substances. But once it is shown that the objects of mathematics are not separate substantial entities *at all*, Aristotle obviously does not feel a need to go on and inquire whether they exist *in* sensibles or *apart* from them—and thus there is this set of subproblems apparently untreated in the subsequent text.

In short, Beta seems to me a typical Aristotelian lecture, with the same properties as *Physics* II. And so far as the match between its initial outline and subsequent discussion is a test, the treatise as a whole seems to be Aristotelian metaphysics after all.[2]

Further, my method of analyzing the character of the lecturer reflected in the text, the development of thought, and the qualities of style, seems to me an application of the art of literary criticism. I sympathize entirely with the critic who finds this prose uncongenial, but not with the attempt to hold that it is critically inaccessible.

The question of locating philosophic works in their proper literary forms is not limited to recognizing the *Parmenides* as deductive dialectic, the *Metaphysics* as didactic lecture course. One of the most interesting cases of location and mislocation has to do with Rousseau's

Émile. Given a low grade by critics expecting logical entailment to unify it, as such entailment should unify a treatise on the principles of education, the book continues to influence educators and find admirers. The reason is that it is unified, but by the development of plot, character, and thought proper to a novel.

I have admitted that philosophy differs from poetry. One difference, apparent in the *Parmenides* example, is that the unifying relation of a philosophic work may be different from the "aesthetic compatibility" that underlies probability and necessity in poetic form. Character is different, too. Unless he explicitly claims the contrary, we assume that the philosopher really believes what he says; in other words, that there is agreement between the way he conducts himself in "real life" and the role he plays as onstage or offstage author and manager in his work. This means that we feel entitled, as we do not or should not with the poet, to introduce biographical material to supplement the character who appears within the given work itself. In doing this, we approach the writer of a philosophic work rather as though he were himself a character in a wider Platonic dialogue, asking him, as Socrates did Thrasymachus, "Do you really believe this?" And unless we are strangely incurious about the interaction of life and thought, about sincerity or dissimulation, we refuse to accept the Sophist's answer, "What does it matter? Your job is to refute the argument."

Looked at in this way, the literary critic, who is at home with questions of consistency of character, is the very expert we should consult in trying to understand the philosopher as he appears in his several roles. I am not saying that inconsistency or insincerity are in themselves a philosophical refutation, but that the analysis of character can be relevant to understanding philosophic writing, and that the relation of the author as revealed in a given work to the author in real life is much closer here than it normally is in poetry.

Perhaps the most difficult and crucial case for testing this idea is that of Socrates. What was he really like? Does it matter whether Plato's picture of him is pure idealized drawing or a study from life with only modest highlighting added? The bibliography of books and articles on this topic is overwhelming proof that the question has mattered to an amazing number of people. In fact, if the literary critic is crucial to the solution of this problem, that alone would justify affiliating him with the department of philosophy.

There is a real enigma in the character of Socrates. Appearing as hero or villain through a wide range of records, refractions of him abound. But somehow, from his first literary appearance in comedy, riding in his basket like a god, each role he plays finds him wearing another mask. Within the classical period, Aristophanes portrays him as a fake scientist and shyster lawyer; Xenophon as a tough, sensible retired soldier; Plato as an ideal philosopher. But we also get Socrates refracted as the hero who advocates a return to nature, the role he is given by the Cynic school; as advocate of calculated pursuit of maximum pleasure, which is the Cyrenaic view; as abstracted master of formal logic, the Megarian version.

In four cases out of this early six, we can see that Socrates is more a symbol than a character. Aristophanes is clearly determined to attribute to his villain every new tendency that the comedian found subversive and objectionable. The Socratic Schools have a portrait of the philosophic hero who is, in each case, a one-dimensional projection of the doctrine which each school believes a hero should hold. As critics, we can show that none of these is convincing as a characterization from life: real persons, at the very least, have more than one trait of character. Further, the discrepancies among the three School portraits can converge in one person only if each has selected a very thin band from the total spectrum. Xenophon's Socrates looks more credible than Aristophanes', until we realize that he is really a projection of Xenophon. That sensible, soldierly projection could never have been the historical figure accused of impiety and staying to stand trial—as Xenophon admits in the beginning of his *Memories of Socrates*. Plato's characterization, in contrast to these others, is historically believable, three-dimensional rather than one-dimensional. Beyond this, Plato argues an implicit philosophic claim: that the historical existence of Socrates disproves the rather shallow Sophistic thesis that men do not ever act against their material interests. If the claim that Socrates is historical were false, Plato's use of this example to prove the possibility of ethics of duty of a Kantian kind, as opposed to an ethics of hedonistic utility of the Sophistic sort, would be unjustified.

I would be happy to rest the case there, embroidering it with analyses of Xenophon's interests and attitudes, Euclides' perverse fondness for formal logic, and the like. But a conversation with a colleague who is a dynamic and distinguished literary critic raised another question: How far does one trust Plato, in spite of his claim to historicity? I had been discussing my reasons for rejecting all but two of the *Letters* attributed to Plato. It seemed incredible to me, I said, that so good a stylist would allow himself to appear in the roles of mystagogue, mendicant, rotarian, and plagiarist, which are the roles of the author(s) of *Letters* II, XIII, VI, and IX. Not at all, said my friend; the mark of a literary genius is to throw himself into those many roles; probably he believes that he is each of them when he is writing; but in any case, this variety of personae should count for, rather than against, the authenticity of the collection. And, in that case, of course, we might have to say the same thing about the role of biographer of Socrates as Plato played it; he may just have been acting when he claimed it was true history.

"My friend," I said, "there is a quarrel from of old between philosophy and poetry; and you just renewed it."

Chapter 19

The Trial of Socrates

The trial of Socrates in 399 B.C. marked a dramatic confrontation between a new idea of human dignity and an old desire for social tranquility, in a legal system where trial by jury was still in a primitive, experimental stage. Socrates was accused of not respecting the religion of the state, and corrupting its youth. His defense, that his insistence on free inquiry made him a public benefactor and not a criminal, failed to convince the majority of the 501 jurors hearing the case, and he was found guilty, sentenced to death, and executed.

Within a few years the strange conduct of both the Athenian statesmen who had arranged the trial, and of Socrates, who had not taken a line of defense that could have saved his life, had produced at least three literary works offering interpretations. And down through Maxwell Anderson's play *Barefoot in Athens* in 1951, reenactments and reinterpretations of the trial continue to enrich Western literature and moral philosophy.

One important account is the *Apology*, recorded by his young admirer Plato. Plato, destined to become one of the great speculative philosophers of all time, saw the real issue as a philosophic one: Socrates' new ideas about justice, the self, and human excellence all ran counter to current common sense, but seemed to him so true and important that he would not deny or compromise them, even to save his life. Xenophon's *Memorabilia* is another, rather different, report. Xenophon, a famous soldier and long-standing friend of Socrates, was absent from Athens at the time of the trial. On his return, three years later, he tried to find out exactly what had happened, but could not fully understand the conduct of either the prosecution or Socrates' defense. Regarding the latter, he finally concluded that Socrates must have wanted to die, but had religious scruples about suicide, and so deliberately provoked the court. From time to time Xenophon quotes someone he calls "The Prosecutor." These quotations are most probably from a third account of the trial, written by a Sophist named Polycrates, which defended the state's conduct and its case. From these quotations it seems "The Prosecutor" saw the real issue as one of guilt by association. Socrates had earlier been on good terms with men who later led the antidemocratic faction, and it is argued that the suspicion that he might be conspiring with these former associates justified his prosecution on the other charges, since, as we will see, there were technical legal reasons why his former associations could not have been introduced as evidence in court.

We could judge better between these three different reports if we had a clear picture of Socrates himself; but, ironically, no figure in the history of thought has appeared in its pages in so many masks. Not only was he a philosopher in Plato, a sensible retired soldier in Xenophon, and a wily conspirator in the mind of "The Prosecutor," but he had already been caricatured as a shyster lawyer and atheistic scientist in a comedy by Aristophanes in 423 B.C. The next generation after his own interpreted him variously as hedonist, cynic, idealist, and logician; since then posterity has assigned him roles that range from a radical existentialist to a withdrawn sage.

To justify my own use of sources in what follows, let me say that in my opinion Xenophon's account leaves no possible explanation for the original prosecution. "The Prosecutor," with his hidden motives for prosecution, leaves no possible explanation for the line Socrates took in his own defense. Plato, however, gives an account that explains both sides of the case, given the historical situation, if we supply a little imagination and draw on our own experiences in the twentieth century.

After the great Greek victory in the Persian War, in the early fifth century B.C., Athens changed abruptly from a small provincial town to a military, cultural, and mercantile capital. Her naval empire spread through the islands of the Aegean; the Acropolis was rebuilt with new splendor; the Agora became an international business center. Pericles, the political leader of this period, was able to compromise and balance the interests of the two main political factions: the oligarchic—made up of the older families of wealth and status—and the democratic. The result was a gradual increase in democracy, a series of experiments in more general eligibility for public office, and new modifications of the system of trial by jury. New ideas came to Athens as well. From the eastern frontier of Greece, Anaxagoras, a young astronomer, brought with him the methods and theories of natural science. From other Greek cities came the Sophists, traveling professional educators who taught young men how to get ahead; our word *sophisticated* reflects the products and aims of their courses in law, public speaking, and urbane manners.

These new skills and ideas were no doubt timely in a city where culture had far outrun the common sense of conservative tradition and training; but the conservatives found them unwelcome. In particular, the new scientific approach to astronomy, with its teaching that the sun and moon were stones, not gods, and that the Reason ruling the world had no human body, seemed to be atheism. The new arts of speaking looked more and more subversive as they proved more effective in winning both votes and legal cases. And, evidently, not just a conservative minority but the public generally were uneasy. At some time between 440 and 430 the young scientist Anaxagoras was summoned to stand trial on the same charges of impiety and corruption of youth that later were brought against Socrates. With Pericles' help his escape was arranged, and he retired to another city. But his new ideas did not leave with him. A group of enthusiastic younger scientists remained, including Socrates, who was a leading member. Because of his part in this group, Socrates was chosen by Aristophanes, a comic poet, as the villain of his comedy the *Clouds*. The play was another attack on innovation; Aristophanes' sympathies were wholly with the conservative far right. In the play, "Socrates" ran a "thought-shop," vending a mixture of naturalistic physics and clever legal tactics. It was a brilliant caricature, which persisted in the public mind for thirty years, creating a confusion between the real Socrates and the villain in the play. This background information is interesting because it shows how the "impiety" charge could be used to get "undesirable" persons out of town, and it also shows what sorts of person the conservatives found "undesirable."

Athenian expansion during the fifth century eventually collided with the interests of Sparta and her allies, and for thirty years there was an alternating period of hot and cold war, ending with the total defeat of Athens in 404 B.C. At this point, with Spartan backing, an interim council of representatives of the conservative faction (the Thirty) took over the government. The more active democratic leaders fled from the city, and the Thirty, led by Critias, instituted a reign of terror. Being short of revenues, they took advantage of a law that the property of traitors could be confiscated by the state. By arresting wealthy foreign residents (and some others) and executing them for treason after secret hearings, they managed to keep the treasury solvent. Criticism was likely to be quieted by assassination.

Here, for a second time, Socrates appears on the stage of history. He had in fact (as we have already heard from "The Prosecutor") been on good terms with Critias and others of the Thirty; but this did not prevent him from making forceful comments on their tyranny. "They are less like shepherds of the people than chefs who barbecue the sheep," he observed. Critias told Socrates his conversations were not only tactless, but that they had become boring; Socrates talked on. Thinking to intimidate him and implicate him in their machinations, the Thirty ordered Socrates to go with a party sent to arrest Leon of Salamis on charges of "high treason" (revenues must have run low again); but Socrates simply went home. What saved him from reprisal was a sudden and successful invasion by the exiled democratic faction, which drove out the Thirty and set up a rather precarious restored democracy in 403. Anytus, a democratic leader, saw that there could be no hope of stability if old feuds and factions carried on; and at his insistence a law was passed that no crimes committed during the civil war (except those of the Thirty themselves) could be prosecuted in court. (This is why "The Prosecutor" could argue that the "impiety" charge was only a formal cover for a real "guilt by association"; for the latter could not have been prosecuted under the law of amnesty.)

Enactment of the amnesty seemed a reasonable and statesmanlike action, and made it all the more incomprehensible that this same Anytus should have been one of the instigators of the prosecution of Socrates in 399. For, all that Socrates had done between 403 and 399 was ask questions. In general these centered around two problems:(1) What is human excellence, and how can one achieve it; and (2) what form of political organization is most reasonable and most likely to produce good citizens? Neither the suave professional teachers nor the pompous political personages of the day seemed to have satisfactory answers to the first question; nor could they defend a number of the procedures of their "democracy" when asked the second. (For example, Athenian legislation was continually being revised by referendum. Nearly all of the executive officers were chosen at random, by a grand lottery. It was assumed that a jury would be impartial if only it were large enough; and there were a number of other procedures equally hard to defend against Socrates' charge of irrationality.)

In later periods of relative peace and calm, Western scholars have failed to understand how anyone in ancient Athens could have been disturbed by mere freedom of speech; and in such periods, scholars—for example nineteenth-century English classicists—have tended to assume that there must be something to the "hidden motive" theory. In our own times, however, the motives behind the prosecution of Socrates are clear enough. Imagine that you are a citizen of a power that has just been defeated; that you have suffered under a puppet government; that you have precariously regained some autonomy, but without the military power to defend it. Might it not seem to you that the one imperative need of the moment is uncritical support of the restored administration, at least until times are better? And if someone keeps insisting on asking questions that imply—or worse, that show—that the leaders are ignorant and the democratic procedures in need of reform, might not this seem a clear and present danger? If we put this together with the precedent, in the case of Anaxagoras, of the use of an "impiety" accusation to frighten someone away, Anytus's action becomes quite intelligible. Whether it was justifiable was one of the issues that the trial of Socrates had to decide, for Socrates, unlike Anaxagoras, refused to run away, and stayed for his trial.

Socrates felt a duty to ask his questions, and to defend the importance of their being asked. And in fact he had made a discovery of such importance to Western thought that "pre-Socratic" and "post-Socratic" are the standard classifications we still use in our histories of Western philosophy. Socrates' discovery was the complex and problematic character of a human "self." "What am I?" was to prove as challenging a question for philosophy as the earlier query. "What is reality?" with which Western science and philosophy had begun. Science, Sophistry, and a common sense shared by poetry and popular religion could barely understand this question, let alone answer it. And yet, until one knew what a human being was, and what really made a person excellent or the opposite, all the bustle of educators and lawmakers was a series of dagger thrusts in the dark. Unless Socrates could at least communicate his question, there was no guarantee that his amazing discovery would be remembered, or that society might not, by law or custom, forever prevent the full human excellence that might be possible.

What was the human "self"? With the new learning of science and Sophistry, it seemed that old religious stories about a "soul" that went to another world at death, and perhaps returned, were out of date. For one thing the stories were mutually contradictory; for another, they made it seem that the gods were able to be bribed and persuaded to overlook injustice. Thus the stories failed to be either moral or credible. As a young scientist, Socrates had already been interested in the physiology of "thought." He had asked whether we think with the air in us, or the fire or blood, or perhaps with the brain? But not too long after the production of Aristophanes' *Clouds*, he realized that natural science could give him no satisfactory answer. It was all very scientific to talk about the soul as a kind of "harmony of the body's functioning," but in fact, in the most obvious cases, this kind of causal explanation reversed the real sequence of events. Whenever an idea or feeling preceded and was followed by a physical response, this thought or feeling certainly seemed to cause the bodily behavior, whereas in the "scientific" account it had to be the other way around. Furthermore, the human soul had the power of knowing necessary and universal truths— the theorems of mathematics were an example. And no physical recording apparatus, simply remembering particular cases, could ever have reached generalizations holding for all possible cases. So if one went by the rule several philosophers had already formulated, that "like is known by like," a soul able to see beyond the particular events in space and time must have some unnatural dimension. Further, there was a concern with what men ought to do; and this is a concern that no machine can feel. So Socrates found himself suddenly aware of his ignorance, of the inability of his scientific learning to answer this fundamental question. Sophistry, with its assumption of universal greed and radical selfishness, did not offer a satisfying answer, either. Yet all the Athenian possessors of unnatural, possibly immortal, souls went about quite unaware of what they were, stolidly convinced that they knew about education and political administration.

This much, at least, had become clear to Socrates: that a self was an inner thing, distinct from the body; and only the sort of inner excellence that justice and honesty represented was intrinsically worth having. In words that seem to anticipate Christian teaching, Socrates believed that it is better, given the choice, to be treated unjustly than to commit an injustice, and that the only real harm that can befall a self is its own decision to become a worse human being. Further clarification of his beliefs would depend on men applying their intelligence to the problem. These convictions were the causes of Socrates' conduct at his trial, as they had been of the behavior that led to Anytus's part in his accusation.

Socrates was not "arrested," as he might have been under the Thirty, but was "summoned" to the court of the First Archon to file his answer to the charges against him. Leaving a discussion of mathematics and logic, he made his way to the portico, where he met Euthyphro, a prophet, seer, and religious fundamentalist. Euthyphro was astonished to hear of the charges: "I dare say that the affair will end in nothing, Socrates. . . ." For once, Euthyphro was a poor prophet.

An executive board received charges, written statements of witnesses, statements for the defense, and set a date for the trial. The trial itself was probably held in a large public building in the marketplace, with the jury of 501 members selected at random. There was a presiding justice and a professional clerk of court; but the outcome was determined by majority vote of the jury. (Here we see a right idea taking a wrong direction: The Athenians wanted impartial juries, and were trying out the idea that a multitude would ensure impartiality.) There were no laws of evidence limiting testimony to relevant matters, but there was a fixed time limit of half a day or less for presenting each side of the case. The defendant had a legal right to cross-examine the principal accuser; and in cases such as this one, could propose a counter-penalty to that asked by the prosecution. The jury would decide which to accept, if their initial vote found the defendant guilty.

The charges were that Socrates did not respect the state religion, and was a corrupter of youth. Once the charges were filed, Socrates would have been free to leave Athens without standing trial, and no doubt this was what Anytus expected him to do. Socrates' friends seem to have been as surprised by the charge as Euthyphro; everyone seems to have been surprised at his decision to stay and stand trial.

One of the greatest writers of legal defense speeches, Lysias, came to Socrates with a written defense. (Another rule of court procedure was that the defendant must present his own case, but it was customary to have a professional write out the speech, which was memorized and recited.) Judging by the other defense speeches of Lysias which we have, this would have been a standard list of proofs that Socrates was a sterling character, an appeal to the jury's sympathy because of his age (he was seventy) and family responsibilities (he was married with three children), and a plea for acquittal. But Socrates refused the offer; he would feel as awkward with Lysias's fine words, he said, as if he walked into a gymnasium in crimson robes. We do not know this, but it is a safe guess that Socrates' friends thought this a mistake; why not take advantage of Lysias' proven skill to gain an acquittal and make his accusers look foolish?

And so Socrates appeared before the court. There are many things we would like to know about the details of the trial that are not recorded. It drew a large audience, in addition to the jury, and Socrates' friends, including young Plato, were among the spectators. But we are not able to know, now, which court had jurisdiction, nor who was presiding judge, nor who was the clerk of court. We do not even know with any certainty what evidence and depositions the prosecution— represented by Anytus's collaborator, Meletus, as main spokesman— had prepared and presented. We can assume that there was evidence concerning Socrates' earlier "atheistic" ideas as a scientist; evidence that his questions had been critical of the government; and as many references to his former association with men of antidemocratic records as could be slipped in without flagrant violation of the law of amnesty of 403.

But our accounts begin with the defense speech of Socrates himself. It was elegantly ironic; he included a standard set of defense topics as neatly as Lysias could have. In the course of his defense Socrates cited his exemplary record as a citizen and soldier, his family responsibilities, and—a telling point against a hidden guilt of association charge—his refusal to be intimidated by the Thirty. But at just this point he told the jury to consider all of this as irrelevant and disregard it, since the true issue was his right to and rightness in his inquiries, and it was on this ground that he insisted the verdict be based. (Neither Xenophon, nor so far as we can tell, "The Prosecutor," could explain this behavior. Only Plato, present but too young to testify, understood it.) After opening with his statement that the jury should not expect great eloquence from him, Socrates proposed to explain why he was being prosecuted. The real issue, he said, was his persistent inquiry; and he proposed to explain why he carried this on. It was, said Socrates, a matter of a divine mission. A friend of his, Chaerephon, had once asked the Oracle of Apollo at Delphi whether any man was wiser than Socrates, and the Oracle had answered "that there was no man wiser."

Perhaps, if Socrates had been a typical professional expert, like his contemporary Hippias, he would have congratulated himself on this endorsement, and used it to collect high fees. But the message came just as Socrates was realizing his own ignorance about what seemed to him the most important of human questions, and he thought there must be some hidden meaning to the Oracle, so he set out to inquire. Oracles were, in fact, notoriously ambiguous; and he had thought, he told the jury, that if only he could find a man wiser than himself, he could go back to Delphi and force Apollo to explain his meaning. (This attitude certainly was not that of an atheist, but neither was it entirely conventional piety to try to prove god a liar, as a pretext for asking him questions!) But—he must ask the jurors not to interrupt—the result was as surprising to him as he was sure they would find it. The poets, inspired, said many fine things, yet were wholly unable to explain their own compositions when he questioned them. The craftsmen were, indeed, skilled in their trades, but believed that this skill also made them authorities in educational and political matters—which further questioning proved they were not. Finally, the politicians, who spoke so eloquently of justice and virtue, were no better off than the craftsmen, though they were more likely to grow angry when shown up before an audience. Socrates at least had the advantage over them of not thinking he knew more than he did, and so he had not been able to disprove the Oracle. That was his main defense. (His three examples were chosen to match the groups his three accusers represented: Anytus, the politicians; Meletus, the poets; and the third, Lycon, the craftsmen.)

After this account of his mission, Socrates exercised his right to cross-examine the prosecution. Anytus, who had experienced Socrates' cross-examinations before, astutely saw to it that it was Meletus, a poet and religious conservative, who answered. The examination was a model of Socratic method. At the same time, Socrates brought out the extraordinary vagueness of both the law and the accusation against him, and demonstrated the truth of the true motivation of the charge: that he asked embarrassing questions of important people.

First, Meletus explained to the jury that Socrates was impious because he was an atheist who believed in strange gods. Socrates responded by asking how anyone who believed in gods could be an atheist. To this sally, all the irate Meletus could find to say in rebuttal was that the jury should not believe Socrates.

Meletus fared no better on the charge that the philosopher was corrupting the youth of Athens. He answered Socrates' questions by saying that the latter deliberately harmed young men, whereas everyone else in Athens helped to improve them. Socrates then inquired whether, if he corrupted the young men, they would become more wicked. Meletus was certain that they would. But surely, said Socrates, Meletus recognized that Socrates knew his fellow citizens would do him harm if he succeeded in making them wicked. The respondent agreed to this proposition.

At this point, Socrates moved in for the kill. Who, he asked rhetorically, would believe Meletus's charge that Socrates would set out on purpose to have himself harmed by the young men he was allegedly corrupting?

Meletus was outraged, but could find nothing more to say.

Socrates' irony and his claim—negatively put, true—to superior wisdom divided the jury. On the ballot to decide his guilt or innocence, he was found guilty by a vote of 280 to 221.

Since the law itself specified no penalty, the prosecution now could propose one, and the defendant in turn offer a counterpenalty. A second vote of the jury would decide which to impose. Anytus, unable by this time to turn back even if he wanted to, asked the death penalty. But it is very doubtful that he expected this to be the final sentence. If there was anything to the "realism" that the Sophists, historians, and politicians held to in their views of "human nature," it would be a certainty that Socrates would admit his guilt and propose something like exile, which the jury—judging from their close division on the first ballot—would much have preferred. After all, it would be a terrible responsibility to have to decide whether to execute a fellow citizen for abrasive eccentricity; whether peaceful society or pursuit of truth is better, if the two collide in a fight to the death; whether, beneath his irony, Socrates' claim to a divine mission might not still be true. So jury and prosecution must have felt confident of the outcome as Socrates came forward to propose his counterpenalty.

The trouble was that the "realists" were wrong again. Socrates really believed what he had been saying. To propose an alternative penalty, he would first have had to admit himself guilty as charged. This would have been a lie, and would have made him a worse person. But if they were to kill him, he would not lose his dignity or deny his vision of the truth. And so Socrates proposed that they give him what he deserved. At the expense of his own time, he had tried to awaken Athens, as a gadfly might a sleeping steed; to awaken her to the sublime ignorance he had discovered through his epoch-making question, "What am I?" Without him, Athens might have remained in an enchanted sleep, in which expediency and quiet were preferred to truth, unless some god should send another gadfly. Therefore, if he got what he really deserved, he thought it should be board and lodging for life, at public expense. But since the jury might not recognize how just the claim was—if the trial had not been limited to one day, perhaps he could have convinced them—and since he had never thought of loss of money as a hardship, he would be willing to pay a fine equivalent to a couple of dollars, with the understanding that this was not an admission of guilt. Urged by his friends, he said he would even pay a larger, though still modest fine; with this same understanding, that he was proud of his activity and would continue it.

The effect of this speech was explosive. The outcome was, predictably perhaps, a vote for execution by a larger majority than the initial vote for Socrates' conviction (we know only this about the second vote). Anytus, Meletus, and Lycon had won; and in their forced, irate ballot upon the nature of man, the jury had decided against Socrates and Apollo. If they had paused to think, as young Plato was to think for many years while writing his imaginary conversations of Socrates, they would háve seen that Socrates' own conduct proved their shallow "realism" wrong. Here was a case where an ideal had become a concrete reality. Socrates would have preferred to persuade the jury, but failing that, he preferred to die rather than betray his search for wisdom and his faith that "no evil can happen to a good man, either in life or after death."

Before the wardens of the prison led him away, to imprisonment and eventual execution, Socrates made a last address to the jury. To the jurors who had voted for his conviction, he expressed understanding; but he wanted to remind them that Anytus, Meletus, and Lycon had not been able to do him real harm, though they had meant to, and for that he blamed them. Nor had the jury vote done what was intended.

Young men, more energetic and passionate, would take up his quest; and it would be said of the Athenians that they had killed a wise man (whether he deserved the title or not).

To the other jurors (whom he addressed now as "Judges" for the first time in the trial, though a plaintiff usually overworked this title desperately to show his respect for the jury) another message was to be given. All through his life Socrates had had an inner "sign" or "voice," which never told him what to do, but would forbid him from doing something wrong. (An ancestor of our Christian and modern "conscience" is clearly suggested by this, though how close the resemblance is we cannot be sure.) Throughout the trial, this inner voice had never spoken; and, therefore, he went from them with confidence that he was right, and no evil would befall him. Perhaps there was an afterlife where he could talk with wise men of the past. "In another life they do not put a man to death for asking questions: assuredly not." Perhaps he was going to a peaceful sleep. His final wish was that the Athenians should question Socrates' own sons as he had questioned the experts of Athens. He felt an unexamined life was not worth living. It is a conclusion many philosophers, jurors, and scholars have pondered since.

The West has never been the same since the trial of Socrates. Young men did carry on his inquiry. Throughout Greece we find "Socratic schools" dedicated to their interpretations of this mission. Plato wrote Socratic dialogues, masterpieces of philosophy and literature, both defending Socrates against the charges made and carrying on his inquiry by facing the reader with Socratic questioning. Athens went on to become a center of science and philosophy, and did not try to restrict the inquiries of her philosophers.

Athenian history in Aristotle's time may give rise to some doubts about a total commitment to freedom, but whenever we discuss the importance of free speech, the duty of an individual to disobey laws that go counter to his conscience, the place that ideals can and should play in our conduct, we realize the importance of this trial. Philosophy would never be the same after Socrates—his new questions became central. Neither would the relation of the individual to the state's authority. Socrates drew the line where respect for justice and conscience must take precedence over social expediency and authority. Ironic, inquiring, uncompromising, Socrates succeeded in convincing the West of the correctness of his views and the justice of his cause.

Present at the trial, but too young to be allowed to speak there, Socrates' admirer Plato heard him prophesy that other, younger men would carry on his mission, and he set out to make the prophecy come true. From writing imaginary conversations which caught the spirit of

Socratic inquiry, his work went on to develop what he thought the speculative answers were to some of its most urgent questions. The *Republic* marks the high point of this search for speculative answers. Throughout his career, Plato seems to have been challenged constantly by one philosophic constraint. Any vision of the world and man's place in it must include the possibility of Socrates.

The end of the trial marked the end of Plato's political ambitions. Broken hearted, he left Athens on the road to Megara, determined to write works that would carry on the spirit of Socrates and his devotion to philosophy. And that determination never altered until Plato died at eighty, as Head of the Academy.

From R. S. Brumbaugh, ed., *Six Great Trials*, copyright Hartford College for Women, 1966, by permission of Hartford College for Women.

Epilogue

All the Great Ideas

Reprinted from *Essays in Introduction to Philosophy*, ed. William H. Brenner and Judith Andre, copyright 1985, by permission of the Editors. This was, however, originally an *epideictic* ("in praise of") lecture at the First International Hellenic Congress, in Norfolk in 1982, offered to a general audience who shared the common property of being enthusiastic Hellenes and Philhellenes. (Socrates, in one of Plato's dialogues, points out that "it is easy in Athens to speak in praise of the Athenians"; perhaps a similar observation is in place here.)

All the great ideas basic to our modern science and common sense, with not more than four exceptions, were the discoveries of the ancient Greek philosophers. At first glance, it is surprising to realize that ideas we have always taken for granted did need to be discovered, and that we can often date and locate their discovery. But it is true; and a sample list shows an amazing clustering of these discoveries in the Greek world between 585 and 322 B.C. Let me just offer some dates and samples for the first appearances of ideas, some great and some not so great. The perhaps not-so-great idea of totalitarian monarchy emerges in the Near East about 4000 B.C.; the great idea of democracy appears in Greece about 500. Use of some sort of calculation seems to go back to marked bones from perhaps 20,000 B.C., found in cave sites; pure mathematics dates from 530 B.C., when it was discovered in the Western Greek world of South Italy. Travel posters go back to an Egyptian expedition to East Africa about 1200 B.C.; geographical maps, and relief maps, date from the sixth and fifth centuries B.C., from Asia Minor. That women are unequal and have no rights is of incalculable antiquity; its opposite dates to about 381 B.C. Matter and the atomic theory are ideas dating from 500 B.C., as opposed to creation myths that go back to at least 3000. And the list can go on.

When you consider it, you will see that these Greek great ideas are still the basic components of our common sense and our science; that it would be very hard to think without them. Whitehead has called this classic achievement the storing up of a capital of ideas that the West has been living on ever since. But our debt is even greater: because even if you don't want to think, but just to talk without thinking, a debt to Greek philosophy is still there. For our ordinary language is chock full of words that were technical philosophic terms in Aristotle's Greek, that have descended into modern Greek directly, into English by way of Medieval Latin, and that are now an essential part of our most everyday ways of talking. For example, if your car has an "accident" you are drawing on a classical notion that each thing, such as a car, has an *essence* which defines it, and then also has various nonessential properties, its *accidents*. Since it is not part of the essential definition of a car that it wrap itself around a lamppost, the collision must be "accidental." And when we look to see "what is the matter" with the "motor," we are still indebted to Aristotelian terminology. From Aristotle's account of the "four causes"—formal, final, efficient, and material—we get our names describing informal dress, inefficiency, material witnesses, and beauty contest finalists.

Our debt is equally great when, instead of ideas and words, we look at systems of philosophy. For the four major types of philosophic explanation that make up Western speculative thought had been established in some detail by 322 B.C.

The story will begin near the city of Miletus on May 28, 585 B.C. That is one of the few firm dates we have in this early period, and it gives us a dating for the man who first invented science and philosophy, making a sharp break with the world of myth and fantasy. On that day in May, a total eclipse of the sun ended a battle between the Lydians and Persians, and as they retreated from the field, some of the soldiers remembered that this eclipse had been predicted by a wise man of the city of Miletus, whose name was Thales. Miletus was then a great cosmopolitan commercial port, and had a record of training civil and military engineers. Thales was an engineer himself, according to report, active, and was engaged in speculation in business as well as in astronomy. We know of his ideas only at second hand, or from further remove; there are many reports and anecdotes, but no direct quotations, and only one important indirect one. That is Aristotle's statement that "Thales said all things are *hydor*." (We usually translate this as "water," but *hydor* could be used more generally to mean "things in a fluid state.") Simple-minded as this sounds, it marks the arrival of a new type of question in the West, and a new kind of answer. Before Thales, explanation had been by way of myth. There were myths of several kinds: *creation myths* told how some god or gods had made the world; *animistic myths* told how the parts of nature were alive, and what kinds of spirit lived in each of them; *genealogical myths* explained things by tracing family trees of ancestors. (Thus, Hesiod explains what nightmares are by tracing their ancestry back to a marriage of the gods of Fear and Sleep.) But Thales is asking about things as they are now; and he is assuming that the discovery of some common material stuff will tell us "what all things are," thus answering the philosophic question, "What is being?" While later thinkers, from Heraclitus to Heidegger, will criticize his answer, they will remain indebted to him for his question.

In two further generations, other Milesian thinkers went on to introduce a new idea of matter, the notion that there are laws of nature, the use of models as aids to scientific research, and the theory that all the causes in the world are forms of *physical* causality. These three generations of Milesian engineers—Thales, Anaximander, and Anaximines—assuming that "to be is to be material," mark the beginning of the scientific mode of thought, and of the type of philosophy later known as "naturalistic materialism."

This actual bit of history is not as clear and straightforward as I may have made it seem. We must recover it from anecdotes, brief direct quotations, and later paraphrase. And we must not be surprised if some of the new ideas were associated with rather primitive traditional imagery. The Laws of Nature, for example, were first described, using imagery from human law, as the work of a goddess, Justice, regulating such things as hot and cold, moist and dry, in a cosmic Court. The opposites "trespass against each other, and are sentenced to pay reparations, according to the order of time," wrote Anaximander. Nor is it surprising that Thales' new ideas seemed strange enough to make him the subject of the first "Absent-minded Professor" story.

The next chapter takes place in the Western part of the Greek world, in Southern Italy and Eastern Sicily. It was here that the Pythagoreans, inspired by their new discoveries in mathematics, next introduced the philosophically challenging idea that what things really are is not determined by their *matter*, but their *form*. This idea originated with the famous mathematician Pythagoras, for whom the "Theorem of Pythagoras" is named. In 530 B.C. he sailed from Samos to Crotona in South Italy, taking new ideas from the East to the Western frontier.

The two worlds were very different: in the East the Persians and the Greeks could exchange coins, commodities, doctors, and soldiers; but in the West, where their neighbors were the Carthaginians, there was almost no such civilized communication—the Carthaginians remained an unknown dark power. And the Western Greeks, probably for this reason—though perhaps for some other—sought for security and vision in the direction of mystery religions, of mysticism, of building Doric Temples like those of the Greek mainland or even larger, of "infatuation with form."

In this setting, it seems that Pythagoras discovered pure mathematics, and extended his discovery in the direction of "formalism" as a philosophy. One simple way to appreciate the difference between pure mathematics and applied is to look at the difference between the *number* two and the various kinds of pairs of things we meet every day. The pairs differ, depending on the kinds of concrete things they represent: two *slices* of bread, two *pieces* of paper, two *teams* in the playoffs. But while the pairs are thus tied down to the couples they represent, numbers are not: they are abstract things in their own right. And the same thing is true with the figures studied in geometry, or the ratios studied in music theory. The discovery was certainly an exciting one. Aristotle sums up the new Pythagorean ideas in two sayings he attributes to the Pythagoreans: they thought, he writes, that *numbers are things* and that *things are numbers*. The first idea, that numbers are real, is clearly a new and correct one. The only reason that it poses a problem is that common sense too often identifies real things with the things we can touch and handle. But by any other test—unchangingess, ability to be seen in the same way by all observers, relations in a logical system— it is certainly true that numbers have being and so are real. For Pythagoras, with this new notion go other ideas about the human soul—which is also real, though it cannot be seen or handled—and the fact that the world has a beautiful mathematical order. Philosophy in the West has begun in this early phase to approach an idealism and a dualism in which being is to be identified, not with physical matter, but with soul or form.

It is interesting to note the effect that the other Pythagorean belief, that *things are numbers*, had on Western science. The Pythagoreans never could agree as to *just how* physical things were made from numbers. But since they saw that, if this is the case, the basis of nature must be mathematical, they measured and they counted. Their results, in almost every area they explored, seemed—and usually were— important new discoveries. Very early, one of these led to the notion of "the music of the spheres," which has captured the fancy of poets and astronomers alike ever since. In measuring the lengths of a lyre string that give notes an octave apart, it turned out that the ratio was exactly 2:1. For the fifth, it was 3:2, and for the fourth it was 4:3. Thus the basis of musical beauty—the concords of the scale—seemed to result from arithmetical simplicity in the scale. But from the periods of the planets established by long observation, the ratios of time for planetary motion were similarly simple, integral ratios; and some of them were identical with those of the musical set. (Later, these planetary ratios were all derived from the numbers 1, 2, 3, 4 [2 squared], 9 [3 squared], 8 [2 cubed], and 27 [3 cubed].) Thus it seemed that "the heavens are a musical scale"—almost as though the planets had been "tuned" like strings on a harp or lyre. And other measurements paid off as well. For example, trying to determine *how hot* and *how dry* patients in the hospital were turned out to be an important medical observation. Work with the ratios that sculptors found most satisfying for human figures turned up some unexpected, simple, proportions. Whitehead, writing about science and the modern world, in his book by that name, says:

> Finally . . . we have in the end come back to a version of the doctrine of old Pythagoras, from whom mathematics and mathematical physics, took their rise. . . .

> Truly, Pythagoras in founding European philosophy and European mathematics, endowed them with the luckiest of lucky guesses—or, was it a flash of divine genius, penetrating to the inmost nature of things?

> > (*Science and the Modern World*,
> > [New York, 1925], pp. 55–56.)

About 500 B.C., back in Asia Minor, in the city of Ephesus, an enigmatic figure, Heraclitus, proclaims *his* insights in epigrams. Whatever his views are, it is clear that he has no patience with mathematicians: he calls Pythagoras' discoveries nothing but "an art of mischief." And he barely mentions the earlier engineers. Even in ancient times, he was known as "The Obscure" (*ho skoteinos*). His short sayings, often with their sense reinforced by sound, deal with a world that is like rivers, strife, and fire. Thus we hear that "All things flow"; that "Into the same rivers we step and do not step; for other waters are flowing on." (The second of these sayings opens with the *sound* of the flow: *toisin autoisin potamoisin.* . . .) "Fire," we are told, "steers all things; Fire will seize and judge all things; all things are exchanged for fire, and fire for all things, as gold is exchanged for wares and wares for gold." (In the last of these, the dark saying ends with a sound of Fire: *hokosper chrysou chremata kai chremata chrysou.*)

The message, modelled on Oracles, not on almanacs or equations, seems to be that both the mathematicians, with their *cosmos* of timeless form, and the natural philosophers, with their world of dead machines, have left something out of account. This something is the fact of violence, change, strife; of individuality and adventure; of a world more like "an ever-living fire" than like a complex metal mechanism or a simple abstract equation. In our own century, one of the few themes common to Western European, British, and American philosophy is that we need to correct too much attention to abstraction by some sort of return to the concrete. In the version of this return offered by Existentialism, we hear an echo of Heraclitus again. (In the Middle Ages, Heraclitus played a different role: with his poetic stress on change, he was known as The Weeping Philosopher; while the more literal and tough-minded Democritus, the atomist, was set up as his opposite, The Laughing Philosopher. We find the two paired in Medieval iconography.)

Now, if real and violent change is not consistent with a world of pure form, may it be that change is unreal? That this is so was the insight of Parmenides, a mystic and logician from the city of Elea in Italy. Thus the next step in our history moves from East to West again. Parmenides wrote an epic poem designed to prove that "Only Being is." This Being that alone is, is undivided, unchanging, ungenerated, and alike throughout. This expresses an insight often found in mysticism—a sense of the unity and permanence of all things. Two things proved particularly important historically in Parmenides' defense of his insight. The first was the use he made of formal logic; the second was the specific proof he gave that change requires some sort of plurality. The use of formal logic is an extension of the Pythagorean patterns of proof that work in geometry to more general patterns that apply to reasoning in any context. (For example, a Pythagorean would reason that "if all multiples of 2 are even numbers, and if 4 is a multiple of 2, 4 is even." This is still arithmetic; to get to logic, we generalize it to the pattern: "if all A is B, and if C is A, then C is B"; now, this holds *whatever* A, B, and C are.) Reality must be logically coherent: "It is the same thing that can be thought and can be," wrote Parmenides. A very similar modern parallel is the development of a logical algebra by letting the x's and y's of standard algebra now stand for any kinds of things in general, not merely quantities.

The power of this new technique was demonstrated by Parmenides' student, Zeno (this is Zeno of Elea, not to be confused with Zeno the Stoic, who came later). Zeno tried to show that neither common sense nor Pythagorean science could give accounts of change that were logical. His paradoxes continue to this day to amuse track fans (they all take place in a stadium) and to baffle mathematicians (our modern Pythagoreans).

As a final outcome of this grand series of ideas, Leucippus and Democritus devised the atomic theory. This was a final, consistent system of philosophy, of the type we call naturalistic materialism. If reality consists of many small bits of being (*atoma*, "uncuttable," because each is indivisible) and these atoms move through empty space, change can be explained by their mechanical interaction. These small particles differ only in "shape, order, and position," and all causal action is transfer of momentum. The atoms themselves do not have flavor, color, or such qualities; those are all "conventional," contributions of the human observer. This type of theory is still basic in our Western science. It offers a simple general rule of method: "divide and conquer." It offers (or did offer until our own century) very simple laws of nature: conservation of matter, conservation of momentum (which is mass times velocity), and necessary causal sequences as momentum is transferred.

There were other attempts to explain change in ways that would avoid logical objections. Empedocles, for example, in Sicily, suggested that there might be six qualitative "elements," which mix and separate. His six were earth, air, fire, and water—built up from hot, cold, moist, and dry—plus Love and Hate. Empedocles' contemporary, Anaxagoras, who first brought science to Athens, argued that nature is a constant process of qualitative mixture in a *continuous* flow of space and time. His model closely anticipates ideas of our twentieth-century "process philosophy."

For all of this time, there was one obvious omission in classical speculation. The emphasis on the objective, outer world was accompanied by an absent-minded neglect of human affairs, and of the human observer. That neglect was corrected, by a violent pendulum swing, when the Sophists appeared on the scene. These Sophists (their name comes from "*sophos*," "wise") were professional educators, who taught "sophistication." By this they meant "the arts of success"—political oratory, legal case pleading, manners and cultural information. They had no patience with philosophy or natural science, which they thought were not relevant to human ambition. They introduced the view that ethical values are not "natural" but matters of convention, varying from one society to another. Their attitudes toward religion ranged from agnosticism to the statement that it was politically inspired superstition. One of the older Sophists, Protagoras, is quoted on these points: "Man is the measure of all things; of things that are, that they are; of things that are not, that they are not"; and "Concerning the gods, whether they exist or not, I do not know, because of the greatness of the subject and the shortness of human life."

The criticism of traditional values became more outspoken with the Sophists of the next generation. Thus we find one of them, Thrasymachus, announcing that "justice is the advantage of the stronger," while another, Critias, says "the gods were invented by rulers to

frighten their subjects into obedience." Thus the attention of philosophy was redirected with a vengeance; and for a time it was not at all
clear how human greed, self-interest, and political "pragmatism" were
related to, or could be learned from, study of geometric figures or
remote stars. (One constructive contribution that these men made, was
to recognize that language is a tool, not a god-given sort of instinctive
power; and that we can study language and improve it.) Some of our
twentieth-century pragmatists, who like the idea of identifying what is
true with what is useful, have claimed these sophisticated Greek teachers as their ancestors. But if they take a closer look at them, I think they
will want to find their roots in a different genealogy.

Partly as a result of the joint impact of science and Sophistry in
Athens in the fifth century, we find Socrates asking a question that
proves as basic as Thales' "What is being?" with which Western philosophy had begun. Socrates' question was "What is a human self?" or,
more simply, for each of us, "What am I?" The medical men had been
working with the idea that a "self" was a physical organ; the Sophists
had based their whole program on an appeal to "self-interest." But
neither group had a satisfying answer to Socrates' seemingly simple
question. The medical notion could not explain how thoughts and in-
tentions, which are not material, could cause our bodies, which are, to
act. The Sophistic notion couldn't explain how anyone ever could be
altruistic, or idealistic, or even friendly—but Socrates thought people
often were. That people sometimes do put their ideals ahead of their
immediate interests was dramatically shown by Socrates himself. Once
the importance of his new question dawned on him, he realized that
until it found some plausible answer, teachers, statesmen, and Sophists
were all working in the dark. But when he tried to show his fellow
citizens that what they thought they knew was mistaken, they remained indifferent or became angry. (One later portrait pictures Socrates at the entrance to the Market, trying to get the racing businessmen
to pause and think; rather as though he had taken over the public
address system in New York's Grand Central Station for his message,
and with about the same result.) Socrates showed that though they
spent their time *praising* justice and other virtues, they had no idea of
how to *define* them. At this time, with the political situation desperately unstable, a democratic Athenian government tried to frighten
Socrates into giving up his "mission of inquiry." They accused him of
"impiety and corrupting the youth," probably expecting that this threat
of prosecution would make him leave Athens or at least stop talking.
But Socrates would do neither: he had done nothing unjust, and did
not propose to go into exile, which would seem a tacit admission of

injustice. And he felt he could not give up asking his questions, either—for, if he did, his mission would have been in vain. So he stayed, stood trial, and was convicted and executed in 399 B.C. (The memory of Socrates has never left the neighborhood of the Agora. During the Middle Ages, a Roman weather station was shown to tourists as "The School of Socrates"; in the nineteenth century, a dry reservoir was exhibited as "The Prison of Socrates"; in our own time archaeologists have found the site of the real prison, with a shelf of vials for hemlock in the prison storage room.)

At his trial, Socrates predicted that some of the young men of Athens would keep his mission alive; and he was right. After his death, his young admirer, Plato, set about writing Dialogues, imaginary conversations in defense of Socrates. Plato first defends his hero against the charges at the trial; then tries to show how different he was from the Sophists (with whom the public had apparently confused him); then Plato goes on to develop a philosophy of formalism and idealism which he believes offers the answer to Socrates' questions. Plato's philosophic vision has been central ever since in Western philosophic and religious thought; so has his design of the Academy, the first Western university, and the ancestor of all of our subsequent institutions of higher education. Plato's vision of reality sees it as a hierarchical system, like a pyramid, converging at the top. There is the changing physical world we live in, but there is also, above it, an unchanging world of "forms." (This is an extension and combination, in a way, of earlier ideas, with the Eleatics and Pythagoreans supplying the world of form, the Milesians and Heraclitus describing the world of change and flow.)

The "forms" that Plato talks about are sometimes structures: blueprints and types of the individual instances we encounter. (For example, there is a single form of right triangle, "shared in" by all right triangles.) Things get their identities through "sharing in" these forms, while philosophy and science work by "generalizations" that go to the forms from particular things. But at least some of the Platonic forms are more than structures; they are "ideals"—justice, beauty, and truth are forms of this kind. These ideals inspire us to *achieve* them; they are part of reality, and indeed the most important part for explaining our human pursuit of excellence. At the top of this world of form, giving order to its levels of value, structure, and process, Plato believes that there is a single organizing form, which he calls the Form of the Good. (Later Western religions will include this idea as part of their definitions of God.)

The final insight of Platonisms is that the Ideal inspires the actual, and that Reality is organized by principles of value. Thus, counter to the Sophists, who urge us to be "realistic," meaning by that that we should be completely selfish, Plato argues that it is the idealist who is in fact behaving realistically, that is, in tune with Reality.

Plato's work offers a final systematic statement of a philosophic position that combines formalism, idealism, and a vision of One Reality as an ordered whole. It leads us to expect that human intelligence, correctly applied, can design ideal societies and educational systems. It assumes, also, that proper grasp of forms can lead us to objective solutions of problems of value: of truth, justice, beauty, and the like. Plato's importance can be seen, in part, from the role he still plays—not only as hero, but as gadfly and villain—in our contemporary discussions, not only of speculative theory, but even more of social and political philosophy. Plato's idealism pictures the world as we hope that it is, and the persistent impact of his philosophy to some extent confirms our hope. Regarding his importance, I can do no better than to cite two comments, one Hellenistic and one modern. The modern comment is Alfred North Whitead's remark that "the best general characterization of Western philosophy is that it is a series of footnotes to Plato." The Hellenistic comment is by Plutarch: "Plato is philosophy, and philosophy is Plato."

One might think, now, that the possible contributions of Greek philosophy have all been made. But there remains a great attempt to reconcile Plato's formalism and the materialism of the atomic theory. This is the system of Plato's student, Aristotle. Aristotle, a doctor's son and a great zoologist, saw the value of Plato's forms: in fact, in nature, these seemed to him to be the *species*, the natural kinds that run true to type. But Aristotle was also very sure that forms required a proper matter if they were to be forms of actual things. And the way in which matter takes on form was, he thought, quite well explained by the sort of experiment and analysis that marked the atomic theory. Fairly early in his career, it occurred to Aristotle that perhaps being, or reality, is four-dimensional. That is, there may be four different kinds of explanation of what things do and what they are, even though the philosophers before Aristotle had each paid exclusive attention to only one of the four. He called these four dimensions "causes" (*aitiai*): the formal, final, efficient, and material. (The word *aition* is not our modern "cause"; it is a legal term, meaning some factor or agent that is liable or responsible; Aristotle's vocabulary here reminds us of the vision of natural law in the Court of *Dike* described by Anaximander.) With the aid of these four causes, Aristotle set about organizing the whole of knowledge and reality.

We usually think—as Mary Renault portrays him in her novels—of Aristotle's one-time student, Alexander, as a great adventurer and conqueror. But neither his project nor his success matches the ambition and achievement of his teacher's campaign in the intellectual domain. Aristotle's astronomy was to dominate Western thought until the seventeenth century; his biology was not improved on until the nineteenth century; his logic was modified—not replaced—only in the twentieth century. His poetics, politics, and ethics remain up-to-date, authoritative sources in their fields. Dante, we may recall, referred to him as "Master of those who Know."

And with this final synthesis, the proposed compromise of ideal and actual, matter and form, Hellenic philosophy drew to its close. Platonism was to survive: Plotinus, St. Augustine, Proclus, the Greek Church Fathers mark its way. So was Aristotelianism: Aristotle has been admired by Averroes, Albertus Magnus, St. Thomas Aquinas, with W. D. Ross and Richard McKeon carrying on the tradition in our own century. The atomic theory remains the foundation and triumph of natural science: Democritus returning to Athens today, far from finding a city where "no one knew him," could enter from the North past the imposing "Democritus Research Laboratory." Heraclitus and Anaxagoras would find themselves at home, I think, with Existentialism and with a process philosophy in which—over a sufficient span of time—"All things Flow."

The Great Ideas have been found, admired, and systematized. And the pictures of the world central to later human efforts at controlling it, appreciating it, living well within it, and reaching beyond it, had been found as well. They had been systematized in the materialism of the atomic theory of Leucippus and Democritus, in the "process" or "existential" view of Heraclitus and Anaxagoras, in the idealism and formalism of Socrates and Plato, and in the balanced scheme of the four causes proposed by Aristotle. These four approaches to philosophy—Platonism, Aristotelianism, speculative process thought, and atomic analysis—have in fact continued to be the main systems of philosophy throughout later Western speculation. And so my anthology of "all the great ideas" is practically completed here, in ancient Greece, by the year 322 B.C.

A Postscript

My Final Lecture on the History of Ancient Philosophy

It seems strange to be planning the final lecture that, after decades of final lectures summing up the history of ancient philosophy, will be my last. My hope has been, all along, to present the rise of philosophy in ancient Greece as an introduction to philosophy itself, and as a source offering insights to our contemporary thought.

It is human nature to look for a metaphysics, that is, for a general philosophic system, and to be far too quick in accepting one. The search generally takes the form of generalizing from one special area of experience or one set of concepts to conclusions about all concepts and all experiences. When such generalizations have become dominant in a culture, they begin to become exclusive and entrenched, and at that point, they may pass into "common sense," so that no alternative seems "sensible." They project themselves into political thought, so that they set limits to the alternatives that are imaginable. (Thus, for centuries the social and political thought of the West assumed a hierarchy converging at absolute authority; the only question was who should be at the top.) They become more precise at the hands of intellectuals. Then, slowly or suddenly, they lose their rights and privileges and go out of date.

I have suggested that the four main paradigms of later Western thought appeared in ancient Greece, selected from a world of boundless energy, flawless love of form, constant competition, and inveterate curiosity. It was also a world of political experimentation: Plato could have observed at first hand each of the five types of state he lists in Book VIII of the *Republic;* Aristotle's general kinds of city-state were subdivided into 158 individual varieties. From our distance, the Roman world can be seen to have had these same paradigms, but now paradigms in collision. The Roman Schools, their philosophic motivation narrowed to topics of consolation and escape, interpreted philosophy in ways the Roman public found less than satisfactory. (Still, I suppose

251

one might say that Stoicism came closest to expressing the orientation of the Empire, Epicureanism that of its individual subject.)

Probably the period from the fifth century through the twelfth should be seen as an age of Platonism in the Latin West—Plato as interpreted by Plotinus, by Augustine, by Chalcidius in science, by Galen in medicine, by pseudo-Dionysius in theology. The dangers of this scheme, with its origins in mathematics, astronomy, speculative natural theology, and formal music theory, are its underrating of Becoming, its overdependence on the ideal, its rigid hierarchy on every base, its elitist class bias, and its conviction that fine art should be allegory. In addition, Christianity added a religious doctrine of salvation in another world which seemed to remove any necessity of care for this one: such salvation depended on attitudes and sacraments, not at all on public health and adequate nutrition. (John Dewey was particularly eloquent in his comments on the this world-other world dualism.)

The Aristotelian interlude of three centuries, the thirteenth through the sixteenth, marked a new tolerance for decentralization and specialization. Experience came to be considered important, nature worth study, authority divisible among specialized authorities. Philosophy, though critical of Platonic idealism, still retained final causes (but now as one dimension out of four), and respect for authority (but now more for special authorities than for great generalists.). The Aristotelian Scholastic theory, at least, left room for study of interfaith common philosophy, new dialogue and new toleration. Further, it guaranteed a new freedom to the arts and science, since "faith and reason can never conflict." And it put a largely new emphasis on observation, since it held that "there is nothing in the [human] intellect that was not first in the senses." The individual began to stand out against the universal. (Somehow, there is a foreshadowing of what is to come when in the Fourth Crusade, in 1204, the Crusaders had sacked Byzantium instead of rescuing Jerusalem.) Philosophers began to question the existence—at least, for access by our minds—of Platonic forms, advocating the position we know as Nominalism. The higher learning was dominated—to the point of being stifled—by respect for the past: this, too, was a function of the Aristotelian orientation, with its promise of intellectual certainty. (Of course, we do find major exceptions to every point I have made. As regards tolerance, for example, we find Roger Bacon advocating experimental science as "a means to removing unbelievers as a threat to the Christian commonwealth." As regards authority, we find William of Ockham writing his treatise *On the Errors of Pope John XXII*, and Giles of Rome his inventory *Of the Errors of the Philosophers*. And throughout—in contrast to the scholars—

alchemists, fortune tellers, magicians, viol players, enhanced local fairs [often without benefit of much Latin, as the words "hocus pocus" attest].)

The change to modern mentality took a common non-Aristotelian direction in the new Platonic humanism of the fifteenth century, the new natural science of the sixteenth and the secular psychology of the seventeenth. Of these three factors, it was science that came to set the tone. Though not explicitly going back to the past for inspiration (though it did with Copernicus and Kepler at its inception), it became a reincarnation of the materialistic paradigms of the classical and Roman atomic theory, abetted by new mathematical sophistication and new technology for observation. In a way, the Aristotelisn emphasis on observation contributed to its own displacement. But Aristotelian "observation" was human in scale, qualitative, ordinary—not telescopic, quantitative, and exotic. And with the new scientific attitude went a belief that final causes could not be observed, hence, not known, either.

This modern viewpoint scored amazing successes, culminating with Newton, but it scored them within the selective range of physics and astronomy. For stupid particles and mindless planetary masses, the scheme could hardly have been better. But even in the seventeenth century there was an uneasy feeling that "mind" might be an exception. (Thus Descartes fell back on a non-Aristotelian but Platonic psychology.) But when the eighteenth century generalized this physics into a metaphysics, disaster was at hand. For now the mechanistic model claimed to exhaust reality and to define "realistic" methods. Spilling over into common sense, it suggested unsentimental value-free realism as its models for economics, social theory, population expansion, and other areas of social science. Perhaps the final logical outcome, deduced with sheer consistency, is found in the work of B. F. Skinner in our own century, titled *Beyond Freedom and Dignity*. There is no mind-body dualism there, since there is no mind. Meanwhile, however, a very little reflection on this materialistic scheme shows that it is untenable as a metaphysics. Whitehead is wryly amused at the experimenter designing his work for the purpose of proving that there are no purposes or final causes. An educational theory or industrial production line that accepts the notion of space as essentially an insulator—as the modern metaphysics does—functions badly. (I have discussed this in my book on *Whitehead, Process Philosophy, and Education*.) The idea of sovereign states colliding at their frontiers, on the analogy of material particles or tectonic plates, offers seriously misleading suggestions for political thinking. And if the material world has no value, it is just waiting for our own advantageous exploitation—suicidal in some racial future, but pleasant in the present.

As the twentieth century developed, dissatisfaction had begun to be expressed. In general, there has been a proposed return to concreteness over against the detached and abstract model of the metaphysics generalized from seventeenth-century science. Thus we have pragmatism looking at practice and how things work; existentialism concerned with how agents decide; process philosophy developing a theory of continuity between feeling and thought. My own guess would be that our present lifetime will see a change in the accepted philosophy in the direction of Heraclitus and Anaxagoras: a new stress on continuity, vital force, flow, and the presence of some degree of mind throughout matter. This return, too, has its Greek ancestors—Heraclitus, Anaxagoras, Plato, the Sophists—even if we don't always appeal to their authority, and it has its dangers. For example, if one generalizes Heraclitean violence without restraint into a philosophy, I can't imagine what will happen. But if we can modify Democritus and Epicurus by some accomodations with Plato and Aristotle, the next century should be a better one—one in which, to quote the end of Plato's *Republic*, "we will fare well." This present awareness of alternatives and tensions is perhaps the most important virtue of the study of past philosophy.

Whitehead makes the general point I have been aiming at far better than I can, in the final paragraph of his *Science and the Modern World*, a book devoted to the history of philosophy from the seventeenth century to the twentieth century.

> I have endeavored in these lectures to give a record of a great adventure in the region of thought. It was shared by all the races of western Europe. . . . Half a century is its unit of time. . . . The moral of the tale is the power of reason, its decisive influence in the life of humanity. The great conquerors, from Alexander to Caesar and from Caesar to Napoleon, influenced profoundly the lives of subsequent generations. But the total effect of this influence shrinks to insignificance compared to the entire transformation of human habits and human mentality produced by the long line of men of thought from Thales to the present day, men individually powerless, but ultimately the rulers of mankind.

On a more modest scale, I have my own Epilogue, summarizing what I have intended and where we have been in my course in ancient philosophy.

This course has been, I hope, an adventure of ideas, a voyage of discovery through classic space and time. The story begins with philosophy itself emerging in Ionia—a springtime of great insights and new ways of thought. One thinks of Thales, first to break with mythology; Anaximander, with his poetic vision of the laws of nature (as in the spring, the hot begins to win its legal contest with the cold). There, too, is Anaximines with his vortex cosmic model; later Ionia finds Heraclitus, his dark sayings carrying the insight that all things flow. Then it is a summer for Greek philosophy, mainly in Sicily and Italy. Pythagoras and his mathematical-religious Order in Crotona are followed, to the northwest, by Parmenides and Zeno. Their city is Elea, famous not only for its austere logicians but for its beautiful women, for its roses, and for its wine. In Sicily, Empedocles composes medical observations and cosmological poetry, in a landscape where Mount Etna's fire replaces Mount Olympus's ice and snow.

Next on to the Athenian autumn, the time of ripeness and maturity of thought as well as olives and of grain. Here in the marketplace stands Socrates; a generation later, autumn remains, with Plato writing the *Parmenides* in his Academy; still later, then, a cooling autumn season finds Aristotle working in the great Museum of his school.

The winter comes in Alexandria and Rome. The Roman circus runs with blood, recalling the wildflowers of an earlier Aegean season. The philosophic schools—Stoic, Epicurean, Academic, and Peripatetic—now counsel resignation without adventure; there is a pause of darkness and of rain.

Of course, true history does not exactly match this story of a direct Heraclitean downward way, from sunlight into damp and dark. For example, even in the autumn of philosophy's maturity, we could have seen a sinister troop of Sophists in the Agora. Their sardonic humanism makes us recognize them as precursors of our own masters of advertising and schools of charm. In fact, they are the earliest advocates of a theme that comes back in vogue periodically in the West: that since what counts is success, and this is quite distinct from thought, there is no reason for young people to study ethics, let alone ancient, or modern, or future, philosophy.

Perhaps the true heroes of the age are those who opened the way for later Athenian mastery. These were men with inspired insight into the heart of things, too engaged and too preanalytical to map great systems or to sharpen fine distinctions. One thinks of Heraclitus, irascible, enigmatic, prematurely existentialist; Pythagoras, a second Prometheus for science in the West; the great Parmenides; and Thales, sober to a fault but the first man to break with superstition.

Sometimes I feel the ages of philosophy do not match well with Hesiod's Ages of Man—Gold, Silver, Heroes, Iron. Our Heroic Age of philosophy is first onstage, followed quickly by the Golden. We ourselves seem living in a perpetuation or renewal of Hesiod's Silver Age—that of a quarrelsome race at war with gods and fellow men. Yet I remain an educable man, and perhaps in my retirement I will learn and change my mind about the present age. My current thought, though—and I want you to take this seriously as I end my lecture—is that the future of American philosophy lies less with American philosophers than with philosophical Americans, and I count you among that number.

The Divided Line, the four causes, the Heraclitean epigram, and the Pythagorean formula have served us well. So well, that an observer from *alpha centauri* or *tau ceti*, writing our human history, will see no reason—other than advanced technology—to mark a break between pre-Socratic Greek and contemporary American philosophy. The divisions of races, of parties, and of schools look much less impressive if we, like Socrates in the *Phaedo* Myth of the True Earth, step out in space and look back from the stars.

Notes

Chapter 2

1. Aristotle, *Politics* II, 1260b36-1266a31. For "what Socrates says in the *Laws*," see 1265a19-27.

2. N. R. P. Murphy, *An Interpretation of Plato's Republic*, Oxford, 1952; Nicholas White, *A Companion to Plato's Republic* (Indianapolis, 1979).

3. *Euthyphro* 15E3, *Diogenes Laertius, Lives. . . . ,* II. 29.(Vol. I, pp. 159-161 of Diogenes Laertius, *Lives and Opinions,* trans. R. D. Hicks, 2 vols. (New York, 1938)).

4. *Meno* 85D2-E5.

5. R. S. Brumbaugh, "Plato's *Meno* as Form and as Content of Secondary School Courses in Philosophy," *Teaching Philosophy I* (1975): 107-114.

6. Thus the cast of the *Charmides* has a temperate Socrates, an intemperately irascible Critias, and an intemperately indolent Charmides. The *Lysis* has two older and two younger boys, one of each pair gentle and rather shy (Hippothales and Lysis), and the other forward and aggressive (Ctesippus and Menexenus).

7. *Statesman* 286D3-287C2. See R. S. Brumbaugh, *Plato for the Modern Age* (New York, 1962; reprinted Weston, Conn., 1979), pp. 163-168, and Fig. 9, p. 168.

8. V. Tejera, "Plato's *Politicus:* an Eleatic Sophist on Politics," *Philosophy and Social Criticism* V (1978): 86-104; 107-125.

9. *Epistle VII,* 342A1 ff.

10. *Epistle VII,* 342B1 gives the *names* of the three tools for acquiring knowledge ("name, definition, and image"; and "knowledge" is named as a fourth thing). From 342B3-C1, we get the image—the example of the "circle." This is named in B3, defined in B5-C1, imaged in C1-C4. The *definition* of these tools results from the generalization of the circle example, which the reader is directed to make in B5. From C1 on, the question is reexamined from the standpoint of *knowledge,* the "fourth thing" of the B1-B3 list.

11. Herman Sinaiko, *Love, Discourse and Knowledge in Plato* (Chicago, 1965).

12. Above, p. 19.

13. *Ibid.*, Figures, pp. 26–27.

14. For the historic Cephalus, see Lysias, *Orations* XII. ("Against Eratosthenes"; translated in K. Freeman, *The Murder of Herodes and Other Trials from the Attic Law Courts* (New York, 1963), pp. 54–62.)

15. Cf. Lysias, loc. cit.

16. See R. K. Sprague, ed. and trans., *The Older Sophists:* A Trans. of Diels-Kranz *Fragments* (Columbia, S.C., 1972); also K. Freeman, *Ancilla to the Pre-Socratic Philosophers* (Oxford, 1948), pp. 141–142.

17. A. E. Taylor, *Plato: The Man and His Work* (New York, 1936), pp. 10–12.

18. Carl G. Hempel, *Fundamentals of Concept Formation in the Empirical Sciences* (Chicago, 1951).

19. *Republic* II, 358E–362D.

20. *Republic* II, 369B5–372C2 (the "simple" state); 372C2–374E1 (the "state with a fever").

21. A schematic chart shows these relations:

CEPHALUS	EIKASIA	APPETITE
POLEMARCHUS	EIKASIA	SPIRIT
CLEITOPHON	PISTIS	APPETITE
THRASYMACHUS	PISTIS	SPIRIT
GLAUCON	DIANOIA	SPIRIT
ADEIMANTUS	DIANOIA	APPETITE

22. *Republic* VII, 532E1–533A1.

23. *Republic* VII, 531C5–D5.

24. *Republic* VII, 539E1–540A1.

25. See Chapter 3, below.

26. *Republic* VII, 531C5.

27. A. Boyce Gibson, "Plato's Mathematical Imagination," *Review of Metaphysics* 9 (1955): 57–70.

28. *Republic* VII, 533C10. Cf. Liddell, Scott, Jones, *Greek Lexicon*, "hypothesis."

29. *Republic* VII, 537C5.

30. *Republic* V, 449A–480B.

31. *Republic* X, 608D1–612C1.

32. *Republic* IX, 588B6–589C1.

33. Among the many discussions of the contemporary relevance and implications of Plato's *Republic*, the following are an interesting sample: Karl Popper, *The Open Society and Its Enemies* (London, 1945); Ronald Levinson, *In Defense of Plato* (Cambridge, Mass., 1954); R. H. S. Crossman, *Plato Today* (Oxford, 1939); Leo Strauss, *The City and Man* (Chicago, 1964); Nicholas White, *A Companion to Plato's Republic* (Indianapolis, 1979); N. R. P. Murphy, *An Interpretation of Plato's Republic* (Oxford, 1952); T. Thorson, ed., *Plato: Totalitarian or Democrat?* (Englewood Cliffs, N.J., 1963); and G. Vlastos, ed., *Plato II* (Garden City, N.Y., 1971).

34. And see James Adam, ed., *The Republic of Plato*, 2 vols. (Cambridge, 1902), Appendix I to Book V: "On the relation of the fifth book of the *Republic* to Aristophanes' *Ecclesiazusae*" I, pp. 345–356.

35. A table of locations and types of mathematical images in the *Republic* shows this progression; it is discussed in more detail in R. S. Brumbaugh, *Plato's Mathematical Imagination* (reprint, N.Y., 1968).

IMAGE	LOCATION (BY BOOK)	BRANCH OF MATHEMATICS
Factors of 12	I	Arithmetic
Circle	V	Plane Geometry
Divided Line	VII	Plane Geometry
Nuptial Number	VIII	Plane Geometry, then developed into Solid Geometry
Tyrant's Number	IX	Solid Geometry
Myth of Er (Cosmic Ratios)	X	Astronomy (with suggested extension to Harmonics)

36. Paul Shorey, ed. and trans., *The Republic of Plato*, 2 vols. (New York and London, 1930), writes as follows: "The eighth book, one of the most brilliant pieces of writing in Plato . . ." (vol. 2, p. xix); "In this review, history, satire, political philosophy, and the special literary motives of the *Republic* are blended in a mixture hopelessly disconcerting to all literal-minded interpreters from Aristotle down." (*Ibid.*, p. xx). Cp. Aristotle, *Politics* II, 1260B–1266A.

37. Socrates and Glaucon are persuaded to stay in Piraeus by the prospects offered of a banquet, a torchlight race, and intelligent conversation.

38. For some general references to interpretations of Platonic "dialectic," see R. S. Brumbaugh, *Plato on the One* (New Haven, 1961), note 1, pp. 189–90, and pp. 189–206.

Chapter 3

1. Richard Robinson, *Plato's Earlier Dialectic*, 2nd ed. (Oxford, 1953).

2. See below, Chapter 5; but note that this is the "simplified" version discussed below in sec. 5, p. 83. For an "unequal segments" construction, see my *Plato's Mathematical Imagination*, p. 103; for "mean and extreme ratio" divisions, see Euclid, *Elements* VI.30.

Chapter 4

1. *Republic* 509D–511 E. See R. S. Brumbaugh and N. M. Lawrence, *Philosophers on Education*, Boston, 1962, "Plato," pp. 10–48.

2. Bertrand Russell, *A History of Western Philosophy* (N.Y., 1945), "John Dewey," pp. 819–828.

3. *Republic* 521C1 ff. For the suggestion that the ideal curriculum is one of four related accounts of the Good which Socrates gives Glaucon, see Chapter 3, above.

4. The phrase is taken from I. M. Crombie's use of it in his *Examination of Plato's Doctrines*, vol. 2. See my review, *Modern Schoolman* (1966): 274–277.

5. "Many refractions." Among these, I take it, are the "characters and paradigms of lives" that souls may choose among in *Republic* X, the Myth of Er.

6. *Republic* III.

7. I will not go into Aristotle's criticism of Plato's "intermediates." I side completely with Plato; such hypothetical models as "the economic man" are very useful.

8. *Republic* VI. 505A introduces this theme of The Good. Dialectic as the only method by which it can be known appears at 531E.

9. In the *Philebus*, symmetry, truth and beauty are the "touchstones" of The Good.

10. *Republic* 531D1.

11. If this course is to mediate the theoretical study of mathematical method and the practice of politics, it must apply the *forms* of the former to the *content* of the latter. See Chapter 1, above.

12 The education in the *Laws* concentrates on arts of measure and introduces applications of mathematics via games and technology.

13. Nancy Cole, ed., Metropolitan Museum of Art, *Greek Athletic Games*, (School Picture Set), (N.Y., n.d.), Fig. 1.

14. *Republic* VII.

15. See below, Chapter 16.

16. A. Boyce Gibson, "Plato's Mathematical Imagination," *Review of Metaphysics* IX (1955–56), pp. 57–71, especially pp. 61–62.

17. *Republic* 521C ff. The mathematics course at 531D; the need for the philosopher to see "synoptically" at 537C.

18. For the *Republic* as itself an example of "dialectic," see Chapter 1, above. Further discussion of this will be found in Chapter 2.

19. A. N. Whitehead, *Science and the Modern World*, Chaps. 5, 10, 13.

20. See my "Whitehead as a Philosopher of Education: Action, Abstraction, Satisfaction," *Educational Theory*, 1965, pp. 277–281.

21. A. N. Whitehead, "The Rhythm of Education," in *The Aims of Education and Other Essays* (reprint, N.Y., 1967), pp. 15–28.

22. The case is indirectly argued in the final chapter of my *Plato for the Modern Age* (N.Y., 1958).

Chapter 5

1. The passage goes on to have the Muses, who are speaking "high tragic" mathematical prose, describe a three-dimensional model of some sort. Aristotle says that later detail "means when the number of the figure becomes solid." He does not seem bothered by any profound mathematics or astrology, nor does he pause to criticize the mathematics that would result if the Muses were literal. In fact, looking at the context of the eugenic problem, there is a simple diagram that might mediate the Divided Line and the tyrant's number. If we set up a plan of human types as a square, determined by three levels of intelligence and three kinds of character, joining one of these squares for the contribution of each parent gives a cube of possible hereditary types. Put into time, each one of them changes year by year in its appearance throughout a rounded-off hundred-year-span of human life.

Chapter 6

1. A. N. Whitehead, *Science and the Modern World* (New York, 1925), chap. 10, "Abstraction."

2. A contrast frequently noted but not very adequately reconciled; see, for example, R. S. Brumbaugh, *Plato for the Modern Age* (reprint, Westport, 1979), pp. 83–115.

3. *Epistle VII*, 342A ff.

4. For a discussion of the evidence for dramatic and chronological dates, see the discussions in W. K. C. Guthrie, *A History of Greek Philosophy*, vols. 4, 5 (Cambridge, 1971, 1975). Various other orderings are not relevant here, for example, Thrasyllus's organization by philosophic theme, or the several arrangements for maximum pedagogical value reported by Albinus.

5. Marvin Fox, "The Trials of Socrates," *Archiv. fur Gesch. d. Philosophie*, 6 (1956): 226–61.

6. In the summary of the *Republic* that opens the *Timaeus*, the metaphysical section (Books VI and VII) is omitted. Since Proclus, commentators have suggested a connection between this fact and the cryptic "One, two, three, but where is the fourth . . . ," with which the dialogue opens.

7. *Parmenides* 130B6–C1.

8. A. Diès, "Notice," *Platon Parménide*, ed. A. Diès (Paris, 1950), pp. 47–48.

9. The correlation is as follows: *Noesis:* Socrates::*Dianoia:* Theodorus:: *Pistis:*Theaetus::*Eikasia:*Ghost of Protagoras.

10. Gilbert Ryle, *Plato's Progress* (Cambridge, 1966), pp. 275–80, esp. p. 278. On this general approach to Plato's treatments of lawyers and litigation, see my review of Ryle, *Journal of Value Inquiry* (1967): 271–74.

11. F. M. Cornford, *Plato's Theory of Knowledge* (reprint, Indianapolis, 1957), esp. pp. 12–13.

12. *Phaedo* 95A–97C; 99D–107C.

13. Jacob Klein, *Plato's Trilogy* (Chicago, 1977), p. 5.

14. *Phaedo* 99D–107C.

15. *Phaedo* 95A–97C.

16. Aristotle takes the geology seriously—something he does not do for such other Platonic myths as the Myth of Er, the Myth of Metals, the *Gorgias* Myth of Last Judgment; Aristotle, *Meteorology*, II.i, 355b32–356b2.

17. Kant, *Critique of Judgment; Universal Natural History of the Heavens*.

18. *Laws* X.

Chapter 7

1. See Chapter 16, below: "In fact, the Stranger from Elea who is brought in to 'track the wily monster down,' reminds me of the team of

bounty-hunters hired, in another time and context, to gun down Butch Cassidy and the Sun Dance Kid." See also n. 31, Chap. 16.

2. *Philebus* 23B5.

3. See W. Windelband, *History of Philosophy*, tr. J. H. Tufts (Norwood, MA, 1893), p. 103. "Among the doubtful writings the most important are the *Sophist, Politicus*, and *Parmenides.* These probably did not originate with Plato, but with men of his school who were closely related with the Eleatic dialectic and eristic. The first two are by the same author." See also W. W. Waddell, ed., *The Parmenides of Plato* (Glasgow, 1894), pp. i–xix.

4. V. Tejera, "Plato's Politicus, an Eleatic Sophist on Politics," *Philosophy and Social Criticism* 5 (1978): pp. 85–104; 107–25. See also Mitchell H. Miller, Jr., *The Philosopher in Plato's Statesman* (The Hague: Martinus Nijhoff, 1980).

5. Frederick S. Oscanyan, "On Six Definitions of the Sophist: *Sophist* 221C–231E," *Philosophical Forum* 4 (1972–73): pp. 241–255.

6. Jacob Klein, *Plato's Trilogy* (Chicago: University of Chicago Press, 1977). For example, p. 27: ". . . the Stranger says to Theaetetus, similingly, we suppose. . . ."

7. *Statesman* 266A, referred back to at 266C.

8. For the W. Scholion, see R. S. Brumbaugh, "Logical and Mathematical Symbolism in the Plato Scholia," *Journal of the Warburg and Courtauld Institutes* 24 (1961), fig. 1h.

9. See note 5, above.

10. *Phaedrus* 265D–266E.

11. *Statesman* 287C–289B. See the comments of J. B. Skemp, ed., on this division in *Plato's Statesman* (New Haven: Yale University Press, 1954).

12. Tejera, "Plato's Politicus"; Miller, *Philosopher in Plato's Stateman;* A. E. Taylor, tr., *Plato, the Sophist and the Statesman*, ed. Raymond Klibansky and Elizabeth Anscombe (London: T. Nelson, 1961), pp. 3–91; Skemp, *Plato's Statesman;* Gilbert Ryle, *Plato's Progress* (Cambridge: Cambridge University Press, 1966); A. Diès, ed., and tr. Platon, *Le Sophiste*, Budé edn. (Paris, 1925); Edith Hamilton and Huntington Cairns, eds., Plato, *Complete Works*, tr. Lane Cooper et al. (New York: Pantheon Books, 1961), pp. 1018–19; et al.

13. For the importance of this detail of arrival *from Clazomenae*, see R. S. Brumbaugh, *Plato on the One* (New Haven: Yale University Press, 1961).

14. *Sophist* 247E; gods and giants, 246ff.; A. N. Whitehead, *Adventures of Ideas* (New York: Macmillan, 1933), p. 165; see also F. M. Cornford's comment on Whitehead's reading, *Plato's Theory of Knowledge* (New York: Liberal Arts Press, 1957), n. 1, p. 5.

15. *Sophist* 257D ff; an interesting triad here, the members of which are asserted to be real: the Ugly, the Short, and the Unjust.

16. *Phaedo* 76E, ". . . these absolute realities . . . which we are always talking about. . . ." (Tredennick's translation).

17. *Statesman* 299 D–1.

18. *Republic* V 501B.

19. N. P. Stallknecht and R. S. Brumbaugh, *The Compass of Philosophy* (New York: Longmans, Green 1954); R. S. Brumbaugh, "Cosmography," *Review of Metaphysics* 26 (1972): pp. 333–47.

20. Plato could propose alternatives to the atomic theory, but there is no record of a *direct* confrontation with it; perhaps *Laws* X comes closest. What the Sophist in the present dialogue has done is to set up an atomism of sharply insulated phenomena, all on the same footing; thus he believes he has prevented questions of appearance and reality from arising.

21. Unlike Plato, Aristotle has a good deal to discuss with the atomic theorists; it is Heracliteans that *he* fails to communicate with.

22. Regarding the *Philosopher*, see Chapter 6, above.

23. *Statesman* 284E, with what seems the promise of a future detailed discussion of "normative measure" at 284D1.

24. Note the claims implicit in the Myth of the True Earth and the Myth of Er; if these are true in principle, what follows on the level of observation? (The *Statesman* myth makes a rather different point.) Aristotle (*Meteorology* II.1 355b32–356b2) takes the geology of the True Earth myth seriously.

25. Simmias and Cebes, the main respondents, are Pythagoreans from Thebes.

26. There has been considerable discussion of the relative date of the *Timaeus* and the *Sophist*. Stylistically, the *Timaeus* falls into the "later" group; but the version of the theory of forms seems rather to match an "earlier" set of statements. I don't think enough attention has been paid to the fact that an extensive encyclopedia of this sort may not have *a* date.

27. The *Euthydemus* is the clearest case study.

28. In the *Cratylus*, ordinary language turns out not to embody a single, consistent metaphysical view. This is not surprising when we review the list of different "givers of names" who have contributed to it. The list includes scientists and mathematicians, Heracliteans, gods, primitive astronomers, and women.

29. As the theory develops its full scope—for example, as one moves through the educational curriculum of the *Republic*—the forms first appear as

meanings, but then refer beyond these to objective *structures* ("hypotheses"), which also serve, at least in some cases, as *criteria* and which are held together in an ontological *system*.

30. Charles Morris, *Foundations of the Theory of Signs* (Chicago: University of Chicago Press, 1938), introduces this distinction of "designation," which relates a term to the abstract form it refers to, and "denotation," which relates it to the particular individuals it indicates. This suggests an interpretation of Plato's *Epistle VII*, with its "name, image and formula." The image is rather like the denotation, the formula like the designation, the name like the term in Morris's scheme.

31. *Epistle VII:* No one will try to discuss the thing itself in writing, "because of the weakness of language."

32. I am not sure which of the Sophistic devices that he recognizes matches Plato's notion of "upsetting the [Platonist's] argument" in *Epistle VII*. Certainly taking all metaphors literally can be damaging—in the *Euthydemus*, the brothers make fun of Socrates' doctrine of "participation" in that way. Falling back on a supposed Parmenidean argument that rules out the possibility of negation, privation, falsehood, and semblance can neutralize an attempt to establish degrees of reality. Trying to reject arguments by analogy, by appeal to the thesis that "everything is like and unlike every other" *(Protagoras)* would be a third attack.

33. The Stranger's dissent from Parmenides, *Sophist* 258C–E.

34. For the projected "emergence" of the forms from criteria of arts to postulates of science and mathematics to ideals, cf. Chapter 6, above.

35. Here Ryle *(Plato's Progress)* is very perceptive in seeing a development in Plato's thought, as it becomes clear to him that questions of meaning and semantics are more complex than the simpler models that seemed adequate for the middle dialogues. But it is clear, even from the indication at the end of the *Theaetetus* that the *Phaedo* is to be read *after* the *Sophist* and *Statesman*, that Plato did not intend to identify metaphysics with this sort of analysis, nor to give up the former as unnecessary.

36. An illicit conversion of "all meanings are forms" to "all forms are meanings" turns Plato's theory. into something quite different. Plato himself seems insufficiently cautious in failing to stress the nonidentity of meanings and forms in the middle dialogues, particularly *Republic* V and the *Phaedrus*.

Chapter 9

1. L. A. Post, *The Vatican Plato and Its Relations* (Middletown, Conn., 1934), pp. 65–92.

2. J. Burnet, *Platonis Opera*, 2nd ed., vol. 2 (Oxford, 1953); A. Diès, Platon, *Parménide*, Budé Edition, (Paris, 1950).

3. See R. S. Brumbaugh, "Text and Interpretation of Plato's *Parmenides*," *Phil. Research Archives*, 1982 (microfiche), hereafter PRA, chap. 4.

4. G. Stallbaum, ed. *Platonis Parmenides. . . . ,* Leipzig, 1839. Stallbaum's alpha is cod. Laur. gr. 80.7.

5. I. Bekker, *In Platonem comm. critica*, vol. 1 (Berlin, 1823), pp. 101 ff. Bekker's s is the Milan codex Ambros. gr. D 71 sup.; see Post. (By error, the shelf marks of r and s are exchanged in R. S. Brumbaugh, *Plato on the One* [New Haven, 1961], p. xxiii and p. 251. Hereafter this is cited as POTO).

6. A gap in s from 151C5 to 152E1 exactly matches fols. 151v–152r of r.: (See POTO, p. 251.)

7. For V, see POTO, p. 251. The *Parmenides* is copied from V by r, though Paris C is copied by it for the *Gorgias* and *Phaedo*.

8. For more detail on the relations of V, r, and Paris C, see PRA, Chapter IV.

9. POTO, pp. 241–261.

10. See PRA, Chapter III.

11. Post, op. cit., is not sure about the contents of the Prague ms or of its relation to Vat. gr. 1029. For the contents, see R. S. Brumbaugh and Rulon Wells, *The Plato Manuscripts: A New Index* (New Haven, 1968), p. 17; for the relation to the Vatican ms, cf. PRA, Chapter II.

12. For Vienna Y, see Winifred Hicken, "The Y Tradition of the *Theaetetus*," *Classical Quarterly*, 17 (1957), 98–102; and especially her n. 1, p. 98.

13. POTO, pp. 47–52, and figure p. 53.

14. The odd exceptions are cited in passing in the notes to the translation in POTO, pp. 55–186.

15. Proclus, *In Platonis Parmenidem Comm.*, ed. V. Cousin (in *Procli, Opera*) (Paris, 1827); see also Proclus, *Elements of Theology*, ed. and trans. E. R. Dodds (Oxford, 1934); Proclus, *Commentary on the First Book of Euclid's Elements*, trans. G. R. Morrow (Princeton, 1970).

16. See R. S. Brumbaugh, "Notes on the History of Plato's Text: With the *Parmenides* as a Case Study," *Paideia* Special Plato Issue (1976): 67–80.

17. See the figure showing these relations, PRA, Chapter II.

18. Almost certainly a parody of a proof style in vogue among astronomers of the Academy. Three treatises *On the Sphere*, the earliest by Autolycus, trace back to an Academy source. They are written in this pattern: an opening

theorem statement, a division into cases, a case-by-case consideration, and a final q.e.d. theorem repetition. See POTO, n. 2 p. 19.

19. R. Robinson, *Plato's Earlier Dialectic*, 2nd ed. (Oxford, 1953), pp. 270–274; A. E. Taylor, Plato's *Parmenides* (Oxford, 1934).

20. On the other hand, lending some plausibility to Taylor's theory, cf. the splendid free association and the wild etymologies of the *Cratylus*.

21. Taylor is the scholar who reads it as a joke; among others, Wyller supports the Neo-Platonic "revelation" interpretation (see his *Späte Platon* [Hamburg, 1970], and my review, *Class. World* [1971]: 160).

22. A finding summarized by H. F. Cherniss in his "Plato Studies 1950–1957," *Lustrum* 5 (1960): 231.

23 Steph. pp. 138C6, 138E1, 149C8, 152B6, 165B8 are cases in point.

24. Parodies of formal logic *can* be funny.

25. For the *Euthydemus*, see R. S. Brumbaugh, *Plato for the Modern Age* (New York, 1962), pp. 54–55.

26. Paul Shorey, "On *Parmenides* 162A,B," *American Journal of Philology* 12 (1891): 349–353.

27. R. S. Brumbaugh, "A Latin Translation of Plato's *Parmenides*," *Review of Metaphysics* 14 (1960): 91–109, esp. p. 94.

28. E. R. Dodds, *Plato's Gorgias* (Oxford, 1959).

29. See PRA, Chapter IV.

Chapter 10

1. L. Robin, *La théorie platonicienne des idées et d'nombres D'après Aristote* (Paris, 1908); H. F. Cherniss, *Aristotle's Criticism of Plato and the Academy* (Baltimore, 1944). See also N. P. Stallknecht and R. S. Brumbaugh, *The Spirit of Western Philosophy* (N.Y., 1950), pp. 119–124, 148–158.

2. *Physics* VIII. 1–2, (250all–253a21); *Gen et Corr.* II.9–10 (335a25–337a35).

3. A reader's first impulse is to think of the Prime Mover as an efficient, not a final, cause. In my article "Preface to Cosmography," *Review of Metaphysics* (1953), I report the odd sense I had that Aristotle's works made more sense in the twentieth century if, book by book, they were read *backward*. The inverse time relation of efficient and final causality is, of course, the explanation.

4. E.g., *Hist. animalium*.

5. McKeon believes study of the shift in method is the best key to understanding Aristotle's departure from Platonism. Thus he not only emphasizes Aristotle's demotion of Platonic "dialectic" to a second best method (in his "Introduction") but opens his selections in the *Introduction to Aristotle* with the *Posterior Analytics*. The difficulty of that text for the modern beginner makes one assume that a much stronger reason than the tradition that "logic" is the introductory branch of philosophy is responsible.

6. A. E. Taylor, *Aristotle* (London and Edinburgh, 1912). McKeon notes, in the Bibliography of his *Basic Works*, p. xxxvi, "Excellently presented but completely unsympathetic treatment of Aristotle by a great Platonist."

7. Aristotle (*Metaphysics* A) explains that "we think we have an explanation of something when we know its causes." And, since it turns out that any given thing has more than one cause, an adequate explanation must include them all.

8. This summarizes a large set of Aristotle's findings, ranging from poetry to genetics and cosmology.

9. Notice the demotion of dialectic to a second-best method in the *Organon* (*Topics* I), and the rejection of numbers as causes—in any sense of "cause"—in *Metaphysics* N.

10. Aristotle, *Selected Fragments*, trans. W. D. Ross, (Oxford translation of the Works of Aristotle, XII) Oxford. An excellent detailed treatment of Aristotle's early work, though done in a wider context of a theory of development which many scholars do not accept, is W. Jaeger, *Aristotle: Fundamentals of the History of His Development*, trans. Richard Robinson (Oxford, 1934).

11. Compare the fragments of *On the Ideas* (in Ross, op. cit.) with the first part of Plato's *Parmenides*. Aristotle seems to incorporate ideas and parts of this early work in his criticisms of Platonism in *Metaphysics* A.

12. For Aristotle's criticism of Speusippus and Xenocrates, see *Metaphysics* M,N.; also see E. Zeller, *Plato and the Older Academy*, trans. S. F. Alleyne (London, 1876); H. F. Cherniss, *Aristotle's Criticism of Plato and the Academy* (Baltimore, 1944); P. Merlan, *From Plato to Neo-Platonism* (The Hague, 1953).

13. Cf. Aristotle's criticism of "utopian" approaches to political science, the theme of *Politics* II.

14. Aristotle, *Metaphysics*, A.ix, 991b4 ff. Aristotle says that "in the *Phaedo* . . . the forms are said to be causes both of being and becoming. But why could not something, say a ring, come to be without the agency of the forms. . . ?"

15. The *Phaedo*, for example, gains its dramatic power from the attractiveness the forms as ideals hold for Socrates; yet the argument does not show how they can play this role.

16. This contrast of their two gods is sometimes (and I think correctly) taken to epitomize the difference in temperament and appeal of the Platonic and Aristotelian philosophies.

17. Richard McKeon has several times pointed out how Aristotle, by his strategy of distinctions, is able to simplify his treatment of Sophistry. Where Plato, following Socrates, tries to refute Sophistic errors as mistakes in metaphysics and ethics, Aristotle's *Sophistical Refutations* treats their work simply as misunderstanding and misuse of language.

18. *Hist. anim.;* and note Aristotle's favorite illustration of natural efficient causality, "man is the father of man."

19. In the biological works, other species are treated as imperfect human beings; in the practical sciences, education is designed as remedial for the lack of mature skills needed by an adult citizen.

20. *Physics* II 194a27: "But the nature is the end or 'that for the sake of which.' For if a thing undergoes a continuous change and there is a stage which is last, this stage is the end or 'that for the sake of which.' (That is why the poet was carried away into making an absurd statement when he said 'he has the end [i.e., death] for the sake of which he was born.' For not every stage that is last claims to be an end, but only that which is best." (Oxford translation.) See also Aristotle's essays on *Youth and Old Age* and *Length and Shortness of Life.*

21. Book by book, the *Nicomachean Ethics* adds new conditions essential for "full human self-realization." Each one—good childhood habits, citizenship in a Greek state, a circle of close friends and leisure to spend with them, intellectual excellence and a chance to develop it—excludes another large group of persons.

22. *Poetics*, 1448b24–1449a30.

23. Lope de Vega wrote that of his numerous tragedies, only two—and these not the most successful—had been correctly written according to Aristotle.

24. Aristotle tends to identify excellence and *autarchy*, self-sufficiency. On this ground, for example, intellectual contemplation is ranked ahead of political action as a virtue in *Nicomachean Ethics* X. The complete self-containedness of the Prime Mover establishes his excellence as greater than that of the other movers, which are capable of thinking and causing change of place. The best state in general of *Politics* VI is self-sufficient.

25. For the *Philosopher*, see Chapter 6, above.

26. A Roman reaction against school discipline in favor of more immediate intellectual access to something like the Forms surely would have altered any Aristotelian establishment in the same direction that it actually modified the Academy.

27. See above, n. 12; also, P. Lang, ed., *De Speusippi Academici scriptiis* (Bonn, 1911).

28. R. S. Brumbaugh, "Cosmography," *Review of Metaphysics* (1972): 333–347.

29. Chapter 16, below.

30. Charles Bigger, *Participation* (Baton Rouge, 1970); R. Neville, *The Cosmology of Freedom* (N.Y., 1976).

31. F. M. Cornford, *Plato's Theory of Knowledge* (reprint, N.Y., 1957), p. 278.

Chapter 11

1. W. D. Ross, *Aristotle's Metaphysics*, A Revised Text with Introduction and Commentary, 2 vols. (Oxford, 1924), p. xxxii, xxxi, note 2 (hereafter cited as Ross).

2. Aristotle, *Metaphysics*, ed. and trans. John Warrington (New York and London, 1956). Everyman's library No. 1000.

3. Ross, xiv–xxxiii. For the account of Eudemus's reported reaction, see xxxi–xxxii.

4. See below, my summary of the several books.

5. Richard P. McKeon, *The Basic Works of Aristotle* (New York, 1941), Introduction, xviii–xxii (hereafter cited as McKeon).

6. R. S. Brumbaugh, "Aristotle's Outline of the Problems of First Philosophy," *Review of Metaphysics* XVIII (1954): 511–521.

7. A. E. Taylor, *Aristotle* (London, n.d.); John H. Randall, *Aristotle* (New York, 1960).

8. Josef Zürcher. *Aristoteles' Werk und Geist* (Paderborn, 1952).

9. Werner Jaeger, *Aristoteles, Grundlegung einer geschichte seiner entwicklung* (Berlin, 1923). Translated by Richard Robinson (*Aristotle: Fundamentals of the history of his development*) (Oxford, 1934).

10. For this lecture "On the Ideas," see W. D. Ross's comments and translation in *Aristotle, Selected Fragments* (Oxford translation, vol. XII, Oxford, 1962).

11. For example, the "On Ideas" fragments with the criticisms of Plato in Alpha IX.

12. Ross, op. cit., I, 221–250.

13. If this were correct, Book *Lambda*, with its cosmological argument, would not qualify as "metaphysics" proper. But while knowledge, which is the concern of *Epsilon*, is of the universal, existence is particular.

14. The lists are compared in my article, cited above, n. 6.

15. *M* chaps, iv, v (1078b34–1079b3, 1079b12–1080a8) repeats *Alpha* (990b2–991b8); and there seem to be two independent (an earlier and a later?) discussions of Academic theories. See Ross, op. cit., xxi.

16. See my article cited in n. 6, above.

17. McKeon, op. cit.

18. Warrington, op. cit., p. 165. "Passing from the static consideration of substance in Z to the dynamic consideration of change in *H*, Aristotle carries a stage further his doctrine of substance as the cause of being, as that which makes a thing what it is."

19. *Metaphysics* Lambda, 1071a1–b1. See Newton P. Stallknecht and R. S. Brumbaugh, *The Spirit of Western Philosophy* (New York, 1950), pp. 148–158 for discussion of this text.

20. *Physics* II, 197b5–14.

21. See Ross's notes on 1065b35 ("after this, say that" seems a good literal rendering of this lecturer's note); compare 1070a4; and Ross's note to 1071a2. Note also that in the *Organon* Aristotle has a very limited number of stock examples, as though he were improvising them from his audience and lecture setting.

22. So Mary Renault, in her *Mask of Apollo*.

Chapter 12

1. The view that Aristotle was not a mathematician, as stated by A. E. Taylor (*Plato: the Man and His Work*, pp. 506–07), cannot be easily reconciled with Sir Thomas Heath's study, *Mathematics in Aristotle* (Oxford, 1949) and that of Hippocrates Apostle, *Aristotle's Philosophy of Mathematics* (Chicago, 1952). Aristotle seems to have been both well-grounded in pure mathematics and interested in the foundations of mathematics and its application. Still, Taylor's point holds that Aristotle does reject concepts fundamental to our contemporary science of mathematics (cf. W. D. Ross, *Aristotle's Metaphysics*, I, p. lvi, where this same point is noted).

2. Particularly *Metaphysics* M and N.

3. I was first struck by this in connection with the use of matrices and diagrams as educational devices; although this pedagogical tradition was Pythagorean, Aristotle followed it extensively. If our editions of Aristotle were equipped with reconstructions of all the figures he alludes to, the point would be quite clear.

4. *Timaeus* 35, where the construction of the world-soul by proportions can be taken as giving an algebraic pattern of analysis used throughout the first part of the cosmology (to 47).

5. Jan van der Meulen, *Aristoteles: Die Mitte in seinem Denken*, (Meisenheim/Glan, 1951), traces this concept but treats the "mean" in question as in the category of substance rather than of quantity. The result is a bridging of Aristotle's sharp ontological distinctions which is philosophically interesting, but not convincing Aristotelianism.

6. *Prior Analytics.*

7. *De Part. Anim.*, 656a ff., where the heart and brain are harmonized in the organism as a mean.

8. *Physics* II, III.

9. *Physics*, 259a20.

10. *Nicomachean Ethics*, 1106a10, 1131a10 ff.

11. *De Gen. et Corr.*, 337b–338; also *De Caelo*, 304b–307b.

12. *Meteorologica* IV: compare the passages cited in n. 10. The Platonic analogue is found in *Timaeus*, 32–35, where God plans and compounds the three-part mixture of the world-soul.

13 *Poetics*, 1457b ff.

14. Ibid.; *Posterior Analytics*, 89b10–20.

15. *Parva Naturalia*, 464b–467b (On Length and Shortness of Life); ibid., 467b–470b (On Youth and Old Age; On Life and Death).

16. *De Caelo*, 310a–311a; *De Gen. et Corr.*, 335a–327b.

17. *De Motu Animalium*, 703a ff.

18. *De Gen. et Corr.*, 337b–338b; *Post. Anal.*, 95a25–96a25.

19. *Metaphysics*, 986a23.

20. For Platonic uses of this "matrix" device, see *Sophist*, 266A; also my "Note on Plato, *Republic* IX, 587D," *Classical Philology* XLIV (1949): 197–99, and my notes on teaching *Republic* VIII and IX, *Classical Journal*, XLVI

(1951): 343–48; in these, matrices are shown to be involved in *Phaedrus*, 249, *Republic*, 546 and *Republic*, 587. For the basic notion of "verbal matrices," see Scott Buchanan, *Symbolic Distance* (London, 1932), and Leonard Bloomfield, *Linguistic Aspects of Science* (Chicago, 1939), "Matrices." In the Platonic tradition, the device remains a standard one; ef. the scholia to *Republic*, 511 and 534 in W. C. Greene, *Scholia Platonica* (Haverford, 1938), pp. 246, 252–53. The computational use of such a device would be the multiplication table up to ten (*kephalismos*) referred to by Aristotle, *Topics*, 163b17 ff. (see Heath, *Mathematics in Aristotle*, p. 93, for translation and comment on the passage); the table seems to fit Aristotle's comment better if it is set up with the Athenian ("Herodianic") notation (Heath, *Greek Mathematics*, I, pp. 30–31). Again, an abacus provides a model for this use of spatial relations in a matrix; see Heath *Greek Mathematics*, I, pp. 46–52, and compare Plato's reference, *Euthyphro*, 12, and his assimilation of mathematics to checkers and dice, *Phaedrus*, 274C. Other antecedents are suggested by some of the theorems in Euclid, *Elements*, V, and the genetic theories of Empedocles and the Hippocratic school.

21 *Metaphysics*, 1093a26.

22. *Metaphysics*, 986a23, 1004b27, 1054b35, 1058a13, 1072a31–35, 1093b12.

23. See the notes to these passages in Ross, op. cit.

24. This is the way I believe van der Meulen would interpret these ideas; see above. n. 5.

25. To determine this, one need only study the passages cited above, notes 6–19, in their contexts.

26. Heath and Apostle demonstrate Aristotle's basic competence; *Metaphysics*, 1073a–1074b shows Aristotle's interest in the astronomical research of the Academy.

27. See the discussion, below, of Aristotle's treatment of transfinite numbers and sets.

28. *Physics* III (where Aristotle tries to assure the "mathematicians" that he is not depriving them of something by his denial of any actual infinity), *Metaphysics*, A, M, N. See also Apostle, op. cit., Chap. I.

29. Richard Courant and Herbert Robbins, *What is Mathematics?* (Oxford, 1941) is an illuminating discussion of the present relation of "formalism" and "intuitionism" in mathematics. See also W. V. Quine, *Methods of Logic*, pp. 207, 226, 248–50.

30. The reader is invited to verify the fact that neither Protagoras, Berkeley, nor Hume is treated seriously as a mathematician, and Kant is usually dismissed rather abruptly. The great mathematicians are the Platonists: Eudoxus, Euclid, Descartes, Leibniz, et al.

31. *Physics* III, 204a–208a. See especially 208a20–25: "To rely on mere thinking is absurd, for then the excess or defect is not in the thing, but in the thought" (Oxford translation).

32. Ibid.; Also *Metaphysics*, 1051a–1052a (Θ, ix), 1076b–1078b.

33. In its context, I take this to be the meaning of *Metaphysics*, 1087a20: "For if the principles must be universal, what is derived from them must also be universal, as in demonstrations; and if this is so, there will be nothing capable of separate existence—i.e., no substance" (Oxford translation). *Posterior Analytics*, 71b10 f., 93a20–29.

34. See for example, the summary in Courant and Robbins, op. cit., pp. 86–88.

35. *De Interpretatione*, 21b11–15, with the qualification of 22b30–23a25.

36. *De Interpretatione*, 18a28–19b5. The example of the seafight at 19a30 is an illustration.

37. *Categories*, 13b20–35. The distinction of "definite" and "indefinite" subjects and predicates in respect to their existential import, in *De Interpretatione*, 16a30–35, 16b11–20, corrects the erroneous modern notion that the A and I proposition always have existential import in Aristotle's logic.

38. See W. D. Ross, *Aristotle's Metaphysics*, I, p. lvi, and A. E. Taylor, loc. cit., for criticisms of Aristotle's mathematics on this point.

39. Aristotle seems to be avoiding both the theory of types and the set-theory paradox of self-including sets by sticking to the notion that a set is a collection of *units*, and a number the multiplicity of a given set. (For a simple statement of these paradoxes, see Quine, op. cit., pp. 248–52.) But if the elements of a set are actually units, and only potentially subsets, this represents a considerable restriction of mathematics in its present scope.

40. The classic study remains L. Robin, *Théorie platonicienne des Idées et des Nombres d' après Aristote* (Paris, 1908). But the notion that this is a literal quotation of a Platonic "esoteric doctrine" becomes almost impossible to defend satisfactorily in the light of Harold F. Cherniss, *The Riddle of the Early Academy* (Berkeley, 1945).

41. *Statesman*, 284C ff.; *Philebus*, 65–67 are the clearest examples.

42. This statement of the case in A (*Metaphysics*, 988a23–993a27) sets the tone for the problems in B and the whole subsequent discussion.

43. *Metaphysics*, 1038b1–1039b20; Ibid., 1071a18–24.

44. This "fusion" is the point of identity between potentiality and actuality, *Metaphysics*, 1045a20–b25.

45. For Aristotle's notion of measure, see *Metaphysics*, 1052a1–1053b6. Platonic measure at least is often expressed in quantitative terms, as in the *Timaeus* and *Laws;* presumably, its normative aspect would seem to Aristotle irrelevant to his criticism in this context.

46. This is the way the problems of first philosophy are organized in *Metaphysics* B, 1. These problems are the final "knots" to be untied, presumably because their loosening requires untying the others first. The translation of Richard Hope, *Aristotle's Metaphysics: A Postscript to Natural Science* (New York, 1952), follows Aristotle's use of connectives in its paragraphing more closely than other translations, and the result is a much tighter set of coordinate problems (Aristotle uses *men* and *de* to indicate coordination throughout this chapter of B.)

47. *Metaphysics* Z, I, A, particularly.

48. *De Interpretatione*, 23a20–25, and Ross, note ad loc.

49. Cartesian points and moments could be added; note that this list of rejected concepts traces the main stream of our standard mathematical tradition.

50. E.g., *De Caelo*, 308a21–310a10. My summary in the text of what Plato had done follows Aristotle: but one could equally well interpret the "triangles" as sound anticipations of modern calculus (*Timaeus*, 51 ff.).

51. *Metaphysics*, 1092b20–25; 1093b8–12.

52. As a matter of fact, Aristotle's description of the properties which transfinite sets would have anticipates our modern notions, and shows mathematical talent of a high order. He is analogous in the history of set-theory to Saccheri in that of geometry.

53. I have summarized this briefly in "An Aristotelian Defense of 'Non-Aristotelian' Logics," *Journal of Philosophy*, XLIX (1952): 582–85.

54. The dialectic of A is typical of the *Metaphysics*, and appears in the resolution of the final problem of the list in B 1 at the end of N. See below.

55. *Metaphysics*, 1093b12–22.

56. Ibid. See *Metaphysics*, 986a23 for the *systoichia*. If the reader will reread the last chapter of N with the Pythagorean diagram before him, I believe his impression of Aristotle's attitude will be different from that given by the mere text without the figure it refers to—which is certainly very like, if not identical with, the Pythagorean table.

57. *Metaphysics*, 1078a32–b6; see also 1075a25–39.

58. The briefest summary here is the treatment of modality of judgments

in *De Interpretatione*, 23a; *Metaphysics*, 1071a ff. and *Categories*, 2a10 ff. make the same point.

59. *Posterior Analytics*, 75a36–b20.

Chapter 13

1. J. Burnet, *Early Greek Philosophy*, 4th ed. (London, 1930), p. 52, n. 2.

2. W. Darsow, "Die Kore des Anaximandros," *Jahrbuch d. deutsch, Archaeolog, Inst.* (Cambridge, 1962), p. 75, 75 n. 3.

3. H. Diels-W. Kranz, *Fragmente der Vorsokratiker*, 10th ed. (Berlin, 1960).

4. See the "Life of Simon" in Diogenes Laertius, *Lives and Opinions* . . . , II, chap. 13.

5. The American School of Classical Studies at Athens, *The Athenian Agora: a Guide*, revised ed. (1962), p. 112 (the shop), 170 (Simon's cup).

6. A. Winspear and T. Silverberg, *Who was Socrates?*

7. C. Seltman, "The problem of the First Italiote Coins," *Numismatic Chronicle* IX (1949): 1–21. The coin in question is pictured in Seltman's attractive *A Book of Greek Coins*, (London: King Penguin Books, 1952), p. 34 (#93). See also Guthrie, op. cit., 176–7. Guthrie comments, p. 177: "It is scarcely possible (to put the theory in its mildest form) that Pythagoras can have had nothing to do with this apparently contemporary coinage."

8. *Timaeus*, 50C: *typothenta;* cp. the *schemata plasas ek chrysou*, 50A and *ektypomatos*, 50D.

9. Presumably why Plato used this example in *Republic* i. 333C, 353D.

10. A brief list of some of these illustrations from arts and crafts in my "Plato and the History of Science," *Studium Generale* IX (1961): 520–22. It may be that Plato used the four-level scheme of his Divided Line as a criterion for completeness of explanation; in that case, we would expect *techne* to have a place in at least all of the middle and late dialogues. That this would make philosophic sense is shown, I think, in the "Platonic philosophy of education" presented in R. S. Brumbaugh and N. M. Lawrence, *Philosophers on Education* (Boston, 1963), Chap. II.

11. The *Pneumatica* of Heron of Alexandria (first century A.D.), which is the first written classical work on engineering and technology, finds steam power making its debut in the West as a way to make toy birds move and whistle; a perfect illustration of my point.

12. *Athenian Agora*, p. 152; see also p. 173.

13. Sausage grill, *Agora* 17; for this and wine coolers and ovens, see Brian A. Sparkes and Lucy Talcott, *Pots and Pans of Classical Athens*, Athenian Agora Picture Books, #1 (1958). The Amazon was described to me by Prof. Henry S. Robinson; the Minoan "mother-goddess" pitchers are a frequent design. The oil lamp was in a temple on the Acropolis. For the statue molds, see D. B. Thompson, *Miniature Sculpture from the Athenian Agora*, Athenian Agora Picture Books, #3.

14. For the apparatus prescribed by statute for an honest day in court, see Aristotle, *The Constitution of Athens*, trans. w. notes by K. von Fritz and E. Kapp (New York, 1950), #63–69, pp. 142–7, and notes pp. 196–200. See also M. Lang, *The Athenian Citizen*, Athenian Agora Picture Books, #4 (1959).

15. Standard weights and measures, *The Agora*, 45, 165–7; Inspector's seals, ibid., 168; market police (*agoranomoi*), Aristotle, op. cit., chap. 50, p. 125.

16. For the Mint, *The Agora*, pp. 24, 96f., 172; measures, see n. 21, above; justice, see n. 19, above.

17. *The Agora*, p. 35, 57–8; Plate IVa.

18. Plato, *Euthyphro*, 12D ff.

19. See, for example, "*rhyton*", in the Hachette *Greece* (Paris, 1955), 553–5.

20. Henry S. Robinson, "The Tower of the Winds and the Roman Market-Place," *American J. of Archaeol.* 47 (1943): 291–305; also J. Stuart and N. Revett, *The Antiquities of Athens* (London, 1762), I, pp. 13–25, Plates i–ix.

21. See the Plan in Hachette Guides, *Athens and Environs*, (Paris, 1962), p. 229.

22. *Athenian Agora*, 106, 108–10, Fig. 23 p. 109.

23. Ibid., 15, 112, 163 f.; S. Young, "An Athenian Klepsydra," *Hesperia*, 1939, pp. 274–84.

24. Plato, *Theaetetus*, 172 D ff.

25. Aristotle, op. cit., chap. 67 (p. 145); the meaning here is evident in spite of the lacuna.

26. For example, the "twin" of the Agora klepsydra at Oropus, *Athenian Agora*, 108.

27. A good compilation from many sources in Hachette *Guide to Greece* (Paris, 1955), pp. 360–8, Map pp. 354–5; read through rapidly, this description gives the "Oriental garden" impression; and, at least for me, detailed study and leisurely visiting does not change it.

28. Hachette Guides, *Athens and Environs*, revised ed., (Paris, 1962), plan pp. 492–3; pp. 495, 500.

29. Ibid., 154–210; see also N. Perfetos, *The Ancient Agora and Acropolis of Athens* (Athens, 1961).

Chapter 15

1. In what follows, I am not arguing against the existence of a theory-building, speculative *emphasis* in classical science; for better or worse, that is there. But the myth of a total, perhaps deliberate, rejection of all mechanical models or empirical investigation (a myth already well under way by Plutarch's time; witness his "Life of Marcellus") needs demolition. Standard histories of science, the most important of which was George Sarton's, make Plato the baneful spokesman for an anti-empiricism. (On this point, and the weaknesses of its presentation, see James Haden, "The Challenge of the History of Science, Part I," *Review of Metaphysics* VII (1953): 74–88.) But a similar view, without the negative evaluation, occurs in the work of A. N. Whitehead, himself both scientist and Platonist (e.g., in *Science and the Modern World* [New York 1925], chapter 1). And a similar overall appraisal opens S. Sambursky's excellent study, *The Physical World of the Greeks* (trans. M. Dagut, London, 1956), pp. 2,3.

2. Some works, particularly Heron of Alexandria's, suggest a radical change of interest and competence by the second century A.D., just as Sextus Empiricus represents a new theoretical stance favoring strict "empiricism." The conclusive piece of evidence that upsets the application of a "no technology or apparatus" label to the Hellenistic period, however, is the "Antikythera machine" (Derek J. Price, "An Ancient Computer," *Scientific American* (June 1959), cover, pp. 60–7.)

3. New interest in, and appreciation of, the Near Eastern contribution was initiated by O. Neugebauer's work (e.g., *The Exact Sciences in Antiquity* ((Copenhagen, 1951)). For an account of the respective contributions and the confluence of Near Eastern and Hellenic "science," see, for example, Derek J. Price, *Science Since Babylon* (New Haven, 1961). I have no intention of denying that a change of emphasis resulted from the new cultural contacts opened by Alexander; I am denying the sharp dialectical antitheses that oversimplify the picture of the "Hellenic" stream.

4. 467 B.C. is the date of the meteorite that directed public attention to the astronomy of Anaxagoras, attention which may account for his invitation to come to Athens. I think there is general agreement that the *Timaeus* was completed by about the time of Plato's third trip to Sicily. That it is "impure" science if absence of models or detailed observations is the test of "purity" is

argued in my article, "Plato and the History of Science," *Studium Generale* IX (1961): 520–2.

5. It seems quite clear that the Milesians—coming from a city which, as Burnet pointed out, was noted for its engineers—were designers of instruments and builders of models. In particular, the doxographical reports of Anaximander's cosmological ring model, his map, star map, and gnomon, and Anaximemes' "vortex" model of the cosmos make this point.

6. See my *Ancient Greek Gadgets and Machines* (New York, 1966). It is suggested there that enough is presupposed about use of models in psychology and cosmology by Plato's *Republic* to justify the assertion that "pure science," if it existed earlier, had already become considerably less pure by about 385. The hypothesis of a continuing development of techniques, mechanisms, and models without benefit of a literary record is confirmed, for fourth-century Ionia at least, by the identification of a coin reverse as a detailed relief map (A. E. M. Johnson, "The Earliest Preserved Greek Map: A New Ionian Coin Type," *JHS* 87 (1967): 86ff.).

7. The "cooking-bell," with these lines of Aristophanes as caption, is illustrated in B. Sparkes and L. Talcott, *Pots and Pans of Classical Athens* (1958), and discussed by Sparkes in *JHS* 82 (1962), 128f. See also K. J. Dover, *Aristophanes Clouds* (Oxford, 1968), ad loc.

8. Reading in 1. 179 *thumation* with W. W. Merry (The *Clouds*, Oxford, 1879).

9. Merry *ad* 1983.

10. And of course making the *dinos* masculine brings out this antithesis of the two "religious" statues more sharply. Cf. Merry *ad loc*. 380 and Dover *ad loc*. 380 and 1473.

Chapter 16

1. Other Platonists have felt the same way. "One main factor in the upward trend of animal life has been the power of wandering. . . . When man ceases to wander, he will cease to ascend in the scale of being. . . ." A. N. Whitehead, *Science and the Modern World* (N.Y., 1925), Chap. XIII.

2. I had mentioned these as part of a proposed reconstruction of Greek philosophy in its context in a paper read to the Society for Ancient Greek Philosophy in 1963. The project and the paper proved too radical to find many supporters, though bit by bit the shift seems to be underway.

3. *Republic* I, 353A: anticipated at 333C.

4. *Euthyphro* 11A, *Apol.* 17C; cf. Sir Thomas Heath, *History of Greek Mathematics*, (Oxford, 1921) I, pp. 46–52; Parry Moon, *The Abacus* (N.Y., 1971), pp. 21–24.

5. This idea inspired the research project of preparing an "Index of Plato's references to the arts and crafts" by my Yale College Plato Seminar in 1959. My assistant, Mr. Kenneth Freeman, and my students from that seminar will recognize my debt to this shared inquiry, which for better or worse I have continued and written about ever since. (For example, in my book *Ancient Greek Gadgets and Machines* [N.Y., 1962].)

6. This point is hard to document adequately simply because I know of no exception.

7. Aristotle, *Politics* I, VI; Plato, *Republic* VI, VII.

8. Plutarch, "Life of Marcellus." In this account, Archimedes, despite his great inventions, totally disdains the whole material universe, and will not waste time writing about it.

9. W. C. Greene, *Scholia Platonica*, Scholion to *Alc.* i. 111 B.

10. The classical controversy is discussed, with Hippias the Sophist as central character in the reconstruction, in R. S. Brumbaugh and N. M. Lawrence, *Philosophical Themes in Modern Education* (Boston, 1972), Chap. II.

11. Plato (?), *Hippias Minor;* see also the *Hippias Major.*

12. *Sophist* 232D.

13. *Theaetetus* 175E.

14. Diels-Kranz, *Fragmente der Vorsokratiker*, 10th ed. (Berlin, 1960), II, 279–283.

15. Plato, *Protagoras* 318D–E. With his notion that mathematical information is also educational, Hippias comes out as a sort of maverick in this contrast.

16. Sir Thomas Heath, *History of Greek Mathematics* (Oxford, 1921), I, 179, interpreting the reference in Aristotle, *Metaphysics* B.2, 998a2. Hume's treatment of geometry in his *Inquiry Concerning Human Understanding* offers what may be a modern analogue to this dismissal of mathematics as irrelevant to the "actual world." See also R. K. Sprague, ed., *The Older Sophists*, p. 22, Frag. 7a.

17. Isocrates, *Antidosis*, 262; Plato, *Parmenides*, 135D.

18. Callicles, in Plato's *Gorgias*, 485A–486D.

19. Selected from the *Index* of my Yale College Seminar, and verified.

20. A. Winspear and T. Silverberg, *Who Was Socrates?* (1939). An implausible ideological interpretation, now rendered considerably less likely by the American School's verification of the actual existence of Simon's cobbler's shop. See *The Athenian Agora*, 2nd ed., 1962, 112, 170.

21. Eryximachus, "speaking as a scientist," defines "astronomy" as the science of the mixing of hot and cold in the seasons! (*Symposium* 188A.)

22. See below.

23. Though in the *Timaeus* Plato claims to have gone beyond an amateur interest, and in certain cases of psychophysical disorders to have made a new medical contribution. His claim is defended by Dr. Lain Entralgo, *The Therapy of the Word in Classical Antiquity* (New Haven, 1970).

24. One might guess that, just as today carpentry is stylish among upperclass men and women who want to get back to something "natural" and out from under the pressure of intellectual competition, weaving in Plato's time had the same vogue and served the same function.

25. I refer here to Susan Woody, now Professor in the Department of Philosophy, Connecticut College, whose expertise sharpened and enlivened a graduate Yale Seminar on Plato's *Statesman*.

26. There is one remark in the *Protagoras* about the inexactitude of carpenters trying to get the parts of a ceiling to fit even approximately which is quite at odds with the praise of precision of the carpenter in the *Philebus*. A. Trevor Hodge's *The Woodwork of Greek Roofs* (Cambridge, 1960) convinces me that the classical mason and carpenter were *not* at all "exact" in cutting and fitting. Hodge does not explicitly draw this conclusion, but see for example, the measurements of his note 3, p. 25.

27. Chapter 6, above.

28. This culminates in the *reductio* proofs of the *Sophist*, that a flat, one-dimensional projection of all "Knowledge" cannot account for the existent experts, whose predictions do predict.

29. *Theaetetus* 178A–181A.

30. *Statesman* 284C–286D.

31. A little more attention to this "stranger from Elea" is in order before Oxford and Princeton admirers become enraptured by his tidy technical weaving of subjects, predicates, and "othernesses" together. "Who *are* these guys?" the Kid asks Cassidy, as the pursuit goes on. Socrates cannot do the Sophist shooting job that Plato has in mind; perhaps because his strength is in education, not assassination? The weaving lesson, anticipating the *Statesman* is an interlude somewhat like Achilles' stay among the women before his military service.

32. Atlantis is obviously modern Manhattan; the only non-obvious question is whether Plato regarded this as the utopia of a daydream or some precognition of a later purgatory. My own view is stated rather starkly in *Plato's Mathematical Imagination* (Bloomington, Indiana, 1954; reprinted in 1968), pp. 47–58; subsequent adventures in the Aegean have not led me to change this notion.

33. E. A. Havelock, *Preface to Plato*, (Cambridge, Mass., 1963), has done a valuable work of interpretation in comparing the modern reader's perceptions to those which a classical student of poetry would and would not have shared.

34. In fact, Plato himself gives contradictory accounts of the ways in which poetic imagery and wisdom fall short of "higher" kinds of knowledge and action. See Chapter 6 above, n. 27.

35. Any standard guidebook treating the dimensions of the Parthenon has the relevant figures; for example, the supposed "vertical" columns would meet 5,200 feet above the temple, if they were extended in the air. A number of such figures were collected by me to scandalize metaphysicians visiting the reconstructed Parthenon in the Nashville, Tennessee, Memorial Park, in a mimeographed guide: "The Parthenon: A metaphysical Enigma," Nashville, 1967.

36. Plato, *Critias*, 116. The modern reader is inclined to attribute the "barbarity" of the temple to the successive ornamentation with silver, copper, towers, etc., each new accretion more gaudy. But an honest attempt to see the Athenian acropolis as it must have been suggests that it must be the 2:1 ground plan rather than the overkill of tinsel that is objected to. See *PMI*, p. 276 nn. 19, 20, 22, 37. See Ernest McClain, *The Pythagorean Plato* (Stony Brook, N.Y., 1978).

38. This of course equals 7! All the other units of measurement are to be based on a duodecimal system.

39. *Republic* VII, 522C–523B.

40. *Laws* VII, 817A; and compare the characterization of life as "serious play," *Laws* VII, 803C.

41. See Chap. 2, above.

42. A point repeatedly made, from the *Charmides* to the *Philebus*; perhaps most sharply put in *Statesman* 284A ff., the contrast of descriptive ("relative") and normative measure.

43. Cf. the need for applied as well as pure geometry in *Philebus* 62A.

44. See my *Ancient Greek Gadgets and Machines* (N.Y., 1966).

45. R. S. Brumbaugh, *The Philosophers of Greece* (Albany, 1969), pp. 93–100, map p. 94, and illustrations, pp. 90, 91, 114, 127.

Chapter 18

1. In an article, "Aristotle's Outline of the Problems of First Philosophy,"
Review of Metaphysics VII (1954): 511–521, I analyzed Beta. I had two theses
to offer in that article. The first was that Aristotle in fact did use consistent
coordinating devices to mark his main outline, but they were lost in the complex maze of subordinate questions. (For the first listing in Beta, *men* and *de*
mark the main topics; in the more detailed second Beta treatment, *aporia* or
aporeseien do this; in Kappa, a combination of *men-de* and *poteron* does so.)
These indicated topics add up to exactly the set of problems an Aristotelian
would expect, and to a set all of which are resolved in the later text. My second
thesis was that Jaeger's finding of the great variety of dates of composition
indicated by shifts of style probably reflected the practice of a busy lecturer
who kept a file of all his back notes and papers. Then, on the occasion of a new
lecture series to be designed, Aristotle could, for example, insert his *On the
Ideas* notes from his Assos days as part of the history of philosophy he had
projected as the first lecture set (*Metaphysics* Alpha). Since then, I have come
to appreciate a third literary feature. The picture is not complete until Aristotle has introduced all of his four causes. But in his overall organization, he
stops short, in Iota and Kappa, to sum up the interaction of the first three—
formal (from Zeta), material (from Eta), and efficient (from Theta). He ends
by reviewing the initial problems, and his advances toward their solutions, in
Kappa. With Lambda, the introduction of the last, the final, cause snaps the
whole picture into focus. Lambda takes care of "problems about entities" from
the Beta and Kappa sets, leaving a final rejection of forms and numbers for M
and N. This makes the reason for the Beta/Kappa duplication lie in a construction of a climax rather than in an inadvertent repetition. The notes are admittedly rather roughly joined together, and repolished to very different degrees.

2. Organized into problems about metaphysics as discourse, which are
treated in Gamma and Delta; metaphysical ways of knowing, taken care of in
part in Epsilon, in part in Iota; the subject-matter of metaphysics, changing
and eternal substances and their causes. This third set of problems requires a
treatment of each cause, and of the causes together. This is developed in the
formal/Zeta, material/Eta, efficient/Theta scheme mentioned above in n. 1.
The unity of these three is treated in Iota; then Lambda: final cause completes
the picture. M and N dismiss unneeded Platonic forms and Pythagorean numbers.

INDEX

Absent-minded professor story, first, 241

Abacus, 280 n.4

"Accident", verbal ancestry of, 240

Achilles not a Platonic ideal, 72

Academics (Roman), 255

Academy: cosmology, 133; if Aristotle had become Head, 136; included women, 211; represented "liberal education", 197–98; transformation of Plato, 136–39

Adam, J., 26, 259 n.34

Adeimantus: his appetitive man, 35, 74; moves discussion to level of theory, 33, 48; represents appetitive part of soul, 19

Adeimantus and Glaucon, question intrinsic value of justice, 31

Aeolipile ("steam engine"), 185

Agalma ("beautiful work of art") describes cosmos, 137

Agave, 212

Agora: boundary stone, fig. 170; Guide to, 276 n.5; Museum, 167

Aition ("cause" in Aristotle), 248

Alexander, 249

Alleyne, S. F., 268 n.12

Alpha centauri, observer from, 256

American School of Classical Studies, 276 n.5

American philosophy, 256

Analytic philosophy, 67, 79

Analytics (Aristotle), 133

Anaxagoras: 100, 190, 228–29; accused of impiety, 229; arrival in Athens, 190; brought science to Athens, 245; "predicted" meteorite, 278–79 n.4

Anaximander, 241, 255; inventions of, 183; statue of, 166, 277 nn.1,2

Anaximines, 255

Anderson, M., 227

"Ancient Athens" (Plato's Atlantis story): 113; details opposite those of Atlantis, 115; like *Republic*, 115

Ancient Athens (historical). *See* Athens

Anscombe, E., 263 n.12 (Ch. 7)

Antigone, 211

"Antikythera machine", 179, 278 n.2

Anytus: accuses Socrates, 230; and his amnesty, 230; Meletus, and Lycon, 234; teaches by example, 18, 30, 217

Apology (Xenophon), 94. *See also* Socrates

Apology (Plato), 227. *See also* Socrates

Apollo, patron of *Phaedo*, 92

Apostle, H., 271 n.1, 273 nn.26,28

Apparatus. *See* Gadgets, Science

Aristophanes. *See Clouds*, Meton, Socrates, Women

Aristotelian: Administrators, 77; final causes, 176; language, 240; lecture, 148–49; period in intellectual history, 252–53; Scholasticism, 252–53; universals, 59; writing of histories of the Academy, 138

Aristotelianism, in Chicago in 1930s and 1940s, 176

Aristotle: and Alexander, 150–51; anticipated by Plato, 130–31; avoids set-theory paradoxes, 274 n.39; on automata, 180; and borderline cases, 130; competent in mathematics, 156; contemporary appraisals of, 153; Dante's appraisal of, 249; denies excluded middle in some cases, 157–58; fascinated by puppets, 180–81; on dialogue form, 133, 259 n.36; on female cowardice (among cuttlefish), 211; on forms, 248; on happiness, 134; on "intermediates", 260 n.7; on kinds of state, 251; makes Plato more specific, 130–31; as a mathematician, is an intuitionist, 153–62, 271 n.1; neither an idealist nor a materialist, 143–44, 151; on normative measure, 136; *On The Ideas*, 132, 144; on the Nuptial Number, 82; on *Phaedo* as geology, 101, 262 n.16; *Physics II* quoted, 269 n.20; and Platonism, 11, 129–40; on Plato's mathematics, 58;